THE PENINSULAR WAR

Battleground series:

Stamford Bridge & Hastings *by* Peter Marren
Wars of the Roses - **Wakefield / Towton** *by* Philip A. Haigh
Wars of the Roses - **Barnet** *by* David Clark
Wars of the Roses - **Tewkesbury** *by* Steven Goodchild
Wars of the Roses - **The Battles of St Albans** *by*
Peter Burley, Michael Elliott & Harvey Wilson
English Civil War - **Naseby** *by* Martin Marix Evans, Peter Burton
and Michael Westaway
English Civil War - **Marston Moor** *by* David Clark
War of the Spanish Succession - **Blenheim 1704** *by* James Falkner
War of the Spanish Succession - **Ramillies 1706** *by* James Falkner
Napoleonic - **Hougoumont** *by* Julian Paget and Derek Saunders
Napoleonic - **Waterloo** *by* Andrew Uffindell and Michael Corum
Zulu War - **Isandlwana** *by* Ian Knight and Ian Castle
Zulu War - **Rorkes Drift** *by* Ian Knight and Ian Castle
Boer War - **The Relief of Ladysmith** *by* Lewis Childs
Boer War - **The Siege of Ladysmith** *by* Lewis Childs
Boer War - **Kimberley** *by* Lewis Childs

Mons *by* Jack Horsfall and Nigel Cave
Néry *by* Patrick Tackle
Le Cateau *by* Nigel Cave and Jack Shelden
Walking the Salient *by* Paul Reed
Ypres - **Sanctuary Wood and Hooge** *by* Nigel Cave
Ypres - **Hill 60** *by* Nigel Cave
Ypres - **Messines Ridge** *by* Peter Oldham
Ypres - **Polygon Wood** *by* Nigel Cave
Ypres - **Passchendaele** *by* Nigel Cave
Ypres - **Airfields and Airmen** *by* Mike O'Connor
Ypres - **St Julien** *by* Graham Keech
Walking the Somme *by* Paul Reed
Somme - **Gommecourt** *by* Nigel Cave
Somme - **Serre** *by* Jack Horsfall & Nigel Cave
Somme - **Beaumont Hamel** *by* Nigel Cave
Somme - **Thiepval** *by* Michael Stedman
Somme - **La Boisselle** *by* Michael Stedman
Somme - **Fricourt** *by* Michael Stedman
Somme - **Carnoy-Montauban** *by* Graham Maddocks
Somme - **Pozières** *by* Graham Keech
Somme - **Courcelette** *by* Paul Reed
Somme - **Boom Ravine** *by* Trevor Pidgeon
Somme - **Mametz Wood** *by* Michael Renshaw
Somme - **Delville Wood** *by* Nigel Cave
Somme - **Advance to Victory (North) 1918** *by* Michael Stedman
Somme - **Flers** *by* Trevor Pidgeon
Somme - **Bazentin Ridge** *by* Edward Hancock
Somme - **Combles** *by* Paul Reed
Somme - **Beaucourt** *by* Michael Renshaw
Somme - **Redan Ridge** *by* Michael Renshaw
Somme - **Hamel** *by* Peter Pedersen
Somme - **Villers-Bretonneux** *by* Peter Pedersen
Somme - **Airfields and Airmen** *by* Mike O'Connor
Airfields and Airmen of the Channel Coast *by* Mike O'Connor
In the Footsteps of the Red Baron *by* Mike O'Connor
Arras - **Airfields and Airmen** *by* Mike O'Connor
Arras - **The Battle for Vimy Ridge** *by* Jack Shelden & Nigel Cave
Arras - **Vimy Ridge** *by* Nigel Cave
Arras - **Gavrelle** *by* Trevor Tasker and Kyle Tallett
Arras - **Oppy Wood** *by* David Bilton
Arras - **Bullecourt** *by* Graham Keech
Arras - **Monchy le Preux** *by* Colin Fox
Walking Arras *by* Paul Reed
Hindenburg Line *by* Peter Oldham
Hindenburg Line - **Epehy** *by* Bill Mitchinson
Hindenburg Line - **Riqueval** *by* Bill Mitchinson
Hindenburg Line - **Villers-Plouich** *by* Bill Mitchinson
Hindenburg Line - **Cambrai Right Hook** *by* Jack Horsfall & Nigel Cave

Hindenburg Line - **Cambrai Flesquières** *by* Jack Horsfall & Nigel Cave
Hindenburg Line - **Saint Quentin** *by* Helen McPhail and Philip Guest
Hindenburg Line - **Bourlon Wood** *by* Jack Horsfall & Nigel Cave
Cambrai - **Airfields and Airmen** *by* Mike O'Connor
Aubers Ridge *by* Edward Hancock
La Bassée - **Neuve Chapelle** *by* Geoffrey Bridger
Loos - **Hohenzollern Redoubt** *by* Andrew Rawson
Loos - **Hill 70** *by* Andrew Rawson
Fromelles *by* Peter Pedersen
Accrington Pals Trail *by* William Turner
Poets at War: Wilfred Owen *by* Helen McPhail and Philip Guest
Poets at War: Edmund Blunden *by* Helen McPhail and Philip Guest
Poets at War: Graves & Sassoon *by* Helen McPhail and Philip Guest
Gallipoli *by* Nigel Steel
Gallipoli - **Gully Ravine** *by* Stephen Chambers
Gallipoli - **Anzac Landing** *by* Stephen Chambers
Gallipoli - **Landings at Helles** *by* Huw & Jill Rodge
Walking the Italian Front *by* Francis Mackay
Italy - **Asiago** *by* Francis Mackay
Verdun: Fort Douamont *by* Christina Holstein
Walking Verdun *by* Christina Holstein
Zeebrugge & Ostend Raids 1918 *by* Stephen McGreal

Germans at Beaumont Hamel *by* Jack Shelden
Germans at Thiepval *by* Jack Shelden

SECOND WORLD WAR

Dunkirk *by* Patrick Wilson
Calais *by* Jon Cooksey
Boulogne *by* Jon Cooksey
Saint-Nazaire *by* James Dorrian
Normandy - **Pegasus Bridge/Merville Battery** *by* Carl Shilleto
Normandy - **Utah Beach** *by* Carl Shilleto
Normandy - **Omaha Beach** *by* Tim Kilvert-Jones
Normandy - **Gold Beach** *by* Christopher Dunphie & Garry Johnson
Normandy - **Gold Beach Jig** *by* Tim Saunders
Normandy - **Juno Beach** *by* Tim Saunders
Normandy - **Sword Beach** *by* Tim Kilvert-Jones
Normandy - **Operation Bluecoat** *by* Ian Daglish
Normandy - **Operation Goodwood** *by* Ian Daglish
Normandy - **Epsom** *by* Tim Saunders
Normandy - **Hill 112** *by* Tim Saunders
Normandy - **Mont Pinçon** *by* Eric Hunt
Normandy - **Cherbourg** *by* Andrew Rawson
Das Reich – **Drive to Normandy** *by* Philip Vickers
Oradour *by* Philip Beck
Market Garden - **Nijmegen** *by* Tim Saunders
Market Garden - **Hell's Highway** *by* Tim Saunders
Market Garden - **Arnhem, Oosterbeek** *by* Frank Steer
Market Garden - **Arnhem, The Bridge** *by* Frank Steer
Market Garden - **The Island** *by* Tim Saunders
Rhine Crossing – US 9th Army & 17th US Airborne *by* Andrew Rawson
British Rhine Crossing – **Operation Varsity** *by* Tim Saunders
British Rhine Crossing – **Operation Plunder** *by* Tim Saunders
Battle of the Bulge – **St Vith** *by* Michael Tolhurst
Battle of the Bulge – **Bastogne** *by* Michael Tolhurst
Channel Islands *by* George Forty
Walcheren *by* Andrew Rawson
Remagen Bridge *by* Andrew Rawson
Cassino *by* Ian Blackwell
Anzio *by* Ian Blackwell
Dieppe *by* Tim Saunders
Fort Eben Emael *by* Tim Saunders
Crete – **The Airborne Invasion** *by* Tim Saunders
Malta *by* Paul Williams

THE PENINSULAR WAR
A Battlefield Guide

ANDREW RAWSON

Battleground

Pen & Sword
MILITARY

First published in Great Britain in 2009 by
Pen & Sword Military
an imprint of
Pen & Sword Books Ltd
47 Church Street
Barnsley
South Yorkshire
S70 2AS

ISBN 9781844159215

Typeset in Palatino 10pt

Printed and bound in the United Kingdom by CPI

Pen & Sword Books Ltd incorporates the Imprints of Pen & Sword
Aviation, Pen & Sword Maritime, Pen & Sword Military, Wharncliffe
Local History, Pen & Sword Select, Pen & Sword Military Classics
and Leo Cooper.
For a complete list of Pen & Sword titles please contact
PEN & SWORD BOOKS LIMITED
47 Church Street, Barnsley, South Yorkshire, S70 2AS, England
E-mail: enquiries@pen-and-sword.co.uk
Website: www.pen-and-sword.co.uk

CONTENTS

Introduction: Background to the Peninsular War...................... 6

Chapter 1.   Wellington's First Expedition to Portugal..................... 35

Chapter 2.   Sir John Moore's Expedition into Spain..................... 51

Chapter 3.   Wellesley Returns to the Peninsula..................... 73

Chapter 4.   The Withdrawal into Portugal..................... 97

Chapter 5.   Sallying Forth from Portugal..................... 131

Chapter 6.   Opening the Roads into Spain..................... 169

Chapter 7.   Advancing Deep into Spain..................... 199

Chapter 8.   Driving the French from Spain..................... 227

Chapter 9.   The French Attacks in the Pyrenees..................... 247

Chapter 10. Securing the Pyrenees..................... 371

Chapter 11. The Advance to Bayonne..................... 295

Chapter 12. The Final Campaign in France..................... 321

Further Reading..................... 343

Index..................... 345

Wellington and Nelson in the waiting room at the Colonial Office, September 1805.

INTRODUCTION:
BACKGROUND TO THE
PENINSULAR WAR

B Y JULY 1807 NAPOLEON'S armies had defeated Austria, Prussia and Russia, leaving the French in a dominant position across Europe. The signing of the Tilsit treaty and an alliance with Russia allowed the Emperor to turn his attentions to the Iberian peninsula. Some believed that greed and ambition drove him to take Spain and Portugal, but Napoleon himself firmly believed his decision was based on strategic and economic reasons. He did, however, fail to appreciate the military and political difficulties of conquering the area.

Spain had been allied to the French cause, and in 1805 Napoleon had used the Spanish fleet to help his navy take on the British. His attempt to break London's naval supremacy ended in disaster, however, when his ships clashed with Admiral Lord Nelson's fleet off the Spanish coast at Cap de Trafalgar. The British then partially destroyed the Danish fleet at Copenhagen and took the rest of the ships to England, which meant that Napoleon would not be able to secure naval supremacy. Thus he was obliged to follow a land-based strategy and his first step was to introduce the 'Continental System', effectively an embargo on British exports. London responded by ordering its navy to impose a blockade around Europe, a decision that would eventually lead to a war with the United States in 1812. Although the French embargo was enforced across many countries, Portugal did not take part and Spain only half-heartedly applied the rules, to Napoleon's annoyance. The Iberian peninsula was the only gap in the Continental System and it needed to be closed before England's markets benefited.

France and Spain had been on good terms until Manuel de Godoy, First Minister to King Carlos VI, called on the Spanish people to rally against an unspecified enemy. It was a thinly veiled attack on France but the statement was quickly withdrawn after the resounding French victory at Jena. But Napoleon would not forget the threat and as French troops gathered along the Spanish border throughout 1807, he decided to deal with Portugal first while Spain was left to contemplate its fate.

Although France and Spain put pressure on Portugal to join the Continental System, she was reluctant to obey, fearing that Britain would seize her South American colonies in retaliation. Portugal's Prince Regent, John, remained friendly but uncooperative and evasive, much to the exasperation of the Emperor, who took steps to involve Spain more closely by drawing up the secret Treaty of Fontainebleau, an agreement to partition Portugal.

Meanwhile, the Spanish king was troubled by intrigue and plots to seize his throne, and although Prince Fernando was temporarily imprisoned, the problems increased in the autumn months. While Madrid concentrated on its internal crisis, Napoleon made his move as Marshal Junot led 25,000 French troops across the border and marched across Spain. By the end of November they had taken Lisbon, as the Prince Regent fled to Brazil. Portugal's army was unable to offer resistance and attempts by the people to rebel were crushed.

Fernando VII was determined to get Napoleon's support during his short reign in 1808.

Napoleon was pleased with the ease with which Portugal had fallen and he now turned his attentions to Spain; the time to deal with Godoy had arrived. Taking control of Spain would finally put a stop to British trade with Europe, while his new ally would provide a welcome source of fresh recruits; he could also introduce his system of government to raise money. It seemed that seizing control of the Iberian peninsula would be an easy task for his experienced armies and the Emperor confidently remarked: 'If I thought it would cost me 80,000 men I would not attempt it, but it will cost me no more than 12,000.'

During Napoleon's early years in power Count Charles Talleyrand-Périgord, a skilful diplomat, had taken part in negotiations with many European countries and had usually been able to fulfil his Emperor's wishes without resorting to conflict. However, relations between the two men had deteriorated following the alliance with Russia, and Talleyrand finally resigned over the decision to take control of Spain. Although the Spanish army was weak, undermined by poor leadership, corruption and a shortage of funding, the government was still popular and the Catholic Church had a huge influence over the people. Talleyrand was concerned that a sense of national pride and religious fervour would motivate many to rise up and oppose the invaders. He also feared that a disastrous campaign on the Iberian peninsula could bring down the whole empire.

Despite the warnings of his experienced adviser, Napoleon decided to take on the Spanish military, and another 70,000 French troops massed along the border as Godoy's attempts to negotiate a peaceful diplomatic solution were ignored. On 16 February 1808 Napoleon's troops went into action, seizing the passes through the Pyrenees and the city of Barcelona, paving the way for an invasion of Spain.

Godoy responded by recalling Spanish troops from Portugal to defend the capital, and advising the royal family to flee. He was right to be cautious, as riots erupted when the news of the French invasion broke. But Prince Fernando's patience finally snapped and he dismissed the meddling minister, ordering him to be taken into custody to remove him from the political scene; this act probably saved his life, as it kept him out of the reach of angry lynch mobs.

The Spanish capital was now in turmoil and as Marshal Joachim Murat led 20,000 troops into the city, Fernando was invited to cross the French border for discussions at Bayonne. It was a political trap. When he refused to accept that he was going to be replaced by an imperial prince, his parents, King Carlos and Queen Maria Luisa, and Godoy were invited to join the negotiations. Napoleon played on the earlier palace intrigues and finally forced Fernando to abdicate while Carlos himself surrendered the throne.

By early May 1808 Spain was under Napoleon's rule but as he handed over control of the throne to his elder brother Joseph, Talleyrand's fears of a public outcry were realised. Murat had also been arguing with the regency junta appointed to control Madrid during Fernando's absence. The crowds finally took to the streets in protest against the occupation on 2 May and the French troops responded violently, killing many civilians. The province of Asturias called up over 18,000 men and declared war on France, and other provinces followed suit; before long the whole of Spain had risen against the invaders.

While Murat's reserve remained at Madrid the French armies began to tackle each area in turn, but they soon discovered that they only controlled the areas they occupied, while sieges tied up large numbers of troops. While the British expeditionary force was being assembled the Spanish inflicted several defeats on Napoleon's trained troops. The city of Zaragoza under the leadership of José Palafox y Melzi held out stoutly, and the French troops were forced to abandon the siege on two occasions. Gerona was also strongly defended, while Spanish troops in Valencia forced Marshal Bon-Adrien-Jeannot de Moncey's army to fall back. The first French victory came at Medina de Río Seco, north of Valladolid, in July but a few days later General Pierre Dupont's army was defeated at Bailén in Andalusia and over 18,000 French troops were captured by a smaller Spanish army. Napoleon was furious, complaining that 'there has never been anything so stupid, so foolish and so cowardly since the world began'.

The Emperor's plan for an early victory now lay in ruins and at the end of the summer Joseph and most of the French troops left Madrid and headed north, leaving the Spanish in control of three-quarters of their country. Over 40,000 French troops had been killed, injured or captured and doubtless Napoleon's early boast came back to haunt him. It was the start of five and half years of war in which Spain and Portugal would be ravaged while soldiers and civilians alike died of injuries and sickness. The campaigns across the Iberian peninsula would be a constant drain on the French armies and Napoleon would eventually call them his 'Spanish Ulcer'.

THE ARMIES

The British Army

Sir Arthur Wellesley, Duke of Wellington, fought the 1808 campaign in Portugal with only 18,700 troops organised into nine infantry brigades. Due to a lack of horses, he had only 500 cavalry and just three batteries of guns, a shortage that would plague the British for several years. By the time of the Talavera campaign the following year, the number of troops had risen to over 20,000 grouped into four infantry divisions and one cavalry division, but Wellington could still not count on reliable support from the Spanish armies and the Portuguese troops would not be ready for another year.

By the autumn of 1810 Wellington had seven divisions and three independent brigades operating under his command. The number of

Portuguese troops had risen to over 26,000, making up about half of his army, and their steady performance at Buçaco proved that their training had been a worthwhile investment.

Another two divisions had been added by the autumn of 1811 while the number of cavalry had risen to 6,500, and Wellington could confidently withdraw his army to the safety of the Lines of Torres Vedras if he felt threatened. In the summer of 1812 nearly 52,000 British and Portuguese troops engaged and defeated Marshal André Masséna's army at Salamanca.

In November 1812 Wellington accepted the Spanish authorities' offer to command their armies and the following spring he led his forces across the Portuguese border for the last time, knowing that he had over 120,000 men under his command. Nine divisions, numbering over 79,000 men, defeated Joseph's armies at Vitoria in June 1813 and by the end of the year they had crossed the Pyrenees and entered France. Wellington took the decision to leave many Spanish troops behind, fearing widespread looting and a rise in guerrilla activity, and although his army was thus reduced to fewer than 50,000 men, the inexperienced French conscripts were no match for his veterans.

The Portuguese Army

The Portuguese army had been underfunded and understrength when Marshal Jean-Andoche Junot's army entered the country in December 1808. It was disbanded over the winter and many troops were marched away to serve under the French; many of these later deserted. Some units tried to reform when the British Expeditionary Force arrived, and although Wellington was offered command of these troops, he turned it down.

The energetic General William Beresford was subsequently offered the post in the spring of 1809 and he soon found that the Portuguese army was in a chaotic state, its officers mostly elderly and incapable, promoted by dint of their political connections. Promotion was irregular and arbitrary while pay was very low; corruption was rife at all levels. Beresford soon discovered that the army only numbered around 30,000 regular troops, less than half the size it should have been, so he quickly introduced conscription to bring the numbers up to full strength. Many incompetent officers were removed and British officers took command of poorly performing units while senior officers toured the army, passing on their skills to the Portuguese.

Over the next two years the reorganisation of the Portuguese forces continued unmolested behind the Lines of Torres Vedras, and by 1811 the Portuguese units were ready to serve alongside Wellington at Buçaco. Between 1812 and 1814 they served effectively in most battles and most British divisions had a Portuguese brigade; Portuguese artillery also supplemented the British guns. By the end of the war Portuguese troops formed around 40 per cent of the British army.

Portuguese militia units, led by civilians or by officers expelled from the regular army, were under strict orders not to engage in large-scale combat. Instead, militia outposts watched frontiers and harassed French lines of communication when they crossed the border, attacking detachments, capturing convoys and rounding up stragglers. The Lines of Torres Vedras were manned by militia units. The men did not have uniforms and few units were fully armed.

The Ordenança were companies of levies that were used to prevent the French troops from foraging. Most were armed only with pikes but they waged a murderous guerrilla war against the invaders.

The Spanish Army

By the autumn of 1808 over 200,000 Spanish men had rallied to defend their country against the French and as the ranks of existing regiments were filled, the provincial juntas raised new units. Although there was no shortage of numbers, a lack of funds and interminable political wrangling meant that the conscripts and volunteers were poorly equipped. Robert Blakeney commented:

> Courage was never wanting in Spanish soldiers. They were left barefoot, ragged and half-starved. In this deplorable state they were brought into the field under leaders many of whom were scarcely competent to command a sergeant's outlying picquet.

Leadership was also lacking. Experienced officers might be overlooked because of their political views, while inexperienced but politically well-connected officers were promoted. Wellington later commented:

> The Spaniards make excellent soldiers. What spoils them is that they have no confidence in their officers — this would ruin any soldiers — and how should the Spaniards have confidence in such officers as theirs?

Divisions contained a mixture of old and new regular units and a range of militia units, and although there were plenty of foot soldiers, cavalry and artillery were always in short supply. As well as the Army of the

Centre, they were grouped into regional armies, based in Aragon, Galicia, Extremadura, Catalonia and Granada, and strengths ranged from 11,500 to over 37,000 men. Spanish troops served under Wellington's command after 1809 but Cuesta's 35,000 troops behaved poorly at Talavera, severely damaging the relationship between the British and Spanish commanders.

By the summer of 1811 the number of men serving had fallen to fewer than 100,000 and the Spanish armies were reorganised and numbered as follows: First Army in Catalonia, Second Army in Valencia, Third Army in Murcia, Fourth Army in Andalusia, Fifth Army in Estremadura and Sixth Army in Galicia. The Seventh, Eighth and Ninth Armies were the guerrilla forces fighting across north-east Spain. Despite the reorganisation, poor leadership and poor discipline continued to plague the Spanish troops.

The Sixth Army from Galicia and the Army Reserve from Andalusia, some 30,000 men in all, took part in the 1813 Vitoria campaign but only a small number were engaged in the battle. Only 10,000 Spanish troops entered France after the British army crossed the Pyrenees due to fears of pillaging when the authorities failed to pay the men. Wellington's complaints illustrate the difficulties he faced:

> The discipline of the Spanish armies is in the very lowest state; and their efficiency is, consequently, much deteriorated. Neither officers nor troops having been paid for months, nay, some for years, it cannot be expected that the troops should be in very good order . . . not only are your armies undisciplined and inefficient, and both officers and soldiers insubordinate for want of pay, provisions, clothing, and necessaries, and the consequent endurance of misery for a long period of time, but the habits of indiscipline are such, that even those corps that have been clothed and regularly paid by my directions . . . are in as bad a state.

The French Army

The number of French troops engaged in the peninsula varied tremendously, increasing during the early years as extensive attempts were made to suppress the entire country. Numbers began to fall when Napoleon's interest dwindled and his reserves were recalled to support the Russian campaign in 1812. Thereafter the numbers dropped quickly owing to further reductions, sickness and casualties. The number of troops available for active campaigning fell dramatically as the number of troops required to fight the Spanish guerrillas, as well as maintain garrisons and lines of communication, increased.

When Wellington's expeditionary force landed in Portugal there were some 165,000 French soldiers deployed across the Iberian peninsula. Of these, some 24,900 troops were deployed around Lisbon, while 24,400 troops confronted the Spanish army in Andalusia. There were 12,700 troops around Barcelona and 29,300 troops in Valencia along the east coast, while 19,000 troops covered the northern provinces. Although there was only a small reserve of 6,400 troops at Madrid, another 48,000 troops were scattered in small garrisons across the country.

By the time Sir John Moore's army left the following January, the French army had seven active corps organised into twenty-seven divisions, four reserve cavalry divisions and a reserve at Madrid. However, of the 286,000 soldiers under arms, some 56,000 were sick and another 36,000 were scattered in small garrisons and detachments across the country. This meant that only two corps, supported by two cavalry divisions and half of the Madrid garrison, were free to confront Wellington at Talavera in July 1809.

By 1811 Joseph had grouped his troops into six armies. The Army of the South was tied up around Cadiz and along the southern section of the border with Portugal, while the Army of Portugal held northern Extremadura. The Army of Catalonia and the Army of Aragon were still engaged around Barcelona while the Army of the North remained dispersed across the northern provinces. Again the number of men available for action was limited by sickness and garrison duty. Although Joseph's forces had increased to 354,000 soldiers, only 291,000 were available for action and large numbers of them were tied up on garrison duty.

Around 140,000 French troops were withdrawn from Spain in 1812 in order to take part in Napoleon's invasion of Russia, and large numbers of the remainder were still occupied in keeping open the lines of communication; many more reported sick. The remaining troops were divided into six armies. The Army of the North had 42,900 men, but 17,900 of them were either in garrisons or were sick. The Armies of Aragon and Catalonia, deployed across north-east Spain, had some 66,700 men available for active service after deducting detachments and sick, while the Army of the Centre held a reserve of 17,800 men at Madrid. Wellington himself faced the 50,000-strong Army of Portugal during the Salamanca campaign, while General Hill took on Marshal Jean-de-Dieu Soult's Army of the South, which had over 49,000 fit troops, many of which were tied up in front of Cadiz and across Andalusia. In total Joseph's armies numbered over 260,000 men but 35,600 of these were sick while another 11,200 were deployed in isolated detachments.

At the end of the Vitoria campaign Marshal Soult was forced to retire to the safety of the Pyrenees with nine infantry and one cavalry divisions — a total of 99,800 men including the reserve. Numbers declined owing to casualties, desertions and sickness over the winter that followed and by the time he reached Toulouse in April 1814 his army had been reduced to just 42,000 men.

TACTICS IN THE PENINSULAR WAR

Infantry Tactics

Infantry battalions had three standard formations. The line was for shooting, the column was for manoeuvring and the square was for defence against cavalry. A British battalion of 500—600 men stood in two parallel lines, around 200—250 metres long, and each company covered around 25 metres. French and Spanish battalions deployed in three lines and were proportionally shorter. Men stood almost elbow to elbow but they were able to open their ranks to let other units pass through if they were advancing or retiring.

Battalions from all nations adopted a similar deployment on the battlefield. In the British army, the light company would form up on the battalion's left flank while the grenadier company deployed on the right flank; the eight line companies stood in the centre. The light company would often be out in front, waiting in open order around 200 metres ahead of the battalion, and they would fire at the advancing French columns, skirmishing with the *tirailleurs*, falling back as they came closer.

The two ensigns stood in the centre of the front ranks with their standards, protected by four colour sergeants. The battalion's senior officers were mounted and they stood three paces behind the colour party with the majors and drummers. Company commanders and captains stood alongside the right end of their companies while the subalterns (junior officers) and their sergeants waited three paces behind their company.

Officers had to anticipate what formation would be required so their men had sufficient time to deploy and face the enemy. The drums would sound formation changes and the junior officers and sergeants had to keep their men in order while they changed positions. It required discipline and well-drilled training to carry out such instructions in the noise and smoke of battle, and it took a strong will to carry on while their comrades were falling dead and injured around them. Seasoned campaigners knew that the best way to survive was to follow orders, and this they did almost instinctively.

The line was the classic defensive formation and it was used to enable as many weapons as possible to fire at the approaching enemy. A disciplined line would fire a succession of volleys from each rank, delivering a devastating shock of casualties, noise and smoke, unsettling the enemy before they charged. For maximum effect a steady unit would wait until the masses of infantry were less than 100 metres distant before firing; any further away, and few if any of the musket balls would find their target. Company fire involved each company firing in turn, creating a constant ripple effect along the line. The range of the first volley and the speed with which the muskets were reloaded were critical; a veteran unit could be ready to fire its second volley at point-blank range.

Sometimes the enemy would also deploy into line and a prolonged firefight would ensue, with each side trying to shoot the other into submission. Usually though, one side or the other would waver and the other would rapidly fix bayonets and charge, accompanied by loud shouting and cheering, intended to unsettle the enemy.

Columns were a single company, or 20 metres wide. Companies could be as far apart as twenty paces or as close as three paces, according to circumstance. They typically deployed five paces apart or quarter distance, because at this distance it only took two minutes to expand out into line or half that time to form square. A 500—600-strong battalion created a 50 metre long column; the grenadier company always led and the light company brought up the rear unless it was skirmishing. Officers and sergeants marched in front of their companies while the colour party and the senior officers were positioned at the head of the column.

The square was the typical formation for defence against cavalry. The two leading companies formed the front wall while the two rear companies turned around and formed the back; the middle companies split in half, turning left and right to complete the square. Alternatively the leading company would stand its ground and the rear company would about face, while the centre companies split into two and turned to left and right to form the sides of a rectangle. The men of the front rank would kneel with their muskets planted by their feet and their bayonets pointing up to form a wall of steel. The second (and third) ranks would fire their muskets at passing cavalry. Horses were reluctant to charge at the wall of men and would shy away if riders tried to bring them to close quarters. The square's main danger came from the horse artillery accompanying the cavalry. If the gun crews were brave enough to bring up their guns within canister range, the square would be decimated.

Many times, particularly during the early years of the war, the French commanders in Spain had to decide what formation their troops would use to attack the enemy. The manuals dictated that they should advance in column for speed and then change into line formation close to the enemy. Concentrated artillery fire and swarms of skirmishers would have already reduced the enemy's morale and the charge would finish them off. However, Wellington's reverse-slope tactics deprived the French of these advantages and they were usually faced by a wall of fresh troops just beyond the crest of the hill, all of them loaded and ready to fire. The late deployment into line did, however, leave the advancing troops exposed to fire for about two minutes, enough for a couple of volleys from disciplined troops. Changing formation and returning fire effectively were difficult to coordinate across the division. Their own troops would be disrupted if it happened too late and it would delay the advance if it happened too soon. It was also difficult to judge how much space was needed to accommodate the different frontages between columns and lines.

When the Colonne d'attaque par division was used, the skirmishers led the way, some 100 metres in front. Battalion columns followed, typically two companies wide and three companies deep, or 50 metres square; companies were arrayed in three ranks. The light company deployed to the left rear while the grenadier company was to the right rear. Standards and sergeants were with the front rank while the drummers accompanied the centre companies. The centre companies could turn to the flanks while the rear companies turned around if the battalion needed to form square quickly. Similarly, the battalion line had three companies deployed on either side of the standards in three ranks, covering around 125 metres. Each company had two sections and two companies formed a division.

Although many different formations were used in the battles across Spain and Portugal, the type of attack most fundamentally associated with the Peninsular War was the French column attacking the British line. What follows is an account of a typical advance, illustrating the dead-ground tactics used so successfully by the Duke of Wellington and the difficulties that the French marshals faced in trying to defeat them.

A French division deployed around 1,500 metres from the British line, out of reach of the cavalry and beyond the maximum range of the medium and light artillery. When the general received his orders, he rode to the front of the massed columns and gave the signal to begin the long march. Meanwhile, the British infantry watched impassively as the sea of blue uniforms under their eagles and tricolours advanced to the sounds of drums and brass instruments.

To begin with the troops were eager and confident as they marched forward in lines of companies. The British artillery, which usually amounted to only a few guns in front of each division, was busy firing cannon-balls at the columns, but these caused few casualties, although they did worry some of the inexperienced men. Meanwhile, order was compromised as the soldiers were forced to negotiate walls, gorse bushes, olive groves and stream-beds. Thomas Bugeaud, a French *chef-de-batallion* in 1812, explained how the long march unsettled the men:

> When we got to about a thousand yards from the English line the men would begin to get restless and excited: they exchanged ideas with one another, their march began to be somewhat precipitate, and was already growing a little disorderly. Meanwhile the English, silent and impassive, with grounded arms, loomed like a long red wall; their aspect was imposing [and] impressed novices not a little.

The French soldiers' countered their nervousness with bravado as they marched closer but the numbers of men falling was increasing as the British artillery crews increased their rate of fire, forcing the column to close ranks. Meanwhile, the British line suffered few casualties from the long-range French cannonade:

> Soon the distance began to grow shorter: cries of '*Vive I'Empereur'* and '*en avant a la batonnette'* broke from our mass. Some men hoisted their shakos on their muskets, the quick-step became a run, the ranks began to be mixed up, the men's agitation became tumultuous and many soldiers began to fire as they ran. And all the while the red English line, still silent and motionless, even when we were only 300 yards away, seemed to take no notice of the storm which was about to beat upon it.

The British artillery gunners were also able to fire a final round of grapeshot or canister at the advancing column and the blast felled many of the leading ranks, causing mayhem and terror among the survivors. Meanwhile the gunners, their work done, would run behind the solid red line of infantry and take shelter. By now the confidence of the men in the steady line was in complete contrast to the confused ranks of the advancing column, a fact that did not go unnoticed:

> The contrast was striking. More than one among us began to reflect that the enemy's fire, so long reserved, would be very unpleasant when it did break forth. Our ardour began to cool: the morale influence (irresistible in action) of a calm which seems undisturbed as opposed to disorder which strives to make up by noise what it lacks in firmness, weighed heavily on our hearts.

As casualties mounted, and French officers struggled to get their men to advance towards the thin red line, the English officers gave the order to fire and the carnage began:

> At this moment of painful expectation the English line would make a quarter-turn, the muskets going up to the ready. An indefinable sensation nailed to the spot many of our men, who halted and opened a wavering fire. The enemy's return, a volley of simultaneous precision and deadly effect, crashed in upon us like a thunderbolt. Decimated by it we reeled together, staggering under the blow and trying to recover our equilibrium.

The noise was tremendous and the thick cloud of smoke created by several hundred muskets added to the confusion as the French column reeled. Many in the front ranks would have been killed or maimed, and the following ranks had to push forward over their bodies to advance. Others, particularly inexperienced soldiers, were rooted to the spot by the shock while others fell back, further unsettling the ranks behind.

The column had been halted and its men were either dead, injured or in a state of confusion. All that was left was for the British line to deliver the final blow in the form of a controlled charge:

> Then three formidable 'Hurrahs' terminated the long silence of our adversaries. With the third they were down upon us, pressing us into a disorderly retreat. But to our great surprise, they did not pursue their advantage for more than some hundred yards, and went back with calm to their former lines, to await another attack.

It was a scene that was frequently repeated on the battlefields of the Peninsular War.

Cavalry Tactics

In the early part of the war Wellington suffered from a lack of cavalry. A lack of experienced troopers meant that many were unable to care for their horses properly, severely hampering the effectiveness of mounted squadrons. Both sides quickly learnt that Spanish and Portuguese horses were virtually useless for combat purposes, being too small and weak to carry a heavily armed trooper, and new mounts for the British forces had to be sent over from England.

The plateau of central Spain, and the lowlands of Old Castile and Leon offered plenty of opportunities for mounted engagements but elsewhere the mountainous terrain reduced the cavalry to a supporting role. This meant that Wellington only needed a small mounted force, and while some units scouted for the enemy or information, the remainder protected his flanks and his rear.

The high mountain ranges and poor climate made cavalry a liability in some areas due to the lack of natural fodder. The limited amount of fodder that was available was poor and troopers were sometimes reduced to feeding their mounts on chopped straw and green maize — a deadly diet for the horses. Wellington was forced to request deliveries of hay and oats from England so that his mounts could rest in quarters near the sea during the winter months and regain their strength.

Cavalry leadership was often an issue and squadrons tended to break into an uncontrolled pursuit after delivering a successful charge, rather than returning to regroup. The undisciplined nature of the cavalry sometimes led to disaster and usually deprived Wellington of his reserve. He was often unable to pursue a defeated enemy owing to his lack of rested cavalry at the end of the battle. Wellington was not impressed by the tactical abilities of his senior officers and he outlined the problems he faced in a letter to Lord John Russell written years afterward:

> Our cavalry are so inferior to the French from want of order, that although I considered one of our squadrons a match for two French, yet I did not care to see four British opposed to four French, and still more so as the numbers increased, and order became more necessary. They could gallop, but could not preserve their order.

The cavalry was divided into three categories. The heavy cavalry included the cuirassiers and the carabineers, who wore helmets and breastplates and were armed with swords. Dragoons were also armed with carbines, but they were trained to dismount and engage the enemy on foot. The light cavalry did not wear armour. The hussars and *châsseurs à cheval* were armed with sabres, while lancers carried the deadly lance.

A typical regiment had around 450 officers and troopers organised into three squadrons. At the start of the battle the regiment would be deployed in a close column of squadrons, a tight formation around 40 metres wide and 30 metres deep that was easy to control. The troopers were arranged in half squadron (troop) lines with about 15cm between boots; the lines were half a horse's length apart. The squadron commanders and their subordinates were at the left of the line while senior NCOs deployed in the centre and on the right.

Cavalry regiments fought in lines but it was difficult to maintain control and even the smallest terrain feature would create disorder among the lines of horsemen. Squadrons often deployed in lines of two troops about 250 metres wide or in double lines with one squadron in reserve, narrowing the formation to 150 metres wide. Regiments sometimes attacked in echelons, with squadrons stepped back from left to right or vice versa for staggered attacks, or in chequered line with the centre squadron following the rest of the regiment.

There were very few cavalry against cavalry clashes and one of the few major decisive cavalry actions was the charge of General John Henry Le Marchant's heavy brigade at Salamanca. A successful cavalry charge could wreak chaos in the enemy lines but it took skill and discipline to deliver. The charge started at the walk while the officers and troopers dressed ranks then the whole squadron broke into a trot to maintain order. Horses were spurred into a canter when the unit was as close as 250 metres from the enemy and the speed increased to the full gallop over the final 80 metres. Everyone had to follow the squadron commander and maintain dressing, and faster horses had to be restrained to maximise the shock of the impact.

Mounted units were ordered to advance towards an approaching charge because a line of stationary horses would be scattered immediately; many charges were delivered and received at the trot. Although the two lines seemed as if they would hit head on as the charge came to its climax, some of the horses would swerve to one side and one or other side would break off its charge and become disordered. Individual combats would then begin as the officers and men cut and parried with their sabres.

A successful unit would let a few troopers pursue the broken enemy, but officers were instructed to rally as many men as possible and lead them back to their own lines so they could reform and rest their horses. If a unit failed to break the enemy, the officers and men had to retire as quickly as possible and regroup while the supports went forward.

If cavalry charged into disordered infantry, the rampaging horsemen would rapidly kill or scatter the foot-soldiers. However, a well-formed and disciplined square was impenetrable and riders would not be able to get their horses close to the wall of bayonets. The only solution was to bring up horse artillery so they could unlimber at close range and blast the squares with canister or grapeshot.

Artillery Tactics

Artillery pieces from the Napoleonic era were smooth-bore, muzzle-loading weapons with brass or iron barrels mounted on wooden carriages. The type of cannon depended on the size of the projectile, and while British and Portuguese foot batteries had 6- and 9-pounders, the French had 6- and 12-pounders. The guns were organised into batteries of six or eight guns and they were transported by horse-drawn limbers. Horse artillery had smaller calibre pieces and the crews were mounted so that the battery could keep pace with the cavalry.

Gun crews were led by the commander, who gave orders and aimed the gun; after firing the spongeman cleaned out the barrel with a damp cloth to extinguish any sparks. The loader then put a powder cartridge into the barrel, followed by the chosen projectile. Once the spongeman had rammed home the projectile, the ventsman primed the cartridge ready for the last member of the crew to light the cartridge with a smouldering cord, known as a portfire.

Artillery fired roundshot at long range, aimed low in front of the enemy in the hope that the solid iron balls would bounce though several ranks of men. Soft ground reduced its effect. Canister, also known as case-shot, comprised a thin tin cylinder filled with musket balls and was used at short range. The container disintegrated when it was fired, spraying the immediate area with projectiles like a shotgun. Guns could be loaded with two canisters to increase their effectiveness. Shell was a hollow ball filled with gunpowder, and lit by a fuse. Howitzers fired the shells high in the air, and the perfect shot exploded just above the enemy; such shells were often used during sieges as they could cause havoc inside the walls. Shrapnel consisted of a hollow sphere filled with musket balls. A fuse burst the thin iron casing, scattering musket balls all around. Again, crews tried to time their shot so that it exploded above a dense column or square.

French generals tended to deploy a large number of their batteries opposite the part of the enemy line they intended to attack. A prolonged bombardment with roundshot would cause casualties among the enemy before the skirmishers moved in to pick off their officers. The enemy would be disordered and their morale low by the time the infantry columns moved up.

During the early years of the war Wellington suffered from a shortage of artillery — indeed, he had less than one British battery for each of his divisions in 1809. Many Portuguese batteries joined after 1810. Wellington often preferred to deploy his guns in batteries or sections along his line ready to fire at the advancing enemy.

Siege Warfare

Wellington was involved in several sieges in the Peninsular War and they were all bloody affairs. The Corps of Royal Engineers had only a small number of officers and siege works in Spain were left to a handful of junior officers who were responsible for planning and supervising a variety of projects ranging from surveying terrain, maintaining lines of communication, building fortifications, bridging rivers and supervising sieges. Partly trained temporary 'assistant engineers' from other units helped to supervise the work while the rank-and-file came from the Royal Military Artificers. The Royal Staff Corps also provided a number of officers who had trained both as infantry and engineers; they worked directly for the army rather than for the Master-General of Ordnance and they specialised in supervising large gangs of infantry working as labourers. Engineering was a dangerous task and many men were killed or injured as they worked long hours under heavy fire.

Spanish castles had been built in the days before gunpowder and some were located near hills that were suitable for gun batteries. In such cases the garrison would dig earthworks on these hills in order to delay the siege and keep scouts at bay. They served as useful observation posts and had to be cleared before the siege could begin. With any siege, Wellington himself would first survey the castle walls with his chief engineer before he decided on a plan of attack. Guns had to be sited so they had a clear line of sight to the wall, and decisions had to be made about how his troops would approach the breach when the time came for the assault. The plan was often dictated by previous sieges, so the gun crews could target a weaker repaired section. Low sections of curtain wall were also studied to see if ladders could be used to scale them. When possible the perimeter would be attacked from several directions at once, and diversionary attacks were sometimes used to distract the garrison's attentions away from the real threat.

At the beginning of a siege, a covering force usually reached the fortress first, preventing the garrison from leaving and supply trains from entering, a tactic known as investing. The main force arrived soon afterwards, followed by the siege train, and then work began in earnest. A series of parallel trenches connected by saps was dug by the infantry, supervised by engineers, and the work was hated by everyone, Rifleman John Kincaid included: 'One day's trench-work is as like another as the days themselves; and like nothing better than serving an apprenticeship to the double calling of grave digger and gamekeeper, for we found ample employment both for the spade and the rifle.'

Trenches were dug in a zigzag pattern to prevent the enemy firing into them and battery positions were reinforced by earth-filled baskets called gabions and bundles of wood called fascines; sandbags were soon added. The final siege of Badajoz needed over 2,700 gabions, 1,450 fascines and 20,000 sandbags. As soon as the siege-train had been manhandled into position, the crews began to fire at the wall. They often targeted a weak section of curtain wall, hoping that it would fall into the moat below; alternatively, towers or gatehouses were aimed at, in the hope that the hollow structure would collapse. The aim was to create a navigable route across the castle's defences.

The infantry continued to dig assembly trenches leading towards the walls while the artillery bombarded the wall; these trenches were designed to reduce the amount of time the soldiers would be in the open during the assault. All the work had to be carried out under the very noses of the artillery crews on the walls, who fired their cannon from the castle battlements; they were joined by sharpshooters when the earthworks were in range. When the opportunity arose, the garrison sent parties of men out to attack the siege works (known as sallying out); they attacked the labourers and damaged the trenches as much as possible before retiring, taking with them as many prisoners and tools as they could.

Digging the trenches was very labour intensive and the numbers involved in the first, unsuccessful siege of Badajoz with its 5,000-strong garrison give an indication of the amount of activity around the fortress:

8,000 men working around the clock in the trenches, split into four shifts

11,250 men guarding the trenches from counter-attack, split into three shifts

7,700 men making equipment or carrying materials, split into four shifts

The work was supervised by 21 officers of the Royal Engineers, 25 artificers from the Staff Corps, 11 volunteers from the line working as assistant engineers, and over 250 infantrymen who had a few manual skills; the rest of the men were unskilled labourers.

After the siege of Badajoz in 1812, Wellington demanded reforms and the Royal Military Artificers (or Sappers and Miners) was formed in April 1812; it was renamed the Royal Sappers and Miners later that year. In addition, 2,800 rank and file soldiers were trained in engineering at Chatham and then organised in companies, led by Royal Engineer officers. By 1813 over 300 Royal Engineer officers were serving with the Army.

Suitable artillery was always in short supply during the early sieges and a mixture of Spanish cannon dating from the days of the Armada, several Portuguese naval guns and a handful of makeshift mortars were used. Cannonballs were sometimes in short supply and transport capable of hauling the heavy artillery pieces also had to be found and paid for.

The earthworks continued to be built while the cannon kept up a constant bombardment until the breach in the walls was low enough for men to be able to clamber across the rubble slopes and wide enough to let enough men through. The amount of shot and shell consumed was enormous, as the following statistics show:

Over 30,000 24- and 18-pdr roundshot were fired at the walls of Badajoz in seven days

Another 5,000 rounds of grape, case and shell were fired at the garrison

Over 52,000 24- and 18-pdr roundshot were fired at San Sebastián in fifteen days

Nearly 16,000 shells wreaked havoc in San Sebastián town

As the time for the likely assault drew near, the besieging force would make a final offer to the garrison, promising them a safe passage if they agreed to surrender. Most garrison commanders declined and everyone knew that no quarter would be offered if the subsequent assault succeeded in entering the town.

Each attack was led by a group of volunteers known as the 'Forlorn Hope'. Their chances of survival were minimal but it was well known that any officer who did return had a very good chance of promotion, while the men would also be rewarded.

While the assault troops prepared their weapons and equipment, making it as comfortable as possible instead of conforming with regulations, the garrison was preparing as many surprises as possible at the breach. *Chevaux de frise*, wooden beams studded with sharp spikes and blades, would be scattered across the rubble, while rocks and barrels were hauled on to the parapet, ready to throw down. Men loaded their muskets and cannon while beacons were prepared to light up the area. If possible, mines were buried under the rubble ready to detonate when the Forlorn Hope was approaching. Then the garrison settled down to wait for the cheers indicating that the attack was under way; the cheering would be quickly replaced by screams as the breaches filled with the dead, dying and wounded. Over a thousand men were killed or injured in front of the breaches at Badajoz, an area no larger than a football pitch.

Guerrilla Warfare

The emergence of guerrilla warfare across the peninsula had a significant impact on the campaigning. To begin with, many guerrilla bands were organised by officers leading regular troops who had been forced to flee into the mountains when their units were defeated in battle. Other groups consisted of impromptu groups of homeless civilians, patriotic men or bandits who took to the hills when the marauding French army passed by. Many joined the guerrillas after their villages had been razed to the ground or in response to atrocities carried out by Napoleon's soldiers. Heinrich von Brandt's study sums up why the population of Spain turned against the French:

> Local causes, added to hatred, revenge and other passions, brought the mountaineers together. From corps thus formed the boldest and most determined stepped forward as leaders. As long as the guerrillas were thus constituted, they made no formidable appearance as a body, but were nevertheless extremely dangerous to the French. They formed the basis of an actual armament of the people, and were soon upon every road and path and eagerly

seeking for plunder.

The central junta issued orders in December 1808 authorising the formation of regular bands of guerrillas and some were eventually recognised by the local juntas. While many of the soldiers rejoined the regular army, some civilian groups were given arms and supplies and turned into semi-regular units. In many areas the threat they posed meant that French troops were confined to base unless they were campaigning in large numbers, but as Marshal Jacques Macdonald, commanding the Army of Catalonia, later complained, the bandits were almost impossible to track down: 'The enemy were ubiquitous, and yet I could find them nowhere, though I travelled through the length and breadth of the province.'

Guerrillas operated everywhere and their activities tied down thousands of French troops who would otherwise have been fighting the conventional war against Wellington. They began with isolated attacks on outposts, couriers and supply convoys, but in due course they could effectively halt all French operations in a given area as thousands of troops had to be diverted to garrison duties or to convoy protection. Comte Miot de Melito, Joseph's close adviser, carried out a study on the guerrilla warfare across Spain, noting how the bandits' influence increased as it spread across the country:

> By that time the Junta had adopted the formidable system of guerrillas. Spread out in parties in every part of the territory that the French occupied, they did us more damage than the [Spanish] regular armies by intercepting all our communications and forcing us never to send out a courier without an escort or leave isolated soldiers on the roads. Large parties of guerrillas often advanced to the gates of the capital.

The guerrillas' local knowledge enabled them to assemble in secret, strike quickly and then disappear when the attack was over. French army commanders were often frustrated by the ever-increasing numbers of troops that they had to divert from active campaigning in order to go in search of their elusive hide-outs. The bandits were, however, useless against formed troops, as Wellington noted during the Salamanca campaign: 'The guerrillas, although active and willing, and although their operations in general occasion the utmost annoyance to the enemy, are so little disciplined that they can do nothing against the French troops, unless the latter are very inferior in numbers.'

Attacks by both sides were carried out with cruelty and prisoners were often tortured before they were killed. The number of reprisals often spiralled out of control as the savagery increased and by 1812 many guerrilla groups were taking the law into their own hands, attracting deserters and bandits who were more interested in plunder and murder than in their country's cause. Comte Miot de Melito noted how the constant threat of guerrillas wore down the morale of the French soldier:

The hatred and fury of the Spaniards was carried to the last excess: they breathed vengeance and exercised it on any Frenchman who fell into their hands. This small-scale warfare quietly undermined us. We only possessed the ground actually occupied by our armies, and our power did not extend beyond it. The business of administration ceased, and there was neither order, nor justice, nor taxation.

Many guerrilla bands were brought under control during the later stages of the war, and some were converted into regular units as Wellington's army advanced across Spain. However, some refused to give up their criminal activities and continued to terrorise their area long after the French had left, taking anything they could steal and murdering anyone who stood in their way. An unidentified Spanish artillery officer serving in Zaragoza recorded his disgust:

The guerrillas who go by the name of Patriots should be exterminated: they are gangs of thieves with *carte blanche* to rob on the roads and in the villages. If some of them have brought benefits, the damage that others have wrought is one thousand times greater. Those who believe these bands to be very useful are many, but if they meditate on the desertion from the enemy that has not occurred for fear of being murdered, the burnings and other disasters suffered by the villages, the many highwaymen and bandits who carry out their crimes under this pretext, and finally the manner in which their disorder and independence has caused all kinds of evil, they will understand how far the disadvantages outweigh the benefits.

Although they did not win the war in the peninsula, the Spanish guerrillas certainly reduced the effectiveness of the French armies in many areas, making Wellington's task a lot easier. The countless attacks on messengers, convoys and garrisons ensured that Napoleon's men could never drop their guard and relax.

COMMAND AND CONTROL

Controlling large armies that were dispersed across the huge expanses of Spain and Portugal was a logistical nightmare for any commander. Particularly so for the French marshals who had to organise supplies of food and fodder in an inhospitable country with a lack of natural resources, where vicious guerrillas attacked those foraging parties that did set out. Starvation was a real threat. A study of Wellington's headquarters gives an insight into how armies operated across the peninsula.

Wellington did not have a regular staff and he did not need a regular chief-of-staff to organise his day-to-day activities. Instead, he delegated tasks to three subordinates, his military secretary, the quartermaster-general and the adjutant-general. He also had around ten aides-de-camp who could take messages, compile reports and carry out any other general duties. These were usually young men from politically well-connected families and most were from Guards or cavalry regiments.

The military secretary was a junior officer who dealt with the commander-in-chief's correspondence with London, with his allies and with his subordinates. The quartermaster-general's job was to keep the army on the road. He was responsible for dealing with all aspects of campaigning, starting with the embarkation and disembarkation of equipment at the harbours. Routes had to be agreed each day and camps or billets had to be organised. Spain and Portugal were, for the most part, uncharted territory and the quartermaster-general's surveyors were kept busy surveying roads, bridges and rivers while assessing everything from likely defensive positions to the potential resources of a particular district.

The adjutant-general was the principal administrative officer. He maintained statistical data relating to the numbers of men and horses available, and dealt with casualties, replacements and returning men. He was also responsible for the harsh disciplinary measures needed to keep the men in check, including overseeing the numerous floggings and hangings.

The heads of several departments also reported to Wellington's headquarters. The General Officer Commanding the Royal Artillery controlled all the batteries attached to divisions, the siege train, the reserve artillery and the all-important ammunition columns. The Commanding Officer of the Royal Engineers organised the Royal Military Artificers, including the engineers' park and the pontoon train; this unit was renamed the Royal Sappers and Miners in 1812. A 200-strong group known as the Corps of Guides, made up of both British and Portuguese, acted as guides and interpreters for the army; they also ran the post office and carried letters to and from the front. The provost marshal was responsible for prisoners who were waiting to be tried by general court-martial, detaining deserters and looking after prisoners of war. In 1812 the Staff Corps Cavalry, a 200-strong body of men intended to carry out policing duties, was formed to assist the provost marshal.

The medical department supervised the physicians and surgeons while the purveyor's department controlled the primitive hospitals and acquired drugs for the sick. The paymaster-general delivered money to the regimental paymasters but it was difficult to find a currency that the local population would accept; the controller of army accounts kept a check on expenditure. While the storekeeper-general maintained the stores of field equipment and tents, the commissariat made sure that they were kept well stocked; his staff also dealt with purchasing local goods. Wellington's army always aimed to either carry what it needed via the lines of communication or buy it locally, allowing his divisions to stay concentrated for long periods and to operate in inhospitable terrain. The French armies relied heavily on foraging for food and fodder, a practice that created deep resentment among the native population. It was also difficult to operate in sparsely populated areas or, as Masséna found to his cost in Portugal, when the civilians had pursued a scorched-earth policy, leaving nothing of value behind.

THE ARMY ON THE MARCH

The British army spent over five years marching back and forth across inhospitable lands trying to outmanoeuvre the French. While on the march the troops had to be fed and armed while the horses needed fodder. Stringent steps also had to be taken to ensure that the enemy did not gain the upper hand and make a surprise attack. Procedures for campaigning were laid down in the manuals, but over the years they were altered or changed to improve life on the road. The following extracts from the Selected General Orders illustrate how the Army operated.

A fixed line of command for communicating orders quickly was established, as follows:

> The orders for movement from the Commander of the Forces were communicated by the Quartermaster-General to the General

Officers commanding divisions, who detailed them, through their Assistant Quartermaster Generals, to the Generals of brigades, who gave them out immediately to the battalions of their brigades, through the Brigade Majors.

During the course of each night returns were sent in so that food and ammunition could be distributed and equipment ordered from the stores; replacements for casualties would also be organised. The route march and orders for the next day would also be discussed and distributed ready for morning:

The drum, the bugle and the trumpet sounded the preparation for the march at a certain hour, generally one hour and a half before daylight, in order that the several battalions might be assembled on the brigade alarm-posts, so as to be ready to march off from the ground precisely at daylight. It must be observed that the alarm-post is the place of assembly in the event of alarm; it was generally, and should always be, the place of parade.

Strict discipline was required in order that the soldiers struck camp quickly and were all ready to move off at the prescribed time. Any delays would upset the entire day's schedule and might compromise reaching the night's camp. The following extract describes the hustle and bustle across the huge camp at daybreak as the officers made sure that their men were ready on time:

It is singular to refer to these orders to see how a division of 6,000 men, and so on in any proportion, rolled up in their blankets, were all dressed, with blankets rolled, packed, equipped, squadded, paraded in companies, told off in sub-divisions, sections, and sections of threes, marched by companies to the regimental alarm-posts, and finally to that of the brigade, formed in close columns. All assembled with the same precision and order, ready to march off under the direction of the Assistant Quartermaster General attached to the division or corps, who had previously assembled the guides, whom he attached to the column or columns directed to be marched to the points or towns named in the Quartermaster General's instructions. In the meantime the formidable Provost Marshal attached to the division made his patrols. The report of 'All Present' was made in succession by the Brigade Majors to the Assistant Adjutant General, and by him to the General commanding the column. The word 'by sections of threes; march,' was given.

The weather across the peninsula could range from severe summer heat across Spain and Portugal to cold, rain and winter snow in the Pyrenees. It was important to give the men adequate rest otherwise the number of men falling out due to exhaustion (known as stragglers) rose dramatically. The following passage describes halting on the march and the procedure for collecting stragglers:

> The first halt was generally made at the expiration of half an hour from the departure, and afterwards once an hour. Each halt lasted at least five minutes after the men had piled their arms; this might vary a little, as the weather, distance, or other circumstances of the march might point out. The object of halting was for the purpose of allowing those who had fallen out to rejoin their companies, which, excepting in cases of sickness, usually occurred; as a man wanting to fall out was obliged to obtain a ticket from the officer commanding his company so to do, and to leave his pack and his firelock to be carried by his comrades of his section of threes; he therefore lost no time to return to his rank, and give back his ticket.
>
> In hot or stormy weather there were many stragglers and the ticket system often broke down. The assistant provost marshal and his guard with their prisoners brought up the rear of the column. They were followed by a rearguard that collected any stragglers and returned them to their units at the earliest opportunity.
>
> Drums or bugles sounded when it was time to set off and music accompanied the battalions as they marched off in order, the beat changing to a steady 'march at ease' when they were back on the road. While the soldiers maintained discipline on the march, a multitude of wagons, ox-carts, mules and camp-followers trailed along in their wake. The draught animals consumed large amounts of forage, hay, straw, oats and barley, and Wellington often tried to reduce the size of his baggage trains by limiting the

Sir Arthur Wellesley.

amount of baggage the officers could carry.

Soldiers' wives also followed the army. Each company was officially allowed between four or six women, but numerous unofficial ones tagged along as well, mounted on donkeys or on foot. George Bell of the 34th later recalled how Wellington tried unsuccessfully to keep them under control:

> The multitude of soldiers' wives stuck to the army like bricks: averse to all military discipline, they impeded our progress at times very much, particularly in retreats. They became the subject of a General Order, for their own special guidance. They were under no control, and were always first mounted up and away, blocking up narrow passes and checking the advance of the army with their donkeys, after repeated orders to follow in rear of their respective corps, or their donkeys would be shot.

The women were hardened scavengers who would usually immediately remarry if their husband was killed, so they could stay with the regiment. Many men acquired unofficial Portuguese and Spanish wives on campaign but when the war ended these women had to return home, unless their 'husbands' could afford to pay for their passage home; few could.

A division needed a lot of space to pitch camp and a great deal of planning went into the selection of a suitable location. If the division planned to spend the night in a town, the deputy assistant quartermaster-general went ahead of the column to meet the local junta and arrange billets. After dividing the town into areas, battalion officers allocated specific streets to each company and their orderlies would then go along the street chalking the letter of the company and the number of men who could stay there on each door. A second battalion officer arrived ahead of the battalion with representatives from each company ready to direct the men to their billets.

Out in the country, the general chose a suitable defensive area on his lines of communication which had sources of wood and water for cooking. The first item on the general's agenda was the security of the camp and he would indicate to the two field officers in charge of the outposts where he wanted them to be placed. The outer ring of picquets was controlled by the assistant adjutant-general of the division and they were expected to raise the alarm if the enemy approached the camp. Set procedures had to be followed to avoid false alarms or accidents, and predetermined signals, either using beacons or a set number of musket shots, were used. The inner ring of picquets was controlled by the battalion officers and they were posted at the billets ready to reinforce the outer picquets if the alarm was raised.

While the outposts were being organised, the rest of the men were busy preparing the camp:

> . . . the tent mules were unloaded, and the company's tents pitched in column on the alignment given to the battalion, brigade, and division. If there were no tents, then the bill-hooks came speedily into play: regular squads were formed for cutting branches, others for drawing them to the lines, and others as the architects for constructing the huts.

Working parties were kept busy collecting ammunition and equipment, while fatigue parties collected rations for the night's meal. The quartermaster took these to the issuing point, and each returned with one item, either bread, meat, wine or forage, for the entire battalion for onward distribution to each company's orderly officer.

Before long hot drinks and food would be ready and the men gathered around the camp fires to hear stories and sing songs before turning in for the night. Bivouacs could be warm and cosy in good weather but wind and rain would lower spirits as they huddled around the fires to keep warm.

British hussars charge French cavalry on the outskirts of Sahagun.

Chapter 1

WELLESLEY'S FIRST EXPEDITION TO PORTUGAL

THE ARRIVAL OF THE EXPEDITIONARY FORCE

ARTHUR WELLESLEY LEFT CORK on 12 July 1808 aboard the fast frigate *Crocodile*, and headed for the Iberian peninsula ahead of the British Expeditionary Force. A fleet of ships followed carrying six infantry brigades, several cavalry squadrons and five batteries of guns. The British commander's first port of call was Corunna in Galicia, in the north-west corner of Spain, but it was made clear that the ships would not be welcome there. Despite this disappointing reception, Wellesley learnt that there had recently been a revolt against the occupying French troops in northern Portugal and he was welcomed by the local junta when the *Crocodile* docked in Oporto (Porto). Arrangements were made to use the small harbour at Figueira da Foz, halfway between Lisbon and Oporto, where the fleet could shelter in the river Mondego's wide estuary while the troops were transferred ashore.

The troops of the Expeditionary Force finally began to come ashore on 1 August and were doubtless relieved to be back on dry land after three weeks at sea. Although the force initially numbered only 9,500 men, it soon doubled in size with the arrival of two additional bodies of troops. Major-General Sir Brent Spencer had sailed from Cadiz with 5,000 men, while another 4,750 troops had sailed from Andalucía following the Spanish victory at Bailén.

While Wellesley made plans to advance towards the French, spending his time reconnoitring the countryside, his commissary-general made arrangements for local transport to carry food and ammunition for the troops. But as the British commander prepared to move south to engage Marshal Junot's army, new orders arrived from London, altering the chain of command. Two senior commanders, General Sir Hew Dalrymple and General Sir Harry Burrard, were en route to Portugal with instructions to take over command on their arrival.

Marshal Jean-Andoche Junot.

Despite this news, Wellesley headed towards Lisbon on 10 August with 13,500 men. His infantry had been organised into six infantry brigades, each with two or three battalions. However, the 20th Light Dragoons and the artillery were short of horses and a third of the troopers and two batteries of guns had to remain with the ships. As the British soldiers tried to become accustomed to the hot, dusty climate, Wellesley was met by General Bernardino Freire at the head of a brigade of over 1,200 Portuguese troops at the town of Leiria. The brigade's commander was Colonel Nicholas Trant, a colourful British officer who was serving in the Portuguese military; he was later described by Wellesley as 'a very good officer, but as drunken a dog as ever lived'.

The British army continued its march southwards, reaching Alcobaça on the 14th. The next day three companies of the 95th Rifles encountered French picquets near Obidos. This clash saw the first shots fired by British troops in the Peninsular War, a war that would last for six gruelling years. Two days later the rest of the allied army reached Obidos.

THE BATTLE OF ROLIÇA, 18 AUGUST 1808

Wellesley was by now aware that the French commander, Marshal Junot, had 26,000 troops under his command, some 8,000 more than he had expected. He also knew that they were marching to join General Delaborde, whose orders were to delay Wellesley's advance until General Louis-Henri Loison could join him from Abrantes to the east with another 9,000 men. However, Junot had given his subordinate a difficult task. Delaborde was faced by odds of three to one and there were few defensive opportunities as he moved his 4,500 troops across the valley south of Obidos to the village of Roliça. To begin with he deployed them on a small, low ridge immediately west of the village, blocking the road to Lisbon. Although the ridge stood at the centre of a wide valley, with ridges on three sides, it was a potentially good position providing Wellesley made a frontal attack.

Wellesley's problem was how to avoid being drawn into a costly frontal assault and after reconnoitring the French position on the 17th, he issued his orders for an attack at first light. His plan was to pin Delaborde's troops on the ridge with one column, while a second column

The windmill used by Delaborde stands on the crest of the first French position.

moved behind the range of hills to the east of Roliça. The skirmishers would draw the French into a prolonged engagement, while three of his brigades made preparations to attack. While Delaborde watched developments to his front, the rest of Wellesley's force would make long detours around the French flank, aiming to cut off their escape route.

Soon after dawn, Wellesley's main column advanced steadily across the open plain while the twelve British guns bombarded the hill-top position. Delaborde watched from the top of a windmill as his tirailleurs engaged the advancing skirmishers and his artillery, a single battery of five guns, returned fire. The British brigades led by Catlin, Nightingall and Hill marched along the main road straight for Roliça, following the east bank of the stream. Meanwhile, Colonel Trant's brigade advanced to the west of the stream as General Fane's brigade advanced along the slopes between the central and easterly columns. Ferguson's and Bowes' brigades, a force of some 4,500 troops supported by a battery of 6 guns, marched over the hills to the east, out of Delaborde's sight.

For a while it seemed as though the French were going to fall into the British trap but as the two flank columns moved slowly across the plain, a French detachment watching for signs of General Loison's troops to the east spotted Ferguson and Bowe and reported the threat. Delaborde immediately realised that his position was in danger and gave the order to withdraw before the British cut off his line of retreat. His men fell back over 1.5 kilometres in good order and deployed south of Columbeira. The new French position was centred on top of a steep escarpment and it was much stronger than the first. Wellesley would have to reconsider his plan and find a way to avoid a frontal attack up one of the steep gulleys on the front face of the ridge.

Wellesley planned to repeat his original manoeuvre, letting his two flank columns move around the French flanks, while the rest of his troops made a feint attack in front of Delaborde's line. Ferguson's and Bowes' brigades continued their wide detour to the south-east, engaging the

French unit waiting to meet Loison's reinforcements. To the west, Trant's Portuguese troops made a similar move on the right flank, aiming to cut the French escape route. Wellesley kept back two brigades in case French reinforcements appeared and while Fane's 6th Brigade waited near Roliça, General Robert Craufurd's 5th Brigade remained in reserve.

In front of Delaborde's position Nightingall's 3rd Brigade approached from the left while Hill's 1st Brigade moved forward on the right towards the foot of the steep slope. Hill's skirmishers opened the battle, engaging in a firefight with the French tirailleurs at the foot of the escarpment while the British artillery bombarded the top of the hill.

To begin with it looked as if Wellesley's plan was going to work but as Ferguson's flank column closed in, disaster struck in the centre. One of Nightingall's battalions, the 1/29th Regiment, began climbing the slopes and Colonel Lake (who was dressed in new uniform, hat and boots with his hair neatly powdered and queued) led four of his companies forward up one of the steep ravines to engage the French. Rather than keeping at a safe distance as Wellesley had wanted, Lake's men were being drawn into a trap. They did not spot the danger until they approached the top of the gulley and then discovered to their horror that they were in the centre of Delaborde's position with Frenchmen waiting around the lip of the ravine. Volleys rang out from three directions, killing and wounding dozens of soldiers while Colonel Lake desperately tried to extricate the survivors from their precarious position. Although Hill ordered the 1/9th Regiment forward to rescue them it was too late for many. Lake himself was killed and many of his men were taken prisoner; only a few escaped to the British lines.

Even though Ferguson was still some distance away, Wellesley ordered Fane, Nightingall and Hill to attack with the rest of their battalions and they began to climb the steep gulleys and spurs towards the French. Battalion commanders struggled to keep order as their men advanced up the steep hillside and many were killed or wounded as the French fired disciplined volleys into them. The British were forced to retire several times, but each time they rallied at the foot of the slope and headed back towards the top of the smoke-covered hill. The battle raged for two hours but Wellesley's superiority in numbers eventually began to tell and as hand-to-hand fighting broke out on the crest of the ridge, the French spotted Ferguson's column marching towards their rear.

Delaborde knew that he was yet again in danger of being cut off and he ordered his subordinates to disengage so they could withdraw

Colonel Lake's men climbed the steepest gulley on the right .

towards Zambujeira. Two battalions pulled out of the line to begin with, followed by the remaining two, and they headed south while the French cavalry kept the British infantry at bay. The French retreat was orderly until panic broke out when the men were forced to crowd through a narrow gorge to the south of Zambujeira. As the British closed in a number of prisoners were taken and three French guns were abandoned. Order was restored at the far side of the defile and the French cavalry was able to stop the retreat turning into a rout.

As darkness fell, Wellesley called off the pursuit, concerned that Loison's troops were only a few kilometres away. His men needed time to regroup and rest, ready to march south to Vimeiro at first light to meet two fresh brigades that were waiting to land. The British commander had a lot to consider as night fell across the battlefield. Despite Delaborde's ability to keep his men at bay, his first battle could be considered a partial success. British losses were around 475, a third of them from the 1/29th, while the French had lost nearly 600, many of them during the final withdrawal.

Wellesley's headquarters in the walled town of Obidos.

TOURING ROLIÇA

Start your tour in Obidos. This walled Moorish town stands on a low hill top, alongside the A8 motorway between Coimbra and Torres Vedras. Park in the car park opposite the large Roman aqueduct and collect a map from the tourist information centre before entering the town via the main gate. Follow the main street for 300 metres to the main square. The large white building on the right as you enter the square is the house where Wellesley spent the night before his first battle of the Peninsular War. It now

Wellesley's view of the French positions.

houses the town museum. It is possible to climb on to the ramparts next to the main gate but extreme care is needed: there is no handrail for the narrow walkway and the stones can be slippery.

You may choose to climb the southern tower to view the French positions in the same way Wellesley did but again care is needed; for a less risky alternative, look over the battlements to the right. To the south is the valley leading to Roliça. The second French position was on the ridge in the distance, to the left of the modern wind turbines on the horizon. Their first position was immediately in front. It is the low ridge just to the left of, and behind, the isolated hill in the centre of the valley.

Ferguson and Bowes marched to the left (east), heading past the modern motorway bridge, hoping to get around General Delaborde's flank, while Fane's brigade advanced along the summit of the ridge, overlooking the valley. Nightingall and Craufurd followed the road through St Mamede, heading to the left of the wooded mound. Hill marched along a second road heading towards the right-hand side of the mound with Trant's Portuguese covering his right (west) flank.

Return to your car and take the road south running parallel with the motorway to St Mamede, 5 kilometres to the south. Turn right, signposted for Roliça, at the far end of the village. After crossing the railway note the hill used by Delaborde immediately in front of you as you drive across the long stone bridge over the stream. It is sometimes possible to stop on the right opposite the village sign but access is very limited. Continue into the village, turning right for Pó towards the far end, and the road rises up on to the rear of the French position. Again the land to the right of the road is private. Continue down the far side of the hill and take the first right after 500 metres, following the road to the gates at the end where there is a turning area.

Looking back, the first French position is to the left, with the windmill on the summit. The size of the hill, and its vulnerability to attack, is very apparent. As soon as Delaborde realised he was in danger, he ordered his

men back through Columbeira
and on to the high ridge,
occupying the section to the left
(east) of the wind turbines.

Return to Roliça and turn
right at the T-junction, heading
for Columbeira. Immediately
across from the junction is a
memorial with a tile depiction
of the battle. Just after entering
Columbeira, stop in the lay-by
on the left-hand side of the
road, opposite a concrete
electricity tower. Delaborde's
main position looms above the
houses and the four gulleys are
easy to spot. The French troops
escaped up the gulleys before
deploying on the top and then
waited for Wellesley to make

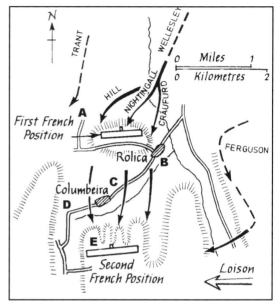

The Battle of Rolica, 17 August 1808.

his move. He planned to skirmish on the lower slopes of the ridge,
drawing French attention away from a second flank attack. Although
Ferguson and Bowes had moved towards the rest of Wellesley's troops,
once Delaborde had left Roliça, the two brigades returned to making their
flanking move to the left (east), hoping to cut off the French line of retreat.
However, the British plan began to unravel when the men of the 29th
found themselves drawn into a prolonged skirmish up the right-hand
gulley, the highest of the four.

Continue through Columbeira and stop at the far end of the village, at
the foot of a steep ravine. It is possible to look back along the face of the
escarpment to understand the strength of Delaborde's position. Drive up
the ravine and turn left for Bombarral at the T-junction after 1 kilometre.
Take the second left after 800 metres, following signs for Picoto and
Lake's Monument. Turn left in front of the church (with the building to
your right) and follow the track across the top of the ridge following signs
for the monument. In poor weather it is wise to walk down the last
section of the track.

Colonel Lake's lonely grave stands at the head of the gulley where 150
of his men were killed, wounded or taken prisoner, drawn into a trap by

Roliça's memorial with its tile relief of the battle.

Colonel Lake's grave.

Delaborde's tirailleurs. The French were lined up along the lip of the shallow valley and would have found it hard to miss the redcoats below.

Continue to walk along the path for 300 metres through the fields, heading into the wood at the edge of the escarpment. It is possible to see across the valley back to Obidos at the far end of the trees.

THE BATTLE OF VIMEIRO, 21 AUGUST 1808

As soon as they were rested, Wellesley's troops moved south to Vimeiro at the mouth of the river Maceira where they could cover the arrival of General Acland's and General Anstruther's brigades, increasing the size of the expeditionary force to 17,000 men and 18 guns. While the troops disembarked, General Jean Junot, the French commander in Portugal, was moving north from Lisbon with 13,000 men and 24 guns, hoping to catch Wellesley off guard. Both General Henri Delaborde's and General Louis Loison's divisions had left Torres Vedras as it grew dark on 20 August, aiming to join Junot by dawn.

Wellesley deployed his troops around Vimeiro, where the river Maceira flowed through a deep gorge, in anticipation of a French attack. Initially his six brigades were deployed along the western part of the ridge, south of the river Maceira, covering the landing beaches at Porto Nova. But the French were not Wellesley's only problem. General Sir Harry Burrard was already waiting to land and take command and Wellesley joined him aboard his ship to brief him on the situation. After the meeting Burrard decided to remain on his ship for the night but Wellesley returned to his headquarters only to learn that Junot's men were on the move.

Junot had wanted to attack at dawn but the march to Vimeiro had taken longer than planned and it was mid-morning before his troops were closing in. As Wellesley and his men scanned the horizon for movement, dust clouds in the distance indicated the approach of the

French columns. What was clearly a considerable number of troops seemed to be heading for Ventosa ridge, north of Vimeiro. The delayed French attack gave Wellesley adequate time to redeploy a large part of his army and by mid-morning several of his brigades were heading for the high ground north of Vimeiro.

Ferguson's and Bowes' brigades were ordered to hold Ventosa and the ridge while Craufurd's brigade and Trant's Portuguese troops deployed in support. The rest of Wellesley's troops were arrayed south and east of Vimeiro. Fane's and Anstruther's brigades, supported by six guns, held a low hill south of the village, while General Ackland's brigade covered their northern flank and General Hill's brigade held the ridge to the west. Wellesley was determined to reduce the number of casualties from artillery fire and a large number of his troops were deployed out of sight on reverse slopes and ordered to lie down.

Marshal Junot's late arrival on the battlefield meant that he was unable to reconnoitre the terrain and he assumed that Vimeiro Hill was the centre of Wellesley's line. Delaborde's division supported by Loison's division would carry out the initial attack against the hill, while General Antoine-François Brennier's brigade climbed Ventosa ridge to outflank the British position. Solignac's brigade followed when it was clear that British troops held the village.

As General Delaborde's columns marched towards Vimeiro to the sound of their drums, the cavalry and artillery moved forward on the flanks of the column. The first shots were fired by the tirailleurs as they engaged four companies of riflemen from the 2/95th and the 5/60th while Fane's and Anstruther's brigades waited silently on the slopes in front of the village. The withdrawal of the British skirmish screen was later described by Rifleman Leach:

> The night before the battle I belonged to a picket of about 200 riflemen. We were posted in a large pine wood. About eight o'clock in the morning a cloud of light troops, supported by a heavy column of infantry, entered the wood, assailing the pickets with great impetuosity, [and] obliged us to fall back for support on the 97th Regiment.

The British guns also joined in, using a new type of artillery projectile called shrapnel. The fuses exploded the hollow casings over the French columns, spraying musket balls on to the men below. The crews changed to canister as the columns drew closer, adding to the carnage.

Charlot's brigade approached Anstruther's men where the 2/97th and the 2/52nd waited silently in two deep ranks, while the 2/9th and the 2/43rd waited in support on the reverse slope. Meanwhile, Thomiére's brigade faced the 1/50th, supported by the riflemen of the 5/60th and the 2/95th. Junot did not realise that his men were outnumbered by nearly two to one until the British troops stood up. The British lines waited silently as the French advance continued until nine hundred muskets and rifles opened fire at close range, decimating the front ranks. Volley after volley hit Delaborde's men and when the moment was right the 1/50th charged, scattering the French soldiers. Leach watched as the columns fell back in confusion:

> Some heavy masses of infantry, preceded by a swarm of light troops, were advancing with great resolution. In spite of the deadly fire which several hundred riflemen kept up on them, they continued to press forward until the old 50th Regiment received them with a destructive volley, following it instantly with a most brilliant charge with the bayonet, which broke in utter dismay and confusion this column.

Wellesley was not entirely complimentary about the 1/50th, later commenting that it was 'not a good looking regiment but devilish steady', but they had demonstrated how a two-deep line could successfully counter an attack by columns.

As the British skirmishers moved to one side, Charlot's brigade found the way forward barred by the 2/97th. Rifleman Leach watched as the 97th and the 52nd brought the French column to a standstill:

> As soon as we had got clear of the front of the 97th that regiment poured in such a well directed fire that it staggered the resolution of the hostile column, which declined to close with them. About the same time the second battalion of the 52nd, advancing through the wood, took the French in flank, and drove them before them in confusion. On the pickets being driven in, I joined my own brigade, which was on the left of the 97th.

Charlot's men tried to return the fire but they too were soon falling back in confusion.

Delaborde's division had been soundly beaten and as the French artillery crews tried to limber up and join the retreat, the British riflemen shot down the horses and gunners. Seven guns were eventually abandoned.

As Wellesley prepared for the next onslaught, he was confronted by a new problem. Sir Harry Burrard had finally landed and was hovering around his headquarters, watching the battle unfold.

Junot was determined to take Vimeiro Hill and ordered Kellerman's grenadiers forward to attack again where Delaborde had failed and two brigades duly advanced towards Fane's position. Colonel Robe's gunners fired roundshot and grapeshot, causing heavy casualties among the French columns, while the 2/9th, the 1/50th and the 2/97th waited for the order to fire. As the French grenadiers closed in, hundreds of muskets and rifles opened fire, killing or wounding many, and St Clair's column shuddered to a halt. Fane's men again charged, sending the French back down the slopes, leaving four more guns in British hands. To the north, General Maransin's column outflanked the 1/50th but entered Vimeiro only to find Anstruther's reserve, the 2/43rd, waiting in the narrow streets. As they engaged in frenzied hand-to-hand fighting with bayonets and musket butts, Acland's brigade attacked the column's right flank. With British troops closing in on three sides, Maransin's men were soon falling back.

Wellesley decided to scatter the French infantry by ordering the 20th Light Dragoons to canter forward and enter the fray even though Lieutenant-Colonel Taylor had only 240 troopers. Sergeant George Landsheit was close by when the order to attack was given: '"Now, 20th! Now!" shouted Sir Arthur, while his staff clapped their hands and gave us a cheer, the sound of which was still in our ears when we put our horses to the speed.'

Taylor's troopers charged over the slopes of Vimeiro hill, scattering one battalion as it tried to form square, while the rest of the French simply ran for their lives. Wellesley's victory was complete. However, instead of rallying at the foot of the slope and returning to the safety of their own lines, Taylor's men charged headlong into the French lines. It was a disaster: the dragoons were quickly intercepted by two regiments of French cavalry. Taylor himself was mortally wounded and over forty troopers were killed or wounded; the rest of the dragoons were able to nurse their tired horses back to Vimeiro.

Although the battle for Vimeiro Hill was over by noon there was another battle to fight on Ventosa ridge, where Generals Brennier and Solignac were bringing up their brigades to attack the British left flank. Combined, the two brigades numbered over 6,000 men, with cavalry protecting their flanks, and a number of guns were also being moved up to bombard the British lines. The three British brigades also numbered over 6,000 men but they had the advantage of surprise on their side as they waited in silence beyond the crest of the hill.

The French attack ran into difficulties at an early stage, partly due to Junot's lack of reconnaissance. Solignac's force climbed straight to the summit towards Ventosa but halfway up the ridge Brennier's men encountered a hidden gulley, too deep to risk entering. They were forced to make a detour to the east and the delay meant that Solignac's brigade attacked Ventosa alone. The French were surprised at how close the British were when they breasted the crest of the ridge and as the three battalions tried to deploy into line to return fire, volley after volley tore though their ranks. Solignac's brigade was shattered in a few minutes and soon fell back, leaving a seriously wounded Solignac and several guns behind.

Brennier's four battalions marched to the sound of guns when Solignac's brigade came under fire and soon ran into the open flank of Ferguson's brigade. The 1/71st and the 1/82nd of Nightingall's brigade tried to redeploy to meet the threat but they were thrown back in confusion and the French infantry recaptured Solignac's guns as they advanced. The 1/29th was the next battalion to turn and meet the threat, firing into the French flank while Piper George Clark of the 1/71st sat wounded on the ground playing 'Up and waur them aa, Willie'. Volley after volley hit the disorganised French column and Brennier's men were

French infantry force their way into Vimeiro cemetery.

soon fleeing down the slopes, leaving hundreds of wounded and killed behind, including their injured commander. Solignac's guns were abandoned for the second time.

It was only midday but Junot was beaten. Each of his brigades had been defeated in turn, resulting in over 1,800 casualties, more than twice the number of British killed or wounded, and 14 guns had been captured — over half the number he had taken into battle. Wellesley could see that Junot's men were falling back in disorder and he wanted to march after them, in the hope of scattering the Frenchmen before they could be joined by reinforcements. However, the decision to give chase was not his to take and the cautious Burrard refused to give permission for the pursuit, thus allowing Junot's men to escape to fight again another day.

Vimeiro was the first occasion when Wellesley displayed his skills as a defensive commander, a skill he would become renowned for. He had an eye for the tactical opportunities offered by the terrain, and had kept his men safely hidden out of sight on the reverse slopes while his skirmishers and artillery engaged the French. These men then opened a devastating fire at point-blank range as soon as Junot's columns advanced over the crest, driving them back with a disciplined charge. The two-deep line, a formation unique to the British Army, had also proved to be an effective counter to the French columns, and time after time Junot's men had been thrown back in confusion.

While Junot withdrew to reorganise, Wellesley found himself embroiled in political problems. General Sir Hew Dalrymple took over from Burrard the following day and took the decision to cancel any plans for pursuit. Instead the two senior commanders decided to negotiate a deal with the French and duly met Junot at Cintra. The resulting treaty, known as the Convention of Cintra, allowed Junot and his army to return to France, taking their arms and plunder with them. Although it brought peace across the Iberian peninsula, there was outrage when news of the agreement reached London. Burrard, Dalrymple and Wellesley were recalled to England to face a court of enquiry, leaving General Sir John Moore in command of the 30,000 British troops in Portugal.

Back in London the three generals were ordered to explain why they had allowed the French army to escape unmolested when they clearly had the opportunity to destroy it. Burrard and Dalrymple were found to be responsible for negotiating the Convention, but Wellesley escaped censure because he had not been involved in drawing up the details of the treaty and had only signed it on Dalrymple's orders.

Touring Vimeiro

Vimeiro is 20 kilometres north-west of Torres Vedras. Follow the IC11 towards Lourinha and the village is to the west of the road. Just before the village church in the centre of the village, turn right up the hill, signposted for the monument. Continue to the right after 200 metres to the top of the hill. Many of the key features of the battlefield can be seen from the top of the hill and it is a good place to get your bearings before starting your tour. The obelisk stands on the top of Vimeiro Hill, which was held by Anstruther's and Fane's brigades. A series of ceramic tiles around the memorial depict scenes from the British landing in Portugal until the battle.

Walk to the south end of the small plaza, to the top of the steps looking west. The Western Ridge, where many British troops were initially deployed to face an anticipated attack from the south, is on the horizon. Its craggy slopes drop down steeply to the southern banks of the river Maceira. As soon as Wellesley realised that General Junot was trying to outflank him, moving to the east around the opposite end of Vimeiro Hill, he moved four of his brigades through the village to counter the threat. Ferguson's and Bowes' brigades led the way, followed by Craufurd's and Trant's, and they marched up the ridge to the north-east towards Ventosa, where there are modern houses along the skyline.

Walk around to the east side of the park and look east from the pergola. Fane's brigade held the low ground in front, covering the east side of the village, while Anstruther's brigade held the slopes to the south and east.

Now walk or drive the short distance to the cemetery, passing to the left of the perimeter wall, and park at the far end next to a water tower. It is possible to see from here the British view of Delaborde's division as it advanced to attack, supported by Loison's division. While Charlot's brigade advanced up the slopes immediately in front, Thomiére's brigade crossed the low ground to the left (north). A short walk down the road to the bottom of the slope gives a better understanding of the significance of Vimeiro Hill.

Return to your car and drive back into the village, turning right at the T-junction at the bottom of the hill, in front of the church. After crossing the river, immediately take the left fork up the hill to reach Ventosa. Ackland's brigade held the lower part of this slope and his men made sure that the French could not enter the village from the north.

Drive up to the top of the steep ridge, turning right at the T-junction at

The hidden gully that stopped the French advance.

the summit. Ferguson and Nightingall led their men up this slope to defend against the outflanking manoeuvre against Ventosa. The brigades formed up below the crest (modern housing occupies this area) and waited for the attack to develop while the French found their way blocked by a ravine. Meanwhile, Kellerman's troops advanced along the valley floor to the right towards Vimeiro.

Follow the right-hand fork in the road, signposted for Pregança, and then go straight on at a mini-roundabout, turning right at a second mini-roundabout before the brick chimney. Head down the slope and after 200 metres stop in the pull-in on the left to view the ravine that blocked Brennier's and Solignac's route to Ventosa. From this viewpoint it is clear how the terrain conspired to thwart the French attack. It looks as if there is a constant slope from Toledo to the top of the ridge, and the steep-sided ravine is invisible. The French commanders had no option but to change direction and march around the perimeter of the obstacle, giving the British time to prepare for the attack.

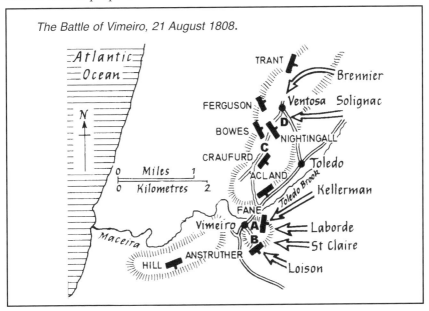

The Battle of Vimeiro, 21 August 1808.

Continue down the hill and turn right at the T-junction in Toledo village, heading back into Vimeiro. Kellerman's men advanced parallel to the road, but on the opposite side of the stream, heading for the church. Fane's brigade halted this second attack on the outskirts of the village. Return to Vimeiro to complete the tour.

Wellesley's Army at Roliça: 12,735 men

1st Brigade	Rowland Hill	1/5th, 1/9th and 1/38th	2,650
2nd Brigade	R. Ferguson	1/36th, 1/40th and 1/71st	2,450
3rd Brigade	M. Nightingall	1/29th and 1/82nd	1,520
4th Brigade	B.F. Bowes	1/6th and 1/32nd	1,800
5th Brigade	Catlin Craufurd	1/45th and 1/91st	1,850
6th Brigade	H. Fane	1/50th, 5/60th and 4 Coys 2/95th	2,000
Cavalry	C.D. Taylor	20th Light Dragoons (part of)	240
Artillery	W. Robe	Three Batteries	225

Wellesley's Army at Vimeiro: 16,785 men

As above, but the following troops joined Wellesley's army before the battle:

7th Brigade	R. Anstruther	2/9th, 2/43rd, 2/52nd and 2/97th	2,700
8th Brigade	W. Acland	2nd, 1/20th, 2 Coys 1/95th	1,350

Junot's Army at Vimeiro

Solignac	2,800	Thomiére	1,400
Brennier	3,000	Charlot	1,100
Kellerman	2,100	Cavalry	2,000

Delaborde's Division

Infantry 4,400   Cavalry 300

The monument on top of Vimeiro Hill.

Chapter 2

SIR JOHN MOORE'S
EXPEDITION INTO SPAIN

FOLLOWING THE BATTLE OF VIMEIRO and the controversial signing of the Convention of Cintra, General Sir John Moore took command of the 30,000-strong British Army in Portugal. The French army was in retreat and the Spanish were looking to their ally to help drive the invaders back across her borders. The decision was taken to move the British army to the Spanish frontier ready to conduct operations, and one of the first objectives was to secure the north-west corner of Spain, including the provinces of Galicia and Léon. General Moore also needed to consider how to address the problem of Almeida and Elvas, where French troops had laid siege to the Portuguese border fortresses. It was a case of too many objectives and too few troops in very difficult terrain.

Initially Moore decided to march through Extremadura, the desolate border province, and concentrate his troops in the fertile plains around Salamanca, where he hoped his commissariat could obtain food and supplies a little more readily. However, the problems experienced on this first foray into Spain highlighted the problems that Wellesley would encounter during his future campaigns across the Iberian peninsula.

The roads were poor and Moore took the controversial decision to send his infantry on the direct route into Spain while his artillery and cavalry made a long detour, a decision made on poor intelligence about the state of the roads. It left his army in a vulnerable position for some

General Sir John Moore.

time, but it was a small problem compared with the one he faced when he reached Salamanca. He entered the city on 13 November only to find that the new Spanish authorities were either unwilling or unable to cooperate. His army was now short of transport, severely limiting his options:

> If I had had sooner a conception of the weakness of the Spanish armies, the defenceless state of the country, the apparent apathy of the people, and the selfish imbecility of the government, I should certainly have been in no hurry to enter Spain, or to have approached the scene of action until the army was united. There seems to be neither an army, generals nor a government. I cannot calculate the power of a whole people determined and enthusiastic if persons are brought forward with ability to direct it, but at present nothing of this kind appears.

The lack of assistance meant that his troops had to rely on an overstretched supply line and it would take another month before the tail of his army reached Salamanca, while the rest of his men found themselves among an apathetic and occasionally hostile people. It appeared that the Spanish were not going to welcome the British with open arms.

Despite the lack of cooperation from both the government and the population, the British commander received numerous appeals for help from the Spanish authorities, none of which were realistic. Moore's complaints' continued: 'We are here on our own in complete ignorance of the plans and wishes of the Spanish government. Indeed, as far as I can learn, the Junta are incapable of forming any plan or coming to any fixed determination.' The only good news was that Sir David Baird's division had recently disembarked at the port of Corunna, nearly 500 kilometres to the north-west, and was just setting out on an arduous trek across the Galician mountains to meet him.

While Moore contemplated his exposed position at Salamanca, reports were received about the varying fortunes of the Spanish armies operating across the peninsula. On 28 November rumours reached British headquarters to the effect that 45,000 Spanish troops had been scattered at Tudela, between Zaragoza and Pamplona in north-east Spain. While Moore contemplated the deteriorating situation, optimistic reports about the Spanish Army of the Left rallying under General La Romana arrived at his headquarters, and there was news that Madrid's garrison was preparing for a siege. The conflicting reports about the fortunes of the

Spanish military meant that the British would have to remain around Salamanca in a show of solidarity and wait for developments. To withdraw while the Spanish were still fighting back would result in a serious loss of face in front of their ally.

By 11 December Moore's supply problems had been alleviated and he was ready to move north-east from Salamanca. As his men passed through the city of Valladolid, news of French movements came in. A captured dispatch, one of many seized by Spanish guerrillas from French messengers, pinpointed Soult's army for the first time, and it was north of the city. Moore acted quickly, advancing north towards Léon, his numbers boosted by the arrival of General Baird's division at Maygora on 20 December.

It looked as if the British were about to take the French army by surprise as plans were made to carry out a night attack on its picquets, in the hope of scattering the French cavalry and causing havoc in their camp. The following night General Hon. Henry Lord Paget led two regiments of hussars out to engage the French light cavalry screening Soult's camp. As they approached Sahagun, Paget ordered General Slade to lead the 10th Hussars through the town, driving the French before them, while he took the 15th Hussars around the outskirts to cut off their escape route.

The 15th Hussars quickly overpowered one outpost but one of the French troopers was able to escape and as he galloped back to the main camp to raise the alarm, Paget ordered his men to charge:

> As soon as the enemy's order of battle was formed, they cheered in a very gallant manner and immediately began firing. The 15th then halted, wheeled into line, huzza'ed and advanced. The interval betwixt us was perhaps four hundred yards, but it was so quickly passed that they had only time to fire a few shots before we came upon them. The shock was terrible; horses and men were overthrown, and a shriek of terror, intermixed with oaths, groans, and prayers for mercy, issued from the whole extent of their front.

General Debelle had twice as many men as Paget, but the British still had the advantage of surprise on their side as they galloped through the camps, scattering the 8th Dragoons and 1st Provisional Chasseurs. By the time Slade's 10th Hussars joined the mêlée, the French were already beaten; 13 officers and over 150 troopers had been killed, wounded or taken prisoner for the loss of only 14 British casualties.

After this success Moore allowed his men two days' rest before giving the order to attack Soult's 16,000-strong army now 24 kilometres to the east. However, just as his 25,000-strong army was breaking camp, dramatic news arrived at his headquarters: Napoleon had discovered his whereabouts and 80,000 French soldiers had marched through the mountains north of Madrid, braving horrendous weather, and were now heading north from Valladolid towards his exposed lines of communication. The British commander had no option but to change his orders and head for Corunna to the north-west in the hope of finding the British navy waiting, ready to evacuate his men. It was the start of an infamous retreat, one which would take his army north-west into the Galician mountains in the depths of winter.

As the French soldiers marched through the Sierra de Guadarrama, battered by ferocious blizzards, Napoleon believed that the British were still camped at Sahagun; while his men regrouped for twenty-four hours at Tordesillas, he confidently announced 'should the British pass today in their positions they are lost'. But Moore's men were already heading west towards Benavente. They had started out on Christmas Day in torrential rain at the start of what would become a desperate race for survival, an episode that would later become known as the retreat to Corunna.

RETREAT TO CORUNNA, 25 DECEMBER 1808 TO 10 JANUARY 1809

By 27 December it appeared that the British had an unassailable head start on the French as the rearguards made their way across the flooded river Esla around Benavente, destroying all the bridges before they left. However, the British soldiers were cold and wet and their morale had plummeted. To make matters worse, it was impossible to obtain supplies and many were dressed in little more than rags and walking barefoot along the muddy roads. Outraged at their predicament, many went on the rampage in Benavente, venting their anger against the inhabitants who refused to give them food or shelter. One officer noted how low morale had fallen as he was powerless to stop his men running riot:

> This is no longer a campaign that we are conducting; it is rather a devastation by bandits in uniform. And although [we officers] lament the situation, risking our lives to contain the soldiery, we are turned into murderers. The towns and villages half-burned, the farm animals and mules killed or stolen, all the tools and instruments of the peasantry and artisans used as fuel because it is easier to throw them on the fire than cut down trees, all the

churches sacked and profaned; this is all that is left of this Kingdom.

Even as the British rampaged through Benavente, Napoleon's cavalry was in hot pursuit and General Lefebvre-Desnouettes was determined that his Imperial Guard cavalry would stop them. The British cavalry managed to hold them at bay outside the village of Castrogonzalo while engineers destroyed the last bridge over the Elsa but the French commander rode downstream looking for a ford. He eventually led four Guard squadrons of chasseurs through the icy waters while the rest of his men continued to look for other places to cross.

Lieutenant-Colonel Otway led a squadron of the 18th Light Dragoons to meet the French chasseurs, and although Otway's men were outnumbered four to one, they managed to link up with a squadron of the 3rd Dragoons, King's German Legion (KGL). As the two squadrons fell back, Lefebvre-Desnouettes's men moved in for the kill only to find Lord Henry Paget and the 10th Hussars, followed by the 7th and 18th Hussars, waiting for them. The chasseurs rapidly turned tail and fell back to the river but for many it was too late; over fifty were cut down while another seventy were rounded up and taken prisoner. The injured Lefebvre-Desnouettes was taken prisoner by Trooper Grisdale of the 10th Hussars when his exhausted horse refused to swim across the river. News of the defeat reached an exasperated Napoleon at his headquarters in Valderas as Moore's army marched north-east. The French had failed to inflict a decisive defeat, but although the British soldiers were safe for the moment, they still had nearly 500 kilometres to go before they reached the port of Coruña. En route they would have to march through the Galician mountains, lashed by rain, frozen by snow and harried by French cavalry. Only stamina, bravery and discipline could save them from capture or death.

The main body of the British army reached the town of Astorga on 30 December. Here the troops encountered La Romana's army as it fell back from Léon ahead of the French, but the appearance of over 9,000 starving soldiers, many of them ravaged by fever, only added to the difficulties Moore faced. The Spanish soldiers had no supplies and few weapons following their defeat at Mansilla and the sight of the British baggage led to inevitable scenes of disorder. Some of the hungry British soldiers joined the starving Spanish as riots broke out across the town.

Despite the fact there were ample stocks of food, weapons and ammunition in Astorga, Moore decided against holding the fortified town. It stood in the centre of an open plain and the French cavalry would easily stop his men leaving again once they were trapped inside. He was also concerned that the isolated incidents of mutiny could spread. He *had* to reach Corunna if he was going to save his army from destruction, even if it meant souring further the already poor relations with the Spanish. After ordering Craufurd and Alten to take their brigades west to the port of Vigo, the rest of his men marched north-west towards the snowy summits of the Galician mountains.

Discipline was already on the verge of collapse when the army entered Bembibre on 31 December but it gave way completely when the soldiers discovered the town's wine vaults. Many drank themselves into a stupor to forget their predicament, while others went on a drunken rampage. Robert Blakeney, a subaltern with the 28th Regiment, later recorded the disgraceful scenes in the town:

> Bembibre exhibited all the appearance of a place lately stormed and pillaged. Every door and window was broken, every lock and fastening forced. Rivers of wine ran through the houses and into the streets, where lay fantastic groups of soldiers; women, children, runaway Spaniards and muleteers, all apparently inanimate, while the wine oozing from their lips and nostrils seemed the effect of gunshot wounds.

Officers struggled to rouse the men the following morning and around a thousand of them, too many to discipline, refused to rejoin the march into the mountains. They were eventually left to their own devices, along with many of the women and children who were too ill to continue. The French attacked the stragglers the following day and many were killed and wounded before the survivors surrendered.

By now, Moore's command barely resembled an army and while a few battalions maintained a degree of discipline, the rest resembled a horde of beggars, dressed in rags, barefoot and starving. Many fell by the roadside, unable to continue, and they either died from cold or were killed or taken prisoner by the equally hard-pressed French cavalry following close behind.

Village after village was torn apart as the soldiers foraged furiously for food, shelter and fuel, in a desperate attempt to stay alive, and many went on the rampage after ransacking the depot in Villafranca del Bierzo. At this, Moore's compassion for his suffering men finally ran out and he took steps to restore discipline. One soldier was shot for mutiny and the rest of his men were made to file past the corpse. He then forced the subdued crowd to march continuously for thirty-six hours through blizzard conditions in a desperate attempt to save the men from themselves. Many collapsed from exhaustion and the road to Lugo was soon littered with sick, wounded, women and children, as described by Stephen Morley, a private in the 5th Regiment:

> We had neither an adequate supply of food or clothing, and our feet were dreadfully hurt from want of shoes; many were actually barefooted. The poor women were deeply to be pitied. One of them, with no covering but her tattered clothes, gave birth to a son. The road all the way was strewed with men unable to proceed. Discipline was forgotten, none commanded, none obeyed.

Although Moore could try to enforce discipline among his troops with the threat of corporal punishment, he did not have similar powers over the Spanish troops driving the baggage train. Wagon after wagon had to be left behind on the steep slopes of Monte Cebrero when many muleteers deserted. A large part of the baggage train had to be abandoned and the wagon carrying the army's supply of cash — some 25,000 pounds in silver dollars — was tipped into a ravine so it would not fall into French hands.

While the infantry trudged on, behind them Lord Paget's cavalry and General Sir Edward Paget's reserve division fought numerous running battles with the French. The largest rearguard action occurred at Cacabelos on 3 January, and the British defiance made Marshal Soult a little more cautious. Three days later Moore realised that his men were at the end of their tether and he called a halt at Lugo so they could turn and fight. Although morale rose as the men prepared to take out their frustrations on the French, they too were exhausted and their commander declined the offer to attack. After a forty-eight hour rest the retreat continued in earnest on the night of 8 January, when the refreshed men slipped away under cover of darkness. Unfortunately, several regiments lost their way in the heavy rain and over five hundred men were taken prisoner when they stumbled into the path of French cavalry patrols.

Over the next two days the pace increased as the road began to descend from the mountains into open terrain, and on 10 January the sea could be seen glinting tantalisingly on the horizon. Although the end was in sight, the French cavalry could once again harry the British stragglers and they were mercilessly hunted down. A few groups turned to fight, taking refuge in enclosures and buildings, and a hundred men led by Sergeant William Newman of the 43rd held the village of Betanzos against an attack by French dragoons.

During the early hours of 12 January the first of the survivors trudged into Corunna at the end of an appalling journey of some 500 kilometres. One after another, the 1st, 2nd and 3rd Divisions marched, or rather hobbled, through the streets as their commander looked on. Sir John Fortescue was with General Moore when the 1st Division passed:

> A brigade caught the General's eye, for they were marching like soldiers. Those must be the Guards and presently the two battalions of the 1st Guards, each of them still 800 strong, strode by in column of sections, with drums beating, the drum major twirling his staff at their head, and the men keeping step as if in their own barrack yard . . . The senior regiment of the British infantry had set an example to the whole army.

While the men settled into their billets, General Sir Edward Paget's Reserve Division carried out one last rearguard action, stopping at El Burgos to guard the Roman bridge while Soult's cavalry spread out to find a ford. The engineers finally destroyed the bridge but French scouts

Sergeant Newman's rearguard of the 43rd stop French dragoons entering Betanzos.

found another crossing upstream at Celas. Paget's division was the last to march into Corunna and Sir John Fortescue again watched in admiration as the men of the rearguard entered the town:

> They had done harder work, they had endured harder marches and they had undergone greater privations than the rest of the army, and they had been more frequently engaged in petty actions with the enemy. Yet there were relatively fewer men missing from their ranks than from any other Division, for, like the Guards, they had faced the high ordeal of the march like disciplined men.

By 12 January the survivors of the retreat had reached Corunna's harbour, where they were greeted by General Alcedo's small Spanish garrison. They had made it to the sea but the navy was nowhere to be seen and Moore had no means of finding out when the ships would come. His men were exhausted, but Sir John would have to ask them to stand and fight the French, before they could finally leave Spain for the safety of England.

TOURING THE RETREAT TO CORUNNA (A CORUÑA)

Sir John Moore's men crossed the river Esla in the vicinity of the village of Castrogonzalo, 5 kilometres south of Benavente, destroying bridges as soon as the last man had crossed. As the infantry went on the rampage in Benavente, the British cavalry held their French counterparts at bay at Castrogonzalo, leaving Napoleon furious at the news that they had failed to stop the British escaping; he was waiting for news at his headquarters in nearby Valderas.

Take the E70, the Autovia del Noroeste, heading north-west to Corunna some 500 kilometres to the north-west. To begin with the road crosses open rolling countryside between Benavente and Astorga. The town of Astorga, where the British met General La Romana's demoralised army stands in the centre of an open plain and would have been impossible to defend so Moore continued north-westwards, following the winding muddy road into the bleak mountains. The mountain tops are covered in snow even in April and the entire area would have been snowbound when the British trudged across the bleak moors in December 1808.

The countryside climbs into the hills and beyond Ponteradda the snow-capped mountains dominate the skyline. The terrain becomes extremely rugged after Villefranque and although the modern viaducts, tunnels and cuttings carve an easy path through the mountains, the old road twists its way along the foot of the narrow valley. The only

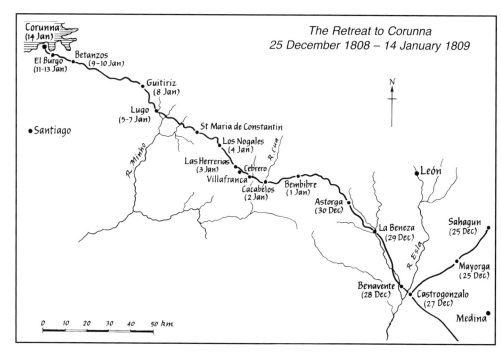

The Retreat to Corunna
25 December 1808 – 14 January 1809

consolation for Sir John Moore was that the narrow confines of the gorge and the patchwork of thick forests and rocky outcrops severely limited the activities of the French cavalry.

The mountains peak at over 450 metres near Bezantos and the road then drops steeply for the last 30 kilometres towards Corunna. Although the end was in sight, the French cavalry was able to take advantage of this open country, moving in for the kill against scattered groups of stragglers. Many died within sight of their destination, having gazed at the tempting

The bridge at O Burgo, site of the last rearguard action before Corunna.

sight of the sea shimmering in the distance.

The village of O Burgo is south-east of Corunna and it was the scene of the final rearguard action. The original bridge, the Ponte Medieval, is close to the main road and there is a memorial stone nearby telling the story of General Moore's retreat in Spanish. Continue along the E70 into the centre of A Coruña heading for the harbour.

The Battle of Corunna, 16 January 1809

Despite their predicament, the British had two factors in their favour. The first was that the range of hills blocking the main road south-east of Corunna could be defended. Moore did not have enough men to secure the Palavea or Peñasquedo Heights but Monte Mero did offer a good defensive position between the mouth of the Rio del Burgo river and Elviña village. The second was that the town's depots were full of arms and ammunition. Many soldiers exchanged their worn muskets and replaced missing items of equipment before filling their pouches with ammunition. Once everyone had replenished their stocks, the quartermaster's staff had to destroy what was left. Even if there was room for the spare stores on the transport ships, there would be no time to load everything and tonnes of equipment and clothing was destroyed or burnt to prevent it falling into French hands. Over four thousand barrels of gunpowder still left in the magazine were destroyed on the 13th to prevent them fakllling into French hands; the huge explosion smashed thousands of windows across the town.

While Moore waited for the French to make a move, Soult was advancing cautiously towards the port, giving the tired British soldiers time to recover from their ordeal. Their spirits soared when the fleet was spotted on the horizon on 14 January and the news spread like wildfire; at last the end was in sight. Twelve ships of the line anchored out to sea as over a hundred transports waited their turn to draw up alongside the harbour wall. The sick and the wounded were carried on board first and although they were followed by the artillery and cavalry, many horses had to be destroyed owing to the lack of space.

On 15 January the Duke of Dalmatia probed the rearguard at El Burgo, forcing it to withdraw, but he decided against attacking General Hope's 2nd Division position at Piedralonga. Although he had some 15,000 men, about the same as Moore, the duke called off the attack, having decided to wait for the arrival of Marshal Soult. This would increase the attacking force to 24,000 men in three divisions, supported by 36 guns including a battery of heavy 12-pounders. In contrast, Moore had only 9 guns ashore. It was going to be an uneven battle if Soult decided to conduct a prolonged artillery duel.

Moore deployed his men on Monte Mero with the 2nd Division on his left flank, overlooking the Rio del Burgo estuary. General Hope placed Hill's and Leith's brigades on the forward slopes while their light companies occupied the houses and enclosures in the valley below; Catlin Craufurd's brigade was in reserve to the rear. The 1st Division held the centre of Moore's line and Manningham's brigade held the western slopes of Monte Mero, while Bentinck's brigade held the slopes overlooking Elviña where the light companies were deployed; Warde's Guards brigade was in reserve. General Sir David Baird's position was overlooked by the Heights of Peñasquedo and his men would be exposed to heavy French artillery fire.

Embarkation had continued throughout the night and by the morning of 16 January all the British cavalry and all but nine of the guns were on board the transports. As the sun rose, Moore rode to Monte Mero to inspect his lines and assess Soult's plans to attack. The French marshal had spotted that Moore's right flank was his weak point and planned to attack Elviña in force but it was taking some time to get his men into position. As there had been no serious developments, Moore decided to continue loading the ships and he returned to Corunna to order General Fraser and General Paget to move their divisions (both of them only of brigade strength) down to the harbour. While Paget's reserve division moved back to Oza covering the road into Corunna, Fraser's 3rd Division deployed on Santa Margarita Hill, covering the south-western approaches to the port.

As the hours passed, the two armies faced each other across the Palavea valley while hundreds of men boarded the transports. The peace was finally shattered just before midday when the French guns began bombarding Elviña as their infantry prepared to advance. News of the imminent attack reached Moore when a report arrived from General Hope, and as Moore cantered back towards Monte Mero, the rising crescendo of gunfire from the Peñasquedo Heights confirmed the news.

Soult had placed a 12-pounder battery opposite the 1st Division's positions and it bombarded the troops around the village of Elviña for two hours while Delaborde's and Merle's tirailleurs forced the British skirmishers back across the Palavea stream and towards the main line. Soult's plan was to pin down the British troops holding Monte Mero on

Moore's centre and left. Delaborde's and Merle's two divisions would feint attacks across the Palavea valley to prevent Moore moving reserves across to where the real threat lay, his right flank. Mermet's division, some 7,500 strong, would then carry out the main attack, capturing the village of Elviña and the western slopes of Monte Mero, while Lahoussaye's cavalry division, some 1,300 dragoons, advanced on Mermet's left and Franceschi's light cavalry covered the open flank. While Mermet's troops rolled up the British right flank, the dragoons would swing around the British rear and cut off their line of retreat into Corunna. The final attack would clear the whole of Monte Mero, destroying Moore's army once and for all.

However, Soult's plan was taking time to unfold and as Moore noted the tirailleurs struggling to drive the British skirmishers back across the Palavea valley, he commented to his aides, 'Now, if there is no bungling, I hope we shall get away in a few hours.' He was sadly mistaken. Shortly afterwards Soult made his intentions known as Mermet's division advanced down the steep slopes of Peñasquedo Heights towards the right of the British line.

Three columns of French infantry marched towards the 1st Division as their guns fired overhead. While the 31st Regiment was heading directly for Elviña, it was clear that the 47th Regiment was aiming to turn General Baird's position. The advance was fraught with difficulties owing to the difficult terrain, and the French artillery was forced to stay at the summit of Peñasquedo Heights while the infantry struggled to maintain formation across the rough ground. One soldier of the 42nd later reported that 'The French Army did not advance very rapidly, on account of the badness of the ground.'

Bentinck's brigade was holding the Elviña area and the 31st Regiment quickly drove the 1/50th's light company out of the small village as it advanced up the slopes of Monte Mero. The few remaining British guns fired canister into the columns, while the French guns fired back at long range; one of the first casualties was General Baird, who was severely wounded, forcing Lord William Bentinck to take command of the 1st Division. (Baird was eventually loaded on to a ship where surgeons amputated his arm.)

The combination of the rough terrain and skirmishing fire disorganised the ranks of the 31st Regiment but they continued to advance through Elviña towards the 1/50th and the 1/42nd who were waiting in two-deep lines beyond the village. Moore was close by when

'Remember Egypt, think on Scotland': the 42nd retake Elviña from the French.

the two battalions opened fire at close range, bringing the French columns to a shuddering halt. As they reeled back from the effects of the British volleys, the general ordered the 1/42nd to charge, and as they drove the 31st Regiment back through the village, the 1/50th followed with Moore's shouts of 'Well done 50th! Well done my Majors' ringing in their ears. (The majors were the commanding officer, Major Charles Napier, who was wounded and taken prisoner, and Major Stanhope.) The counter-attack had the desired effect and after brisk hand-to-hand fighting, the French were forced to retire from Elviña and regroup.

While the 31st Regiment made the frontal attack against Bentinck's brigade, the 47th Regiment had been advancing to the west of Elviña, before turning to attack the British flank. Moore had already spotted the French manoeuvre and had taken steps to counter it, ordering General Paget's division forward from Oza. While Anstruther ordered the riflemen of the 95th and the 52nd to advance in extended order to confront Lahoussaye's dragoons, the 28th would follow in support. Disney's brigade extended the British flank when the 20th and the 91st occupied the San Cristobal Heights. Moore had also ordered General Fraser to abandon his plans to embark on the waiting transport ships and his division headed out of Corunna and occupied Santa Margarita Heights.

Meanwhile, as the 47th Regiment moved slowly around Bentinck's flank it found that the 1/4th Regiment had deployed half its companies at right angles to its main line in order to face the attack. As the 47th Regiment turned to face the British line, their officers found that the ranks became disordered and men began drifting to the rear. According to Sir Robert Ker Porter, 'the numbers of the enemy augmented their own consternation; they fell back on each other, making a confusion as successful as our arms'. Bentinck's brigade had won the battle even before the first volley had been fired and the 47th Regiment was soon falling back in disorder alongside the 31st Regiment.

Soult's first attack had ended in disaster. While Mermet's division regrouped on the lower slopes of the Peñasquedo Heights, Anstruther's men were engaged in a furious firefight with Lahoussaye's dragoons. The dragoons were unable to get their horses across the Monelos stream and many had dismounted and taken cover among the stone walls, rocks and gorse bushes scattered along the valley floor. It was an unequal contest. The British infantry were used to fighting in extended order and their rifles had greater accuracy and a longer range than the troopers' carbines. Lahoussaye's men would be forced to fall back slowly over the hours that followed.

By mid-afternoon Mermet's division had regrouped and made a second attempt to take Elviña from General Baird's division. The 50th and the 42nd were driven from the village by this renewed offensive but Moore rallied them with the words 'Remember Egypt, think on Scotland.' For once his words of encouragement did not work, and Warde had to send two battalions of foot guards to halt Mermet's men in the village. While the fighting raged around Elviña, General Merle sent his remaining regiment forward to support the attack. Baird countered by sending forward the 3/1st and the 2/81st of Manningham's brigade, supported by the 2/59th of Leith's brigade, to strike the French column in the flank. After prolonged fighting, the French finally fell back from the slopes, leaving Elviña in British hands once more.

Moore had directed the fighting from the slopes for most of the afternoon but as the battle was finally swinging in his favour, disaster struck when a cannon-ball hit him in the left shoulder. As aides carried the mortally wounded general to safety in a blanket, he asked to take one final look back over the battlefield with the words, 'I always wanted to

Moore's aides rush to their general's assistance as he falls mortally wounded.

die this way'. He was taken to his headquarters, a house close to the harbour, where he died soon afterwards. The general was buried late that night on the southern ramparts of Corunna.

Meanwhile, on the battlefield, Sir John Hope was finding it difficult to assert himself as the focus of the battle turned away from Elviña and towards his left flank where General Henri-François Delaborde's division was about to make the final French assault against the summit of Monte Mero. Until now Marshal Soult had avoided attacking the 2nd Division's positions astride the main road into Corunna, but General Hope had been forced to send several of his battalions west to support the battle for Elviña, thus weakening the hill-top position. French skirmishers had also spent the day forcing their British counterparts from the valley and Soult now decided that the time was ripe to sweep the British from Monte Mero. As Delaborde's division began to descend the steep slopes of the Heights of Palavea in the late afternoon, the tiralleurs surged forward to clear Piedralonga.

As three columns of infantry crossed the Palavea stream and advanced up the slopes towards Hope's division, Hill moved two of his battalions, the 14th and 92nd, to take up a position astride the Corunna road to reinforce the only battalion remaining under Leith's command. Several volleys and rounds of canister from the two guns covering the road brought the leading French regiment to a halt and it was soon falling back to regroup. Although the three British battalions were outnumbered, Craufurd's reserve brigade was waiting in support only a few hundred yards away, out of reach of the French guns. Soult called off further attacks, and as Delaborde's troops withdrew across the Palavea stream, darkness began to fall across the battlefield.

As the exhausted men marched back down to the harbour a simple burial ceremony took place on the ramparts overlooking Corunna, as Sir John Moore's body was laid to rest. The embarkation continued throughout the night and the following day, while the French guns fired long-range shots at the ships; only a few were damaged. The last regiment to embark was the 23rd and legend has it that Captain Gomm of the 1/9th Regiment was the last man to step off the quayside.

After the horrendous march and the final battle in front of Corunna, the exhausted men could finally say goodbye to Spain, leaving behind not only their commander but more than 800 men dead on the slopes of Monte Mero. On 18 January Moore's battered army sailed for home while

Soldiers of the 26th stand their ground during the final French attacks on Monte Mero.

Corunna's garrison fought on until the fleet was safely out to sea. General Alcedo, the garrison commander, then surrendered his men.

Although the British soldiers were safe at last, severe weather battered the fleet all the way across the Bay of Biscay on the two-week voyage. When the ships finally began to land on the 31st, there was a public outcry at the state of the dishevelled men scrambling on to the quayside. Concerns were raised across England as the country was embroiled in political turmoil.

Sir John Moore had been instructed to safeguard the only army that Britain had, and he had done so; but the cost had been high. Over 6,000 men had been left behind, either dead or as prisoners of war, many of them suffering from terrible injuries. Although there had been time to save the majority of the army's guns, most of the baggage train had been left behind, often unceremoniously dumped alongside the road to Corunna for the French to plunder.

The departure of the army also further deepened the distrust between Britain and Spain. Moore's troops had done little to endear themselves to the Spanish population as they left a trail of destruction across the Galician mountains, but now they had gone, the people felt abandoned and complaints of betrayal were soon heard across the country. It would take a series of military victories and delicate political negotiations before the Spanish and the British would trust each other again.

Visiting Corunna Battlefield

Drive straight into the centre of A Coruña along the N550, heading for the harbour and the old town, the Ciudad Vieja. Park your car near the small fort overlooking the entrance to the harbour, one of the few features that

Right: The plaque on the house where Sir John Moore died.

Below: Sir John Moore's tomb.

EN ESTA CASA
MURIÓ EL VALEROSO GENERAL INGLE
Sir. JOHN MOORE
EL 16 DE ENERO DE 1809,
Á CONSECUENCIA DE LAS HERIDAS
QUE RECIBIÓ EL MISMO DÍA
EN LA BATALLA DE ELVIÑA
LUCHANDO HEROICAMENTE EN DEFEN
DE LA INDEPENDENCIA ESPAÑO
PRIMER CENTENARIO.
1909

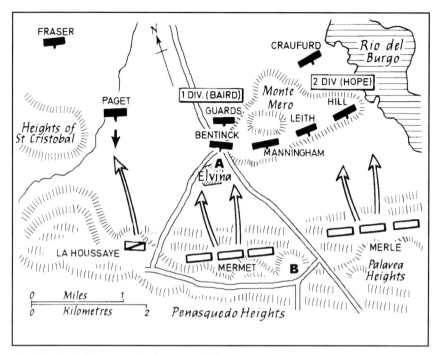

The Battle of Corunna, 16 January 1809.

has not changed since General Moore's weary soldiers embarked on the waiting ships. After Moore's death his body was taken to the nearby Jardin de San Carlos, a small walled bastion next to the Military Hospital, to be buried. His tomb stands in the centre of the small garden. Verses of Charles Wolfe's poem dedicated to Moore can be found on plaques by the gate, while a second plaque inside the gate marks the Duke of Wellesley's tribute to the Galician soldiers.

Head back along the harbour along Avenue la Maritimo to reach the site of the house where Moore died. It stood at 5 Canton Grande, now a bank, alongside a plaza with a small clock tower. A plaque commemorates Moore's death.

Go back to your car and head south out of the town, following signs for the N550 Santiago. The road climbs into a cutting through the Monte Mero, in the centre of Moore's line. The slip road turning for Elviña is 5 kilometres from the harbour, just after the Carrefour supermarket, and it is also signposted for the university. The Heights of Peñasquedo and A

Old Corunna harbour

Elviña Church

British line

Mermet's attack

Marshal Soult attacked General Moore's right flank at Elviña, his weakest position.

Coruña University fill the horizon as the N550 climbs up towards Elviña. It is clear from the view here that the French position dominated the British troops.

After leaving the N550, head straight on along the narrow road signposted Elviña. The church is to the left after 300 metres; take care here as the road is narrow and parking is difficult. There are several plaques near the building commemorating anniversaries of the battle and remembering the men killed here. Although the church was at the extreme right of Moore's line, it became the focus of the initial French attacks both from the heights to the north and from the low ground to the west where the reserve division occupied San Cristobal, a low rocky outcrop, threatening Mermet's flank. Bentinck's position was weak and his men would have felt exposed as the French guns fired from the heights while Mermet's columns advanced down the steep slopes.

Continue to drive up the steep slope, following the narrow road into the university campus, turning left beyond the main buildings at the T-junction near the summit. San Cristobal can be seen to the left. The views across La Coruña show how the French could see Moore's every move and it is difficult to see how he made his men stand and fight one last time.

Turn left on to the main road 200 metres beyond the campus and almost immediately pull in to the lay-by on the left in front of a large tiled map of the battle. The colourful display depicts all the various brigades and indicates the direction of the French attacks, but the orientation is

Mont Mero

British line

misleading. There is another memorial to Sir John Moore alongside.

Follow the path to the right of the memorial (down the hill) across the waste ground and across a field; here you will get a good viewpoint across the British positions. Elviña is immediately in front and the rocky slopes of San Cristobal can be seen to the west. Monte Mero, where General Hope waited for the final half-hearted French attack at dusk, lies beyond the motorway. Return to your car. Continue down the hill from the plaque and rejoin the N550, heading south, to complete your tour of the battlefield.

It is possible to enter Palavea but housing and the motorway make it difficult to locate any landmarks. However, it is clear that Monte Mero dominated Palavea valley and it was pointless trying to advance up the slopes when Elviña was such a tempting target.

Elviña's church was at the centre of heavy fighting.

Sir John Moore's Army at Corunna

1st Division, Sir David Baird, **5,100** men
Warde   1/1st Guards, 2/1st Guards
Bentinck   1/4th, 1/42nd, 1/50th
Manningham   3/1st, 1/26th, 2/81st

2nd Division, Sir John Hope, **5,600** men
Leith   51st, 2/5 9th, 76th
Hill   2nd, 1/5th, 2/14th, 1/32nd
C. Craufurd   1/36th, 1/71st, 1/92nd

3rd Division, Fraser, **2,600** men
Beresford 1/6th, 1/9th, 2/23rd, 2/43rd
Fane   1/38th, 1/79th, 1/82nd

Reserve Division, Hon Sir Edward Paget, **1,500** men
Anstruther   20th, 1/52nd, 1/95th
Disney   1/28th, 1/91st
Robert Craufurd 1/43rd, 2/52nd, 2/95th, 1st Flank Brigade
Charles Alten 1st and 2nd Light Bttn KGL, 2nd Flank Brigade

Cavalry, Hon Lord Henry Paget
7th, 10th and 15th Hussars, 18th Light Dragoons, 3rd Light Dragoons KGL

Soult's Army at Corunna
Infantry Brigades:
Merle 6,200
Delaborde 5,500
Mermet 7,500

Cavalry Brigades:
Lahoussaye 1,600
Lorge 1,600
Franceschi 1,300

Chapter 3

WELLESLEY RETURNS TO THE PENINSULA

THE FRENCH ADVANCE INTO PORTUGAL, 9–28 MARCH 1809

FOLLOWING THE DEPARTURE of the British army from Corunna, the armies of Marshal Soult and Marshal Claude Victor were free to retake Portugal but it took time to occupy the ports of Corunna, Ferrol and Vigo. After handing over Galicia to Marshal Michel Ney's corps, the two marshals gathered together their scattered divisions and gave their tired men time to recover before heading into the mountains where La Romana's men were hiding.

The fiery Michel Ney.

As Victor's army marched east to Mérida, Soult's army headed south along the coast, finding Valensça's fortress blocking the crossing over the river Mino. The march inland to Orense added an extra 80 kilometres to their journey, lengthening the march by several days, and the French did not cross the border into Portugal until 9 March. By now Soult's problems were increasing as he headed deeper into enemy territory. He had some 20,000 men and 20 guns, but supplies were limited and his men were forced to forage for food far and wide across the inhospitable countryside.

The Portuguese armed forces looked impressive on paper but in reality they were no match for the French. Although the regular Portuguese army numbered 25,000 men, they were poorly led, inadequately trained and lacked arms and equipment. The country's militia and home guard were in an even worse state; many had no weapons and few had had any form of military training. The only reliable troops in the country were 16,000 British troops led by General Cradock, but they had orders to protect the last remaining British foothold in the country, Lisbon and its port.

As Soult's army advanced southwards, the 12,000-strong garrison holding the border area east of the Sierra Gerez mountains withdrew ahead of them, leaving the fortress at Chaves in French hands; they had not fired a shot. As the French turned west towards the sea, they faced a formidable line of redoubts along the hills east of Braga, held by 25,000 members of the home guard. Soult sent his cavalry forward on 20 March to test their nerve and, as expected, the Portuguese fled ahead of the French horsemen.

As the French infantry began the final stage of their long march towards Oporto, 50 kilometres to the south-west, the city was in a state of chaos. A second line of redoubts had been built on the hills north of the city and the 30,000-strong garrison was expected to hold out for some time. But once again, when Soult's army approached on 28 March the majority of the home guard simply abandoned their positions and headed into the city in search of loot or drink.

Two days later Soult's army advanced towards the city. General Mermet's troops led the centre of the advance, while General Merle's and General Delaborde's divisions approached from the west and the east respectively; all three divisions found little to stop them. As news of the approaching French spread around the city, panic set in as marauding mobs of home guard troops turned and ran towards the river alongside thousands of terrified civilians. The crowds were heading for the river bank, pushing and shoving towards a temporary bridge of boats, the only crossing over the wide and fast-flowing river Douro. The weight of bodies, horses and wagons squeezing on to the bridge eventually pushed the temporary structure under the water. With their only means of escape gone, thousands of Portuguese soldiers and civilians headed back into the city, only to find Soult's men already rampaging through the streets, committing murder, pillage and rape. The French soldiers were indiscriminately shooting or beating to death soldiers and civilians alike, and by the time the carnage ended approximately eight thousand men, women and children had lost their lives. In contrast, only five hundred French soldiers had been killed.

When the rioting eventually came to an end, Soult was pleased to hear that large stocks of supplies had been seized, along with dozens of artillery pieces of various vintages and calibres. The conquest of northern Portugal had been achieved relatively easily, but the widespread and unnecessary violence in Oporto turned the local population against the French invaders. In future Portuguese soldiers and civilians would retaliate at every opportunity, leaving Soult isolated in a hostile country and far from his supply depots. His army was too weak to take Lisbon and Victor was too far away to provide assistance. It was time for Soult to reassess the situation. But even as his army moved south, Sir Arthur Wellesley was returning to the peninsula with a new British Expeditionary Force.

WELLESLEY'S ADVANCE ACROSS PORTUGAL, 22 APRIL–12 MAY 1809

Wellesley returned to Lisbon as the British Expeditionary Force's new Commander-in-Chief on 22 April 1809. The number of troops now in Portugal had risen to 48,000 but 12,000 of them had to be left behind under General Mackenzie to protect the port of Lisbon. The rest could be deployed against the French and spies reported that Marshal Soult was deployed along the Vouga river, 50 kilometres south of Oporto, blocking the main road to Coimbra, while General Victor was still 240 kilometres to the east around Mérida.

Wellesley's plan was simple. He would move north quickly to Coimbra with 26,000 British troops supported by over 2,000 Portuguese. He would then lead 18,000 men north, driving Marshal Soult towards

The view along the Douro, looking east towards the Bishops' Seminary.

Oporto, while General Beresford's division headed north-east towards Lamego, cutting off the French line of retreat along the river Douro towards the Spanish border. Once Soult had been isolated and defeated, Wellesley could gather his troops and head east to attack Victor's army.

While Wellesley's men marched north, Royal Navy ships followed their advance along the coast. The troops entered Coimbra on 1 May, Wellesley's 40th birthday. A few days later they were heading north towards Soult, while Beresford turned north-east at Buçaco, heading across the Sierra Alcoba mountains for Lamego. As Wellesley approached Sardoa, General Hill was ordered to move west through Averio, before heading north along the coast, in the hope of outflanking the French positions.

A two-pronged attack at Albergia Nova on 9 May failed to trap Soult and his troops fell back towards Oporto. Although General Hill's men used boats to cross the Lake of Ovar, in an attempt to cut off the French line of retreat, the marshal was one step ahead and his men entered Villa Nova, on the south bank of the river Douro opposite Oporto, on 11 May. Soult's divisions immediately began crossing the bridge of boats and had reached the north bank by the early hours of the following morning, setting up camp west of the town by dawn. As Wellesley's troops approached, the bridge of boats was destroyed by French engineers while Portuguese sailors were forced to sail their wine barges across to the north bank to prevent the British commandeering them.

CROSSING THE RIVER DOURO, 12 MAY 1809

Wellesley reached the south bank of the Douro a few hours after the last of Soult's troops had crossed. He studied the city's layout from the Monastery de Serra do Pilar, a large complex sitting high on a promontory on the south bank. He could see that the river was in flood and the bridge had been destroyed, and that there was no sign of any boats along the south bank. Scouts were dispatched with orders to search for alternative ways to cross, while the British commander studied the French camp on the far bank and looked for a solution to a difficult problem.

The first good news he heard was about the ferry at Avintas, just 3 kilometres upstream. Although the boat had been scuttled and left half-submerged in the river, it could be salvaged. It was a start and General Sir George Murray was ordered to take two KGL infantry battalions and the 14th Light Dragoons to the village so they would be ready to cross as soon as the vessel was repaired.

Wellesley knew that the majority of Soult's 11,000 troops were deployed on the open heath north-west of the town, so they could march north at the earliest opportunity. He had also noticed that the Bishops' Seminary, a large structure on the eastern outskirts of the town, was unoccupied and out of sight of the French camp. The walled enclosure surrounding the building would make an excellent base for a bridgehead once his men were across the Douro, and there was even a hidden beach, suitable for embarking troops on the south bank. All he had to do now was to find boats to take his men across the river.

The answer came from an unexpected source a little time later. Colonel John Waters, one of Wellesley's scouts, had spoken to a Portuguese barber who had rowed across the river in a small boat. He had seen four wine barges hidden on the river bank below the seminary; he was also able to confirm that the seminary was unoccupied. It was the news the British commander had been waiting for and he greeted it with the exclamation 'By God! Waters has done it!' Waters crossed the river with the barber, taking the Prior of Amarante to act as a guide. Once on the far bank, four local boatmen were enlisted to help sail the barges across to the south shore.

An accurate depiction of crossing the river Douro; the seminary is on the skyline.

Although Wellesley now had the means to cross the Douro, it was going to be a dangerous operation, requiring organisation, luck and, above all, bravery from the men chosen to lead the crossing. They would have to cross the fast-flowing river, thirty men at a time, in the slow-moving barges and in broad daylight. Even if the operation went ahead without French interference, it would take an hour to carry Hill's brigade across to the far bank.

A platoon of the 3rd Foot crossed first, without the French picquets in Oporto noticing, and after climbing the steep steps to the seminary, they secured the gates to the adjacent cemetery. As the wine barges brought across more of the Buffs, some fortified the large building while others took up positions behind the cemetery walls. They were followed by the 2/66th (Berkshires) and 2/48th (Northamptonshires), and by the time the French raised the alarm, over six hundred men were waiting for them in and around the seminary. Wellesley had also had the foresight to provide artillery support for the bridgehead, deploying three artillery batteries on Serra Heights, part of the convent gardens, to cover the approaches to the seminary across the river.

Marshal Soult had been up all night reorganising his troops after their hurried retreat and when he was finally roused from his sleep around midday with the news that the British were crossing the river, he dismissed the claim with the words: 'Pah! It is just a party of red-coated Swiss going down to bathe.' When the alarm was eventually raised, General Maximilien Foy was instructed to investigate the situation at the seminary. He ordered three battalions of the 17th Léger Regiment to approach the British stronghold, expecting to retake it easily, but he was mistaken. Many of Hill's men opened fire from the cemetery walls while others took aim from the building windows. Meanwhile, the eighteen guns deployed on the Serra Heights fired roundshot across the river at the French columns, knocking out their guns. The combination of heavy artillery fire in the flank and volleys of musket fire from the seminary complex came as a complete surprise to the 17th Léger Regiment and it was driven back in confusion. A second French attack by the three battalions of the 70th Line Regiment, sent forward by General Delaborde, also failed to dislodge the British from their fortress. While British losses were minimal, their leader, Lieutenant-General Edward Paget, was seriously wounded and General Rowland Hill had to cross to take his place as another French brigade gathered to attack the slender bridgehead.

By now, Soult had realised that this was no minor excursion to the north bank and he ordered the troops guarding the quayside to leave their posts and support the assault on the seminary. It was a sensible move in some respects but it did leave the river bank unguarded and the people of Oporto took the opportunity to take their revenge and drive the French from their city. Hundreds of Portuguese civilians emerged from their houses and untied their wine barges, before rowing them across the river. The men of the 1st Division watched in amazement as dozens of boats headed towards them.

With boats of all shapes and sizes now available, Wellesley gave General Sir John Sherbrooke orders to cross and although the Guards brigade was supposed to lead, the 29th Regiment was already waiting on the riverbank and refused to stand aside. Before long, the Portuguese had rowed the Worcesters across and as they assembled on Oporto's quayside, Soult called off further attacks on the seminary so he could reorganise his men to counter the British advance and head east to escape.

As the rest of the 1st Division crossed the river, it seemed that Wellesley would be able to cut off the French line of retreat and inflict an overwhelming defeat on the French. Murray's troops had already crossed the Douro at Avintas and they were well positioned to cut off Soult's escape route. However, although the 14th Light Dragoons captured three hundred prisoners, sending the rest fleeing eastwards in disorder, the rest of Murray's men allowed the French to escape. It was a bitterly disappointing end to an otherwise successful day.

Wellesley's bold plan had worked. As he ate Soult's supper at the Palacio das Carrancas he reflected on how his men had crossed the Douro and seized Oporto for the loss of just 123 casualties. Although Soult had lost only 300 casualties in the fighting at the seminary, another 1,500 sick and injured men were taken prisoner when the town was searched. In addition, some 70 French and Portuguese guns were seized.

Marshal Soult's problems were far from over: he had to escape from Portugal. The shortest route lay to the east, but Beresford's division was waiting near Lamego across his line of retreat. Instead Soult was obliged to race for the north end of the Sierra de Cahrerra mountains before Wellesley could catch him. The two armies turned east near Braga and marched on a parallel course along the river Cávado towards the Gorge of Misarella. Following a brief engagement at Pontenova on 16 May, Soult crossed the border into Spain and headed north, leaving Wellesley behind.

The British could not follow, for two reasons. Victor's army was already moving to join Soult and their combined armies would outnumber the British. Wellesley was also suffering from a lack of transport and he was limited by the amount of food and ammunition that the Commissariat could send north of the river Douro. As his men turned south once again, Wellesley could, however, be content in the knowledge that he had given the French a bloody nose and damaged Soult's reputation.

Wellesley's Army at Oporto

General Sherbrooke's Division **6,700** men
H. Campbell's Brigade   1/Coldstream, 1/3rd Guards, 1 Coy 5/60th
Sontag's Brigade   97th,   1 Coy 5/60th, 2nd Det. Bn, 2/16th Port.
A. Campbell's Brigade   2/7th, 2/53rd, 1 Coy 5/60th, 1/10th Port.

General Paget's Division **5,150** men
Stewart's Brigade   29th,   1st Bn Det., 1/16th Portuguese
J. Murray's Brigade 1st, 2nd, 5th and 7th Line Battalions KGL

Soult's Army

At Oporto
General Delaborde with 5,000 men
General Merle with 6,000 men

South of the Douro
General Mermet with 6,300 men

At Amarante
General Loison with 6,300 men

Ponte de Dom Luis I bridge; while Wellesley watched from the Monastery de Serra do Pilar to the left, Marshal Soult's army was camped behind the cathedral on the right.

TOURING OPORTO

Oporto (Porto) is now a sprawling city built up along the banks of the river Douro, its suburbs a maze of narrow streets and one-way systems. The Ponte de Dom Luis I is an ornate two-tier steel lattice bridge in the centre of the old town, and the dome of the monastery, high on its promontory on the south bank, can be seen from many parts of the city. The upper level of the bridge is pedestrianised but cars can join the long queues to cross the lower level. The modern white concrete bridge known as the Ponte Infante de Henrique crosses from the Observatory promontory on the south bank, a tree-covered hill to the east of the monastery (where Wellesley placed his eighteen guns), in front of the Bishops' Seminary, the large rectangular white building with a red roof on the opposite bank.

After crossing the Douro, the British troops climbed the slope to reach the Seminary.

On the south bank of the river Douro, drive down the Avienda de Republic to the pedestrianised area that begins in front of the upper level of the Dom Luis I bridge. Drive straight on at the traffic lights, climbing the narrow cobbled road called Rampa do Infante Santo, along the foot of the monastery wall. A sign marked 'Monumento' points the way to the small car park at the top. It is possible to see most of the city from the Monastery de Serra do Pilar, and Wellesley studied the French deployment from here on the morning of 12 May 1809. (Alternatively park in the vicinity and walk up the ramp to the view the river.)

French troops had destroyed the bridge of boats the night before the British arrived and Soult was confident that Wellesley could not cross the

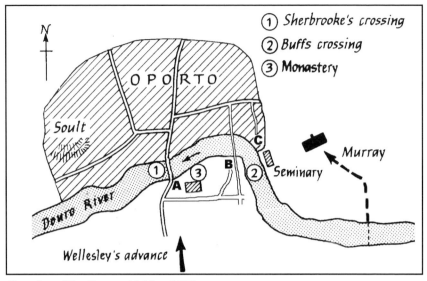

① Sherbrooke's crossing
② Buffs crossing
③ Monastery

O P O R T O

Soult

Murray

Seminary

Wellesley's advance

Crossing of the Douro, 12 May 1809

river. His headquarters and most of his men were based to the west of the cathedral, out of sight of where the British commander decided to cross, upstream in front of the seminary building.

Drive back down the ramp and turn left at the bottom, passing the artillery barracks. Take the third exit from the roundabout signposted for the Observatory and follow the road for 300 metres to a pull-in area on the right, overlooking the Ponte Infante de Henrique. Wellesley placed his eighteen guns on the slope of the hill, looking across to the seminary on the opposite bank.

Turn around and return to the roundabout, taking the third exit signposted for Ponte Infante de Henrique. Turn left at the crossroads and turn right 300 metres after crossing the bridge to visit the seminary. Turn right at the first set of traffic lights and follow the cobbled street to the end where there is parking in front of the seminary.

Follow the path around the front of the seminary and note the small commemorative plaque on the corner of the building. Cross the tennis courts to view the crossing area (if the gates are open). The beach used by Hill's brigade is on the opposite bank of the river, far below, at the foot of the Ponte Infante de Henrique. After crossing the river, the 3rd Foot climbed the steep slope and secured the building and the cemetery gates. High above the crossing area is the hill where the British guns were based, while the monastery and the cathedral can be seen downstream. Sherbrooke's 1st Division crossed at the site of the Ponte de Dom Luis I, next to the remains of the bridge of boats. Finally, upstream to the left was where Murray crossed.

Return to your car and drive across the square heading north. After 500 metres turn left at the traffic lights and head back to the Ponte Infante de Henrique, turning left at the third set of traffic lights to recross the river. Once on the far bank continue straight on at the traffic lights and then take the first right after 500 metres, following the road back up the hill. Turn right at the mini-roundabout after 400 metres and go down the steep slope, turning left for Quai Sebantos under the road bridge. Park at the bottom of the hill, near the river.

The launching area is at the bottom of the hill and it was a perfect place for the troops to cross, being hidden from the cathedral area where Marshal Soult was based. There would have been a few tense moments while Hill's men crossed the fast-moving river and then climbed the hill to the seminary standing high above. Return to the town to complete the tour.

The Battle of Talavera, 27–28 July 1809

After losing Oporto, Soult decided to evacuate Galicia in the spring of 1809, aiming to concentrate his troops. Ney still wanted to remain in the province and use it as a base for future operations but he was forced to withdraw after a bloody encounter with the Spanish Mino Division. With the threat in north-west Spain reduced, Wellesley could move his troops east to attack Victor and his army of 20,000 men concentrated around Mérida.

The British army had agreed to cooperate with the Spanish but Wellesley and General Gregorio Cuesta repeatedly argued over strategy. The British commander was also concerned about the condition of Cuesta's 35,000-strong army, having noticed how poorly equipped and armed the men were during an inspection at Almaraz. Wellesley also needed assistance with food and transport if he were to operate successfully over the border, but the promises of help offered by the Spanish authorities failed to materialise, leaving the British in considerable difficulties.

Despite these problems, 20,000 British troops advanced across the Spanish border in May 1809 and assembled north of the river Tagus at Plasencia. Victor withdrew to avoid confrontation and concentrated his forces north-east of Talavera de la Reina, hoping to rendezvous there with General Horace Sébastiani's army of 22,000 men, while Joseph Bonaparte's 12,000-strong force also moved north-west from Madrid to join him.

Wellesley and Cuesta had eventually decided to concentrate their armies at Oropesa and they assembled some 50 kilometres west of the town on 20 July. They had also agreed to attack Marshal Victor at the first opportunity, aiming to destroy his army before Sébastiani and Bonaparte were able to join him. The two allied armies were supposed to advance together on 23 July but the Spanish general did not move, and to make matters worse, he did not inform the British headquarters. This left Wellesley's men moving forward alone for a short time. As soon as it became clear that Victor was withdrawing the following morning, Cuesta decided to pursue him, in spite of the news that Sébastiani and Joseph were now close by. It was now Wellesley's turn to refuse to cooperate, choosing instead to wait by the river Alberche until his transport caught up. Cuesta found to his cost how close the French were when they attacked on the 25th; his army was driven back and the men were lucky to escape across the river.

It was now clear that the British and Spanish would have to cooperate to avoid defeat at the hands of the French, who now numbered 46,000 troops and 86 guns. Although the allies had superior numbers, 55,000 troops supported by 60 guns, their mistrust of each other was endangering the whole situation. Wellesley had only 20,000 British and German troops and 36 guns, and he did not rate Cuesta's 35,000 Spaniards very highly. Worse still, neither general trusted the other.

The allied plan was to deploy along the banks of the Portina stream, north of the town of Talavera, in the hope that the French would be tempted to attack them. By 27 July they were starting to deploy while Mackenzie's 3rd Division posted troops along the river Alberche to keep the French at bay. An attempt to cross the river took General Donkin's brigade by surprise and it suffered 440 casualties before the French withdrew. Wellesley was watching Victor's movements from a farmhouse called Casa de Salinas when the attack was made. He ran down the stairs from the tower when he spotted enemy cavalry approaching the building and barely escaped capture. The French then decided against making further attacks across the river, allowing the allies to continue deploying.

The right flank of the allied line was fixed on the river Tagus, where Cuesta's two corps, led by General Zayas and General Portago, covered the town of Talavera. General Campbell's 4th Division was deployed immediately north of the Spanish on Pajar de Vergara, a small hill east of the Portina stream, topped by a large farm complex and a redoubt. Sherbrooke's 1st Division was in the centre of the British position, on the southern slopes of a prominent hill called the Cerro de Medellín, with Mackenzie's 3rd Division deployed behind in reserve. The 2nd Division was positioned on the forward slopes of the hill, and General Hill was responsible for holding the allied left flank. North of the hill was a 1.5-kilometre-wide open plain, stretching to the foot of the Sierra de Segurilla, a range of steep, rocky hills. Wellesley echeloned his three cavalry brigades behind Hill's position, ready to counter any attempts to turn his flank.

During the afternoon the French divisions moved towards Cascajal Ridge, the high ground east of the Portina stream, but by nightfall only Victor's four divisions had reached their deployment area opposite Wellesley's left flank. Milhaud's 2,200-strong cavalry was moving towards Cuesta's troops when several nervous Spanish battalions fired a volley at a range of a kilometre or so. No one was hurt but the noise caused panic in the Spanish ranks and many fled into Talavera with shouts of treason ringing in their ears. Some were stopped but many disappeared from the battlefield after plundering Wellesley's baggage train. The British commander was close by when the incident happened and later described how his confidence in his Spanish allies had reached a new low:

> In the battle of Talavera a whole corps threw away their arms, and ran off in my presence, when they were neither attacked nor threatened with an attack, but frightened, I believe, by their own fire. When these dastardly soldiers run away, they plunder everything they meet, and in their flight from Talavera they plundered the baggage of the British army. I have found, upon enquiry and from experience, the instances of the misbehaviour of the Spanish troops to be so numerous, and those of their good behaviour so few, that I must conclude that they are troops by no means to be depended on.

Cuesta wanted to punish his men severely and gave the order for two hundred deserters to be shot; the number was reduced to forty after Wellesley intervened.

As night fell, Wellesley's troubles persisted. Although he had reconnoitred the battlefield and issued strict deployment instructions, he was not able to revisit his divisions to check that his instructions had been carried out before dark. Sherbrooke's 1st Division was in position on the southern slopes of Medellín, but two of Hill's brigades, led by Tilson and Stewart, were a kilometre further back than he wanted, leaving the crest of the hill unguarded.

As luck would have it, Victor took the decision to carry out a night attack on Medellín Hill before King Joseph arrived on the battlefield, and as soon as it was dark General François Ruffin's division moved forward in three columns. After crossing the Portina stream they climbed the slopes towards the deserted summit, eventually running into the 1st Division's flank, held by Lowe's KGL brigade. The two battalions of King's German Legion infantry quickly fell back after a few volleys, but the sound of firing alerted General Rowland Hill, and although he was heard to say that it was 'probably the Buffs as usual, making some blunder', he nevertheless rode forward to investigate. He soon found to his cost that he was wrong when he galloped into the ranks of the French 9th Light Regiment, some of whom seized the bridle of his horse. Hill was a strong man and managed to break free, escaping from the French infantry at the gallop but his brigade major was killed in the struggle.

After raising the alarm, Hill found Stewart's brigade and led it forward on to the crest of Medellín Hill. The 1/29th led the way, firing volley after volley, and the French withdrew back down the slopes in confusion. The brief firefight had only cost around 300 casualties on each side but for a short time the allied position had been in serious jeopardy. Wellesley was soon on the scene, making sure that Hill placed his brigades exactly where he wanted them before settling down among his men on the Medellín Hill and going to sleep with only his cloak for shelter. While he slept, Sébastiani's corps arrived in front of the centre of the allied line and the three divisions completed Joseph's deployment.

The British soldiers were roused from their sleep while it was still dark and as the sun rose over Talavera on 28 July the sound of a single gun opening fire signalled the start of the French attack. Thirty guns bombarded General Hill's positions on the Medellín as General Ruffin's division once again marched forward in three columns and scrambled across the Portina stream. In front, on the forward slopes of the hill, the

2nd Division's battalions lay in the grass arrayed in their two-deep lines while their guns returned fire from the summit. General Hill's deployment meant that the French artillery had little effect while the British artillery was able to fire into the dense columns of infantry as they queued up to cross the stream. The swarms of British skirmishers also engaged the French columns, firing as they withdrew towards the smoke-wreathed crest where General Hill was watching, furiously shouting 'Damn their filing, let them come in anyhow.'

The northern column of Frenchmen moved over the slopes on the north side of Medellín Hill; spotting the British cavalry waiting in the distance, their commander ordered his men to halt and they engaged in a long-range duel with the 29th. This column would not advance any further. The rest of the division marched up the slopes of Medellín Hill only to find Stewart's and Tilson's brigades lying in wait for them, standing up to take aim as the French columns came within range. As Ruffin's men deployed from column into line, volley after volley blasted the mass of men, virtually wiping out the front ranks before they could return fire. In the fighting that followed, the 29th captured two colours (the eagles had been removed from the standards) and before long the French were falling back down the slopes towards Portina stream having suffered over 1,300 casualties.

This early defeat shocked the French commanders and they called a council of war to decide what to do next. Victor wanted to continue the attack but Joseph and his Chief of Staff, Jean-Baptiste Jourdan, wanted to suspend operations and wait for Marshal Soult to arrive from the north. News that General Venegas's army was moving to threaten Madrid prompted Joseph to order a full-scale assault. Victor's corps would make a third attempt to take the Medellín Hill while Sébastiani's corps advanced towards the rest of the British line, simultaneously making a feint attack against the redoubt on Pajar de Vergara.

While the French divisions waited for their new orders, men from both armies gathered along the Portina stream to fill their canteens with water. Although they had been engaged in heavy fighting only hours before, the French and British soldiers exchanged greetings and wished each other well across the stream. One soldier recalled the informal truce:

> The water in the stream, which in the morning was clear and sweet, was now a pool of blood, heaped over with the dead and dying. There being no alternative, we were compelled to close our

Marshal Jean-
Baptiste Jourdan.

eyes and drink the gory stream. The French troops were equally ill off and came down in thousands to follow our example. In place of looking grimly at our enemies, we shook hands with them in the most friendly manner.

In the early afternoon four French divisions moved forward in column down to Portina stream while their guns bombarded the British line along the slopes of Medellín Hill. General Leval's troops advanced towards General Mackenzie's 4th Division on Wellesley's right flank only to be stopped by repeated volleys fired by the 2/7th and the 2/53rd. When these two battalions charged, the French infantry fell back, leaving behind a gun battery. A second attack by Leval's division was stopped by Campbell's division and its artillery was captured when Cuesta's troops joined the counter-attack.

General Sébastiani's division crossed the Portina stream to Leval's right and advanced towards the 1st Division where Sherbrooke's men were once again lying hidden in the grass. As the first wave of French columns drew closer Campbell's and Cameron's brigades stood up, took aim and fired a single volley with devastating effects. Sébastiani's stunned men staggered to a halt and then fell back as Sherbrooke's men charged.

It was too much for us to lie any longer, and, leaping up, we gave the well-known British cheer and charged. This was a movement for which they were not prepared, and we soon broke their front ranks, when they immediately fell back on the dense columns in the rear.

However, while success was close at hand, a lack of discipline in the British lines left Wellesley's line severely stretched. While Cameron's brigade rallied quickly and returned to the safety of the upper slopes of the Medellín Hill, the Guards Brigade and two KGL brigades chased the French across the Portina stream. This was a disastrous move: they ran into a line of fresh French battalions who were only too eager to return the favour, firing volley after volley into the now disorganised ranks of British and German troops. The firefight had stopped Sébastiani's

Campbell's Guards Brigade repels Sébastiani's attack across the Portina stream.

division but a large part of the 1st Division had been reduced to a disorganised mob. Over 600 guardsmen had been killed or wounded. The rest of the three brigades were in no fit state to halt the next French attack. The undisciplined charge had left a large gap in the centre of the allied line and General Pierre Lapisse's division was heading straight for it.

Wellesley was on the summit of Medellín Hill when he heard the bad news, and he ordered General Mackenzie to move one of the 4th Division's brigades forward to fill the gap. The 1/48th also escorted a battery of 6-pounders forward, extending the right of the 1st Division's line. As the 2/24th, the 2/31st and the 1/45th deployed across the gap, they opened their ranks to let the survivors of the Guards and the King's German Legion pass through. Once they had reformed in reserve, they gave out a loud cheer to let Mackenzie know they were ready to rejoin the fray.

Wellesley's rapid redeployment meant that Lapisse's battalions faced a solid wall of redcoats and the four battalions let loose a devastating volley at a range of only 50 yards. Mackenzie's troops then charged Lapisse's stunned men, bringing the French attack to a halt. Fierce hand-to-hand fighting followed and for a time it appeared that the French might break through the British line until a charge by the 14th Light Dragoons stopped the column in its tracks. When the French eventually broke, they fell back across Portina stream leaving 1,700 dead and wounded behind. Mackenzie's three battalions had suffered over 700 casualties and both Mackenzie himself and General Lapisse were killed in the fighting. A breakthrough in the centre of the British line had been averted and

The 23rd Light Dragoons' uncontrollable charge ends at a dry watercourse.

Wellesley later acknowledged the part played by the 1st Division's battalion: 'the battle was certainly saved by the advance, position and steady conduct of the 48th'.

A final attempt to break the allied line was made by Ruffin's division, its third attack in twenty-four hours, and this time it was supported by Merlin's cavalry brigade. The French battalions advanced across the plain north of the Cerro de Medellín, aiming to outflank the hilltop position while Villatte's division was poised to attack the east slopes. Wellesley had already spotted the French movements and had ordered Anson's British and Albuquerque's Spanish cavalry brigades to deploy on the north slope of the hill, ready to cover his flank. Bassecourt's Spanish division had also been deployed on the rocky slopes of the Sierra de Segurilla, overlooking the plain.

Ruffin's men were exhausted even before they began their advance and their attack was half-hearted at best. The eight guns supporting Wellesley's cavalry opened fire on the French columns as they moved forward and as soon as it became clear that the French were wavering, Anson was given the order to advance at the trot, ready to deliver a charge. As the 1st Light Dragoons KGL and the 23rd Light Dragoons advanced into view, the French infantry formed square, presenting an inviting target for the British artillery. While the 1st Light Dragoons broke into a steady canter, jumping a ditch as they closed in, Major Ponsonby's dragoons set off in an uncontrolled gallop. The first rank failed to spot the ditch in time and many horses reared up and threw their riders rather than jumping the obstacle. The rest of the regiment cleared the ditch but failed to break any of Ruffin's squares. While the 1st Light Dragoons rallied and returned to their lines in good order the 23rd ran into Merlin's chasseurs and although they broke through the first rank of French horsemen, they were routed by the rest of the brigade, losing over 200 men out of 480. Although the cavalry attack had been a partial disaster, it had halted the French attack.

The cavalry charge was the last action of the day. With dusk approaching, Joseph called off further attacks despite Victor's protests. Wellesley believed that Talavera had been the hardest battle he had had to face since he had taken command and he was powerless to help his men as grass fires swept across the fields, burning the wounded where they lay. George Napier later wrote: 'I never saw a field of battle which struck me with such horror as Talavera.'

Casualties had been high. The French had lost over 7,200 men and had been forced to abandon 17 guns. While Cuesta's Spanish divisions had lost only a few men before they made their untimely withdrawal, Wellesley's British and Portuguese battalions had suffered heavy losses; over 5,300 men had been killed or wounded, a quarter of his strength. Wellesley could count himself a lucky man, having been hit in the chest by a spent bullet; it was the first of three minor wounds he would suffer in the Peninsular War.

The bulk of Joseph's army had to withdraw, leaving the charred battlefield to the allies. He headed east with the bulk of his army towards Madrid to protect the capital from attack by General Venegas. Marshal Victor stayed behind to defend the crossings over the Alberche river to stop the allies following. However, Wellesley was in no mind to pursue the French towards Madrid. Although the Light Division arrived the following morning, following an extended forced march from the coast (having just arrived from England), his transport system was struggling to cope with the extended lines of communication, leaving his men hungry. He was also wary of relying on his Spanish allies after the incident in front of Talavera and he wanted to withdraw while he had the advantage over the French and his men were in good spirits.

Wellesley was confident that Joseph was fully engaged in defending

Madrid and his army headed slowly west and met up with Cuesta's divisions at Oropesa on 3 August. However, his optimism was soon dampened when guerrillas delivered a captured French dispatch to his headquarters: Soult had gathered over 50,000 men and was heading south towards Plasencia, aiming to cut Wellesley's lines of communication into Portugal. There was no time to lose and his troops crossed the river Tagus the following day at Almarez, heading for Badajoz.

Although the immediate situation had been saved, two Spanish defeats at El Puente de Arzobispo (where most of the guns captured at Talavera were lost) and Almonacid de Toledo, south of Madrid, left Wellesley in an exposed situation once again. Relations with the Spanish junta and the military were also once more at a low ebb, leaving him no option but to withdraw to the Portuguese border. The only consolation was news that Wellesley had been awarded the titles Viscount Wellesley and Baron Douro.

At the end of October the Spanish started a new autumn campaign and while the Armies of the Left and Centre converged on Madrid, the small Army of Extremadura was supposed to draw French attention towards the Portuguese border. The campaign did not last for long. Joseph led a small army south to Ocaña, south of Madrid, and on 19 November decisively beat the Army of the Centre, suffering minimal casualties in the process. The Army of the Left was also overrun by a large group of French cavalry when it camped astride the river Tormes at Alba de Tormes, south of Salamanca, on 28 November.

Meanwhile, the French conquests across Europe went from strength to strength. Austria had been beaten and Napoleon was able to send extra troops to join Joseph, bringing the total under his command in the peninsula to nearly 140,000. This meant that Victor, Mortier and Sébastiani could lead a 60,000-strong force against the remaining Spanish troops. With their two main armies scattered, the Spanish junta had no option but to escape to Cadiz, an impregnable fortress protecting a port at the south-west corner of the peninsula. The Army of Extremadura joined the politicians on 3 February, only two days ahead of French troops. After the successful Talavera campaign, the new Duke of Wellesley knew that he would have to start all over again if he were to conquer Spain.

Wellesley's Army 20,641

1st Division General J. Sherbrooke   **5,964**

Campbell's Brigade	1st Coldstream, 1/3rd Guards, 1 Coy 5/60th
Cameron's Brigade	1/61st, 2/83rd, 1 Coy 5/60th
Von Langwerth's Brigade	1st and 2nd Line Bns and Light Coys KGL
Von Lowe's Brigade	5th and 7th Line Bttns KGL

2nd Division General R. Hill   **3,905**

Tilson's Brigade	1/3rd, 2/48th, 2/66th, 1 Coy 5/60th
Stewart's Brigade	29th, 1/48th, 1st Bn Det.

3rd Division General A. Mackenzie   **3,747**

Mackenzie's Brigade	2/24th, 2/31st, 1/45th
Donkin's Brigade	2/87th, 1/88th, 5 Coys 5/60th

4th Division General A. Campbell   **2,960**

Campbell's Brigade	2/7th, 2/53rd, 1 Coy 5/60th
Kemmis's Brigade	1/40th, 9th, 2nd Bttn Det., 1 Coy 5/60th

Cavalry   **2,969**

Fane's Brigade	3rd Dragoon Guards, 4th Dragoons
Stapleton Cotton's Brigade	14th Light Dragoons, 16th Light Dragoons
Anson's Brigade	23rd Light Dragoons, 1st Light Dragoons KGL

Touring Talavera

Soult's Army

Victor's I Corps

Ruffin's Division	5,250
Lapisse's Division	6,850
Villatte's Division	6,150
Cavalry	1,000

Sébastiani's IV Corps

Sébastiani's Division	8,100
Valence's Division (part)	1,600
Leval's Division	4,550
Cavalry	1,200
Desolles's Madrid Garrison	5,800

Cavalry Reserve

Latour-Maubourg's Division	3,150
Milhaud's Division	2,256
Artillery	**82** pieces

Exit the A5 E90 motorway at the Segurilla exit to the north of Talavera. Go north and after 500 metres turn right into the car park, at the far end of which stands the modern tripod-shaped monument. This marks the centre of Wellesley's position, south of Medellín Hill, and the orders of battle of the armies engaged in the fighting are listed on the legs of the monument. There is a detailed tiled map of the battle, marking the position of the monument in relation to the two armies. Views from the monument are restricted but it is possible to see the old memorial near the summit of Medellín Hill, an area that is now in private hands and is not accessible. Look east towards the French lines, where Sébastiani's division was, and south to Talavera, where the Spanish were deployed along the Portilla brook.

Return to the main road and turn right. Note the two dirt tracks where

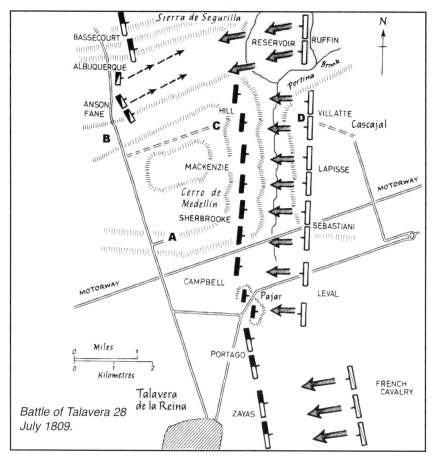

Battle of Talavera 28 July 1809.

The new monument.

the road goes through a cutting after 500 metres. Continue driving north, pulling off to the right into a turning area after 1 kilometre. The Segurilla Hills fill the horizon to the left (north) while Medellín Hill stands to the right (south). The British cavalry charged across this ground, starting near the road cutting, and headed east, coming to grief when they encountered a hidden gulley.

Turn around and drive back towards the monument. It is possible to park on the dirt track to the right at the cutting, and walk up the slope to view the area of the cavalry charge. Cross the road and follow the footpath for 2 kilometres along the northern slopes of Medellín Hill. The track continues around the eastern face of the hill and although a lake now covers the area to the north-west, the vast majority of this area of the battlefield has hardly changed. The area is also covered by trees but it is possible to see a large part of the battlefield and work out where the armies were deployed. Hill's division was lined up on the slopes in front of the crest, while Sherbrooke's division held the undulating ground to the south. The ground drops steeply to the Portilla stream, a serious obstacle to formed troops, and the slopes where the French deployed can be seen to the east.

Return to your car and drive south, past the memorial and over the motorway. Keep going south and take the first turning to the left after 300 metres, following the canal for 2 kilometres. Here the road runs through the area held by Campbell's 4th Division while the Spanish were deployed to the south. At the T-junction 2 kilometres further on turn left on to the main road, which leads up Pajar de Vergara hill where Leval's troops tried unsuccessfully to take a redoubt.

Drive on to the industrial estate and after a kilometre turn back on yourself on to the service road at the roundabout. Make a sharp right turn

The French view of the British deployment; Medellín Hill is to the right.

Ruffin

Cavalry charge

The British cavalry charged across this valley with disastrous results.

on to Calle de Portina and drive up on to the motorway bridge. Stop here to take in the French perspective of the allied line: Medellín Hill and the memorial park can be identified. Continue straight on along the dirt track for 200 metres and park where it widens out. Follow the path to the left (west) for 1 kilometre. This goes through the centre of Lapisse's division's deployment area and can be followed as far as the Portina stream. Return to your car and retrace your route to the industrial estate roundabout, turning right to Talavera.

Casa de Salinas, where Wellesley was nearly captured the day before the battle, is on N502 Avienda de Madrid, the main road running from the centre of Talavera to the A5 E90 motorway. Drive east past the hospital and go straight on at the roundabout in front of the Carrefour supermarket. Turn right into the parking area after 200 metres and park in front of a line of industrial units. There is a signpost for La Torre and the large white farmhouse with its distinctive tower is in the distance, some 300 metres to the south. The farm is private property.

The original monument keeps a lonely vigil over the battlefield.

Wellesley was nearly captured when observing French movements from the tower of this farm.

Chapter 4

WELLINGTON WITHDRAWS INTO PORTUGAL

ESCAPE ACROSS THE RIVER CÔA, 24 JULY 1810

AFTER A LONG SIEGE General Andrés Herrasti's garrison finally surrendered the fortress of Ciudad Rodrigo on 10 July 1810, opening the northern road into Portugal. Eleven days later Marshal André Masséna ordered Marshal Ney to advance west with his VI Corps so he could threaten the Portuguese fortress town of Almeida. General Craufurd's Light Division was holding the border area in front of Ney's corps and rapidly withdrew to the safety of Almeida, destroying the isolated Spanish fortress of Fort Concepcion before crossing the border.

Almeida stands on the east bank of the river Côa, where it cuts through a deep gorge to the west of the fortress, and Craufurd took the controversial decision to deploy his division on the heights covering the southern approaches. He was hoping to delay the French advance into Portugal, but it was a risky decision, and one fraught with potential difficulties.

Ney's corps consisted of more than 24,000 men but Craufurd had only 3,500 infantry spread out across a 3-kilometre-wide front. The 1st and 3rd Portuguese Caçadores were deployed in the centre of Craufurd's line alongside the 1/52nd Regiment. The 1/43rd Regiment and a company of riflemen from the 1/95th Regiment were covering the Valle de la Mula road on the left flank, and it was hoped that Almeida's guns would be able to give them support. The rest of the 1/95th was positioned to cover Craufurd's right, to stop the French turning his southern flank and cutting off his line of retreat to the bridge over the Côa. Craufurd also had 1,200 cavalry at his disposal but the rough terrain limited their deployment.

Ney's corps advanced towards Almeida as darkness fell on 23 July but the soldiers had to endure a long night of heavy rain as Craufurd's picquets strained to see any signs of movement in the dark night. The French commander was determined to take his adversary by surprise and his men were on the move while it was still dark, heading for Craufurd's positions. As the first touch of dawn lit the sky above Almeida, Craufurd's outposts were surprised to see the eastern horizon alive with activity and one by one they sounded the alarm as massed columns of French infantry and cavalry advanced quickly towards their lines.

General Loison's division was leading the advance towards the Light Division, followed by General Jean-Gabriel Marchand's. Craufurd had been caught unawares. The men of his meagre force of five battalions dressed their lines and waited nervously as thirteen battalions marched towards them. Rifleman Verner watched the French advance: 'The whole plain in our front was covered with horse and foot advancing towards us. The enemy's infantry formed line and, with an innumerable multitude of skirmishers, attacked us fiercely.'

The first French attack was driven back by musket and rifle volleys, but this was only the first round of an uneven contest. Loison's men reorganised as Craufurd contemplated his next move. Once again the French columns advanced, urged forward by their officers, and Verner's comrades used their rifles to pick their targets:

> They came on again, yelling, with drums beating, frequently the drummers leading. French officers like mountebanks running forward and placing their hats upon their swords and capering about like madmen, saying as they turned to their men, 'Come on, children of our country. The first that advances, Napoleon will recompense him!'

The centre of Craufurd's line stopped the French infantry for a second time but developments elsewhere along his front placed the Light Division in a very precarious situation. The French 3rd Hussars had cantered towards his left flank, ignoring the cannon on Almeida's walls, and headed straight towards the company of the 1/95th. The riflemen stood no chance against the fast-moving hussars and were soon running for safety, leaving the road down to the river Côa wide open.

Before panic could break out all along the line, the buglers of the 1/43rd sounded the retreat while the officers led their men down towards the bridge, hoping to escape the French cavalry. It was a race against time: if Craufurd's troops could make it down the rocky slopes fast enough, they would be safe from the hussars' slashing sabres. Most made it to the safety of the ravine and took refuge in a walled enclosure, but some were cut down by the marauding cavalry. A sergeant of the 43rd later described how his battalion fell back in disorder down the steep hillside:

> There was no room to array the line, no time for anything but battle; every captain carried off his company as an independent body, the whole presenting a mass of skirmishers, acting in small parties and under no regular command. Having the advantage of ground and number, the enemy broke over the edge of the ravine and their hussars poured down the road, sabring everything in their way.

With his left flank in tatters and the bridge in danger of being captured, Craufurd had no option but to order an immediate retreat towards the Côa. The guns and cavalry led the way down the road, followed by the two battalions of Caçadores. The British battalions brought up the rear, taking up positions on a large rocky outcrop overlooking the bridge. The French appeared reluctant to follow them down into the gorge as musket volleys tore through their ranks, and for a time it appeared as if Craufurd's men were safe. However, disaster struck on the bridge when a wagon overturned as the crew tried to negotiate a tight turn in the centre. The road was blocked and there was no time to remove the

The Light Division withdrew down the rocky slopes towards the river.

Bridge

Almeida

Over 5,000 men had to withdraw down the rocky slopes and across the narrow bridge with the French in hot pursuit.

obstruction. Although the infantry could squeeze past, the rest of Craufurd's guns and limbers had to be abandoned.

While the three British battalions held Loison's men at bay on the east bank, Craufurd began organising a new line of defence on the far side of the river. His remaining guns were deployed along the road, overlooking the approaches to the bridge, while the Caçadores took up positions on the slopes ready to engage the enemy. It was a race against the clock and by the time the order was given for the rearguard to cross, the French were almost upon them and they quickly occupied the rocky outcrop, covering the approaches to the bridge.

For a time it looked as though everyone had escaped but five companies of the 1/52nd had been cut off in the confusion and were now unable to force a way past the French-held outcrop. Seeing his men in trouble, General Craufurd ordered two of his British battalions back up the slopes, hoping that they could drive the French back and secure an escape route for the cut-off companies. Major Charles Macleod led the 1/43rd, while Lieutenant-Colonel Thomas Beckwith ordered the 1/95th forward and the two battalions charged up the slope, driving the French from the summit. With the way across the river secure once more, the 1/52nd companies crossed the bridge, followed by the two battalions that had rescued them. The Light Division had finally slipped the French clutches and Craufurd now ordered his subordinates to hold their fire and wait for the French to make their next move. Over 300 men had been killed or wounded escaping across the Côa and a number of guns, limbers and ammunition wagons had been left behind, but the worst was over. British and Portuguese soldiers now lined the west bank of the Côa while the artillery crews trained their guns on the bridge.

Despite the difficulties posed by the partly blocked bridge, and the inevitable heavy casualties his men would suffer, Ney ordered his men to seize the bridge. The first attempt was made by grenadiers of the 66th Regiment but volleys and rounds of canister tore them to pieces as they advanced down the slope towards the river. It was a massacre, and virtually every soldier was killed or wounded before the advance even reached the bridge. As the grenadiers fell back, dragging their wounded with them, Ney ordered forward an elite light infantry battalion, known as the *Chasseurs de la Siége*. These men were hardened warriors, specially trained to scale fortress walls, but even for them the bridge over the Côa proved too much of a challenge. Oman described the attack: '[They] flung themselves at the bridge, and pushed on till it was absolutely blocked by the bodies of the killed and the wounded, and till they themselves had been almost literally exterminated.'

In just ten minutes 90 men were killed and nearly 150 lay wounded. A final attempt on the bridge by the 66th Regiment only increased the number of dead, dying and injured strewn on and around the tiny bridge to over 500; in contrast, the Light Division suffered only 20 casualties. Craufurd had had a lucky escape but it was cold comfort for his men as they crept off into the darkness later that night, heading for Pinhel. He had gained nothing by attempting to defend the east bank of the Côa, but had risked his division to do so, and by the following day Masséna was making plans to lay siege to Almeida's fortress.

The rocky ground made it difficult to dig trenches and a month passed before the engineers were able to roll the siege guns into position while the garrison settled down for a long siege, confident that they had enough supplies and ammunition to resist the French. They were wrong. A lucky shot set off an enormous explosion in the citadel's main powder magazine, instantly killing 500 of the Portuguese garrison, destroying the medieval castle and devastating many buildings inside the fortress. It was

Portas de São Francisco's inner gate.

a complete disaster, and although the perimeter walls had not been damaged the garrison had been shocked into submission. The British commander, William Cox, tried to organise the survivors but his men mutinied the following night and Almeida was soon in French hands. This left the way open into Portugal.

TOURING ALMEIDA FORTRESS

The Portuguese border fortress of Almeida is on the N322, 13 kilometres north of the A25. Turn left off the N322 on the north side of Almeida's modern outskirts and park outside the Portas de São Francisco. Walk through the outer entrance, cross the moat, and enter the citadel through the second gate, a dark tunnel which follows a dog-leg through the wall. The town's tourist information office is inside the second gate, to the left; obtain a town plan from here before heading inside the fortress.

Almeida is a picturesque town with a maze of narrow streets filled with a mixture of houses, shops and military buildings. The infantry barracks stand to the left of the gate while the cavalry barracks (now a training school) are on the northern edge of the town. The explosion in 1810 completely destroyed the castle and its ruins stand at the top of the hill on the north side of the town. It is possible to study the remains of the foundations from a series of elevated walkways.

The northern gatehouse has two exhibitions. One details the history of Portuguese military fortifications while the other illustrates the development of Almeida from a medieval fortress.

Leave the castle by the northern gate and walk around the ramparts to the left (west) to explore the extensive fortifications. These consisted of two perimeter walls separated by a wide moat and reinforced by gun positions. There are extensive views across the steep rocky valley of the river Côa to the north.

On 24 July 1810 the Light Division was deployed on the ridge to the south of the fortress and it is possible to see their positions from the ramparts (modern housing stands on the highest part of the ridge). General Craufurd's men managed to hold Marshal Ney's corps at bay to begin with but when French hussars charged across the slopes in front of the ramparts, overrunning the company of the 1/95th covering their flank, the 1/43rd sounded the retreat. Guns, cavalry and infantry were soon falling back down the rocky slopes towards the river Côa. Continue around the ramparts to the Portas de São Francisco and your car.

The foundations are all that remain of Almeida castle. Busaço

TOURING THE RIVER CÔA BRIDGE

Head south from Almeida's gate and turn right on to the N332 after 200 metres. After 400 metres turn right on to the N340 signposted to Pinhel and follow the road west as it makes its way down to the Côa. The river winds its way through a narrow gorge with steep-sided slopes covered with rocks, gorse and scrub. The modern bridge crosses above the old stone bridge; continue for 400 metres to find a safe pull-in area on the left. (The first pull-in area after 200 metres is opposite a dangerous blind bend.) Turn around here and then drive back down to the first pull-in where it is safe to pull off the road to the right. Part of the old stone road still exists; follow it down to the old bridge, a narrow stone structure with a dog-leg in the centre topped by a large plaque dating from Roman times.

Craufurd ordered his artillery and cavalry to head down to the river first while his riflemen and the Caçadores kept the French infantry at bay. Gun carriages and ammunition wagons queued up to cross the narrow bridge as the battle raged on the slopes above but several had to be abandoned when one wagon overturned at the dog-leg. British infantry formed a rearguard on the hillock overlooking the approaches to the bridge, while the Caçadores and the remaining guns deployed on the west bank. Five companies of the 1/52nd were cut off by the French advance but a counter-attack spearheaded by the 1/43rd and the 1/95th drove the French back allowing everyone to escape. French soldiers then tried repeatedly to force a way across the narrow crossing, only to be driven back by volleys and canister fire; over 500 were killed or wounded.

THE BATTLE OF BUÇACO, 27 SEPTEMBER 1810

After the disaster at Almeida, Masséna's army was free to advance deep into Portugal but problems lay ahead. It was difficult to keep any army supplied in the inhospitable terrain, but the hostile population destroyed or hid anything of use to the French. Inaccurate maps and poor advice also led the French troops along a number of impassable roads, putting an added strain on their logistics.

While Masséna blundered his way across the Serra da Estrela, spies kept Wellington informed of his movements and by 26 September his army, over 50,000 men and 60 guns, was waiting to meet him on Buçaco ridge, north-east of Coimbra. The ridge was a perfect defensive position consisting of a high, steeply sloping ridge, some 14 kilometres long, commanding excellent views of the surrounding countryside. The allied troops could deploy out of sight behind the crest while Marshal Masséna's men climbed the steep, rocky slopes, forcing their way through the thick heather and gorse. The French could not take Wellington by surprise and he would have plenty of time to watch and wait, moving reinforcements along the lateral road his engineers had built along the western slopes.

Marshal André Massena.

Wellington had organised his troops into seven divisions, supported by six Portuguese brigades who were about to face their first test in battle. All the artillery pieces were deployed along the summit of the ridge, many of them in two-gun sections, supporting individual brigades. In addition, several batteries covered the Coimbra road alongside Craufurd's Light Division. The British army had only two squadrons of British cavalry but the broken terrain severely restricted movement for mounted troops: Buçaco was going to be an infantry battle.

Wellington knew that his adversary was a formidable opponent and later admitted that, 'When Masséna was opposed to me in the field, I never slept comfortably.' He believed that the French marshal would advance up the main Coimbra road and attack Sula village, next to Buçaco's convent, and so four British divisions were waiting astride the road, supported by three Portuguese brigades. In all, there were some 35,000 troops lying in wait, ut of sight of the advancing French columns.

The 4th Division held Wellington's left flank, General Galbraith Lowry Cole having deployed his three brigades on the crest of the ridge, north of the Coimbra road. While Collins's Portuguese brigade held the forward slopes on the extreme left flank, Kemmis and Campbell had positioned their brigades behind the crest in the centre and right respectively.

Wellington believed that the Buçaco convent would be the focus of Masséna's attack and he placed the Light Division astride the road in front of it, where the Coimbra road snaked its way up to the top of the hill. While General Craufurd's battalions and his guns deployed along the mountain road, his skirmishers could use the rocks and bushes as cover and snipe at the French columns as they climbed the steep slopes. The three independent Portuguese brigades commanded by Campbell, Pack and Coleman had been positioned close behind the Light Division and they could rally behind the convent's high walls if the French pushed Craufurd's men back.

General Spencer's 1st Division held the ground south of the convent, the highest part of the Buçaco Ridge, and he had placed his three brigades, led by Blantyre, H. Campbell and Stopford, in line on the reverse slopes out of sight; Von Low's KGL brigade was also holding the crest. Immediately south of Graham's division was General Picton's 3rd Division, deployed astride the track which crossed the ridge between San Antonio de Cantara and Palheiros. This was another place where Masséna might launch an attack. The slope was extremely steep but it was the easiest route to the crest. Lightburne's brigade had been positioned to counter any French troops climbing the slope north of the track, and was joined by the 1/88th and part of the 1/45th from Wallace's brigade (a temporary command). The rest of the 1/45th and the 1/74th, supported by Champlemond's Portuguese brigade, held the summit of the ridge overlooking San Antonio de Cantara in the valley far below.

Wellington did not believe that Masséna would try to assault the centre of his position. There were no roads to speak of and the ridge was extremely steep, and the French marshal knew that the British commander could turn against his flanks if he managed to reach the summit. Even so, the 5th Division, led by General Sir James Leith, had been spread rather thinly to guard the 3-kilometre-wide gap separating the two wings of the allied army. While Spry's Portuguese brigade covered Picton's right flank, Barnes' brigade covered the rough track connecting St Paulo and Palmases. Wellington also had three battalions of the Lusitanian Legion to deploy and while several companies were stationed in front of General Hill's position, the rest were placed between Leith's two brigades.

The rest of Wellington's army, two divisions led by General Rowland Hill, was holding the summit of Buçaco ridge 3 kilometres to the south, near Penacova, to prevent Masséna's troops climbing the gentle slopes overlooking the river Mondego.

General Sir Thomas Picton.

General Stewart's 2nd Division covered Penacova at the southern end of the ridge, and his three brigades, led by Willson, Inglis and Colborne, were deployed alongside General Hamilton's 6th Division and his two Portuguese brigades led by Fonseca and Campbell.

General Sir Rowland Hill.

All along the line Wellington made sure that as many of his men as possible were kept out of sight, to prevent Marshal Masséna studying his deployment. Dense lines of skirmishers covered the important areas, using the rough terrain for cover, with orders to harass the French columns as they advanced; the sound of their musket and rifle fire would alert Wellington to the approaching danger.

While Masséna had neither the time nor the opportunity to study the allied dispositions, Wellington watched from the hillside above Buçaco convent as two French corps deployed around Moura and a third drew up in front of Picton's division. The duke had made his plans, and the lateral road behind the crest of the ridge would allow him to move troops quickly if any part of his line was threatened. The initiative now lay with the French.

Marshal Masséna was confident that his three corps, numbering over 66,000 men and 114 guns, were more than capable of smashing through the allied line and he confidently deployed his troops in front of Buçaco Ridge on 26 September. Marshal Michel Ney's VI Corps assembled around the village of Moura astride the Lisbon road and Masséna established his command post at a nearby mill which had a commanding view of Sula and Buçaco. Marshal Jean Reynier's II Corps gathered to the south, assembling around San Antonio de Cantara, unaware that Picton's division was waiting at the summit.

Masséna was so confident about the outcome of the forthcoming battle that he remarked, 'I cannot persuade myself that Lord Wellington will risk the loss of a reputation by giving battle, but if he does, I have him. Tomorrow we shall effect the capture of Portugal, and in a few days I shall drown the leopard.' But he had seriously underestimated Wellington's abilities as a military commander. In Masséna's defence, he had seen how poorly the Spanish troops had performed in previous battles, and he firmly believed that Wellington's 10,000 Portuguese troops would do no better. The allies would be the weak link in the duke's line and their presence would undermine the confidence of the British soldiers. Wellington thought differently, and later recalled how he wanted to give them 'a taste for an amusement to which they are not before accustomed and which they would not have acquired if I had not put them in a very strong position'. However, he was not taking any chances and the majority of his Portuguese brigades had been deployed behind the Light Division at the strongest part of the line in front of Buçaco convent.

Masséna's plan was simple. Reynier's II Corps would advance from San Antonio de Cantara, seizing the centre of the ridge, and then roll up Wellington's flank. Then VI Corps would attack the north end of the ridge while VIII Corps waited in reserve. However, this plan was based on out-dated information. Masséna was unaware that General Hill had just joined Wellington, allowing him to hold the centre of the ridge in strength. This meant that II Corps faced a strong adversary and Reynier's men would have a tough fight to reach the top of the ridge instead of making a simple outflanking manoeuvre.

As the French troops settled down for the night around their fires, Masséna retired to his tent with his mistress, Madame Lebrerton (who was often disguised as a dragoon officer to keep the marshal's romantic activities a secret). Meanwhile, a short distance away beyond the crest of Buçaco Ridge the allies camped in darkness to keep their strength and the extent of their positions hidden. As the British and Portuguese troops huddled together, eating cold food, Wellington shared their discomfort, sleeping out in the open with his cape as a blanket.

The men were roused in the early hours of 27 September to prepare for the day's battle, but as dawn broke it was clear that the early morning mist would hinder operations for some time. Wellington waited on the San Antonio road with Picton's 3rd Division, where he expected the first attack to fall. Far below he could hear the sounds of drums and bugle calls in the valley as Marshal Reynier's II Corps began to advance, and the sound of musket fire indicated that his skirmishers were engaging the French. General Etienne Heudelet's division, advancing astride the San Antonio road, reached the crest first. The columns of infantry emerged from the mist, panting with exhaustion after the steep climb, only to find Mackinnon's brigade and Champlemond's Portuguese brigade waiting for them. Orders rang out along the crest of the ridge as musket volleys and grapeshot raked the French columns, sending many of the survivors fleeing back down the slopes to safety.

Reynier's men faced a steep climb from San Antonio de Cantara before they reached Picton's positions on the crest of the ridge.

Wellington's view of Reynier's attack.

Many of Heudelet's men swerved south to escape the hail of lead, moving beyond the 3rd Division's right flank. Picton (who was still wearing his night-cap) saw the danger and responded by moving his reserves to cover the gap. Part of the 1/45th led by Lieutenant-Colonel the Hon. Meade and two battalions of Portuguese deployed immediately in front of the French while the 1/88th Regiment led by Lieutenant-Colonel Wallace and the rest of the 1/45th wheeled round to face the French flank. As the four battalions opened fire, raking the dense column with musket balls, they drove Heudelet's men from the crest of the ridge. William Grattan later described the Connaught Rangers' charge:

Wallace, with a steady but cheerful countenance, turned to his men and said; 'Now Connaught Rangers, when I bring you face to face with those French rascals don't give the false touch, but push home to the muzzle! I have nothing more to say, and if I had it would be of no use, for in a minute there'll be such an infernal noise you won't be able to hear yourselves.' This address went home to the hearts of us all, but there was no cheering: a steady and determined calm had taken the place of any lighter feeling. Wallace then threw the battalion from line into column and moved on at a quick pace. On reaching the rocks, he threw himself from his horse and ran forward into the midst of the terrible flame in his front. All was now confusion and uproar, smoke, fire and bullets; officers and soldiers knocked down in every direction; British, French and Portuguese mixed together; while in the midst of all was to be seen Wallace fighting at the head of his devoted followers and calling out to his soldiers to press forward.

The Connaughts' charge brought Heudelet's attack to an end and Wellington later praised their colonel for their actions: 'Upon my honour, Wallace, I never witnessed a more gallant charge than that just made by your regiment.'

General Merle's columns struggled up the steep slopes north of the San Antonio road, where Lightburne's brigade and two 6-pounder guns waited silently near the summit. Once again volleys of musket fire and grapeshot brought the French advance to a halt as they emerged from the mist on to the crest of the ridge.

As the leading men of the columns reeled back down the hillside, Reynier ordered both his divisional commanders to renew the attack, leading their men up the steep slopes for a second time. As the mist cleared, General Foy led the rest of Heudelet's division forward north of the San Antonio road, where they ran into the battered 1/45th and three battalions of Champlemond's Portuguese brigade. Seven French battalions topped the crest of the ridge and their sheer weight of numbers soon threatened to drive Picton's division from the summit. Fortunately

The French reach the summit of Busaço only to find Picton's division waiting for them.

Wellington had taken steps to counter just such a threat when it was clear that the French did not intend to attack 5th Division's sector, having ordered General Sir James Leith to send troops north along the lateral road to reinforce Picton.

As Heudelet's men moved across the summit of the ridge, believing the day was theirs, they found Barnes' brigade waiting for them on the reverse slopes. The 1/9th and the 2/38th fired volley after volley as they advanced towards the shocked French troops. Lieutenant-Colonel Cameron of the 1/9th had his horse shot from beneath him, but he continued at the head of his battalion on foot, ordering his men to fix bayonets as they closed in. The charge that followed scattered Heudelet's battalions and they fell back down the slopes leaving some 2,000 casualties behind. The wounded General Foy had to be carried to safety. After two hours of fierce fighting, the five British and seven Portuguese battalions had stopped II Corps' attack in its tracks, although the French outnumbered them by two to one.

As the fighting in Picton's area died down, heavy skirmishing could be heard on the slopes north of the Lisbon road, indicating that VI Corps had begun to advance towards Sula and Buçaco. Wellington, confident that Picton no longer needed his presence, galloped along the summit of the ridge to direct the defence. Marshal Ney had deployed General Loison's division north of the Lisbon road while General Marchand's division was to the south, and the two would smash into the allied line at the same time. As the two divisions advanced towards Sula village Masséna watched from Moura mill, unaware that General Reynier's attack had already failed.

Loison's two brigades approached the village in columns of six battalions, the right under General Simon and the left under General Ferey, while their tirailleurs fought a running battle with 1,300 riflemen of the 1/95th led by Lieutenant-Colonel Beckwith, and the 3rd Caçadores in the village of Sula. The riflemen had the upper hand as they conducted a fighting withdrawal and the French columns were quickly disorganised as they climbed the rock-strewn slope. Hew Ross's battery of guns added to Loison's difficulties as their crews fired grapeshot at the advancing columns, only running for cover at the last minute.

Tired and disorganised, Loison's men still thought victory was theirs for the taking as they reached the summit of the hill, where a lone figure waited motionless on his horse by Sula mill. But this was General Robert Craufurd, commander of the Light Division, and he was waiting for the right moment to strike with the two battalions lying silently in the grass alongside him. The 52nd (Oxfordshires) were north of the road while the 43rd (Monmouthshires) were south of the road, and when the moment was ripe the general gave the order to rise, with the words 'Now, 52nd, avenge the death of John Moore!' It must have been a terrifying sight as 1,800 men suddenly rose to their feet, shouldered their weapons and opened fire on the French columns with deadly effect. The front ranks were decimated by the initial volleys as Craufurd's two battalions advanced their flanks, forming a semi-circle around the head of the reeling column. When the moment was right the two battalions sounded the charge, sending the French running for their lives back down the slopes. Sergeant Anthony Hamilton of the 43rd later recalled how Craufurd's men stopped Loison's division:

> No sooner did they crown the height than he found us drawn up to receive him, and his column became exposed to a most destructive fire, both of musketry and artillery. This was but of short duration, yet the leading regiments of the assailants were almost totally annihilated. A charge of bayonets followed: the whole column was routed and driven down the hill with prodigious slaughter.

It was a disaster for the French. Loison's division suffered no fewer than 1,200 casualties, including 68 officers; General Simon was also taken prisoner by Privates Hopkins and Harris of the 52nd. The Light Division had suffered 132 casualties, the majority of them in Sula village, while the two leading battalions, the 43rd and 52nd, between them lost only 3 men killed and 2 officers and 18 men wounded.

General Marchand's division was close behind, clambering up the ridge south of the Lisbon road under heavy artillery fire. Lieutenant-Colonel Hill's skirmishers from the 4th Caçadores were quickly driven back and the French columns advanced towards Pack's Portuguese brigade. Wellington reached the brigade as Marchand's men closed in for the kill and Auguste Schaumann of the British Commissariat looked on as he gave out his orders:

> His orders were communicated in a loud voice, and were short and precise. In him there is nothing of the bombastic pomp of the commander-in-chief surrounded by his glittering staff. He wears no befeathered hat, no gold lace, no stars, no orders; simply a low plain hat, a white collar, a grey overcoat and a light sword.

The four Portuguese battalions, two from Lieutenant-Colonel de Regoa's 1st Regiment and two from Major Armstrong's 16th Regiment, were outnumbered three to one but they stood their ground bravely and opened a devastating volley fire at close range. Despite heavy casualties, the French continued to advance and their weight of numbers threatened to overwhelm Pack's brigade. Although the Portuguese soldiers fell back, they quickly rallied in front of Buçaco convent and delivered another burst of volley fire. This was the final straw for Marchand's men and they withdrew down the slopes. It was a defining moment for the Portuguese soldiers: they had stood their ground and fought the French columns to a standstill.

By late morning the battle was over. It had been a perfect example of Wellington's use of reverse-slope tactics, of which he was becoming a master. Masséna had underestimated the tenacity of the British commander and the resolve of the Portuguese troops, and his overconfidence had cost him dearly. Although he still had some 20,000 fresh troops available, including all of Junot's VIII Corps, Masséna called off the attack having suffered 4,600 casualties in four hours. Five French generals and nearly 300 officers had fallen, 'the highest proportion of officers to men that the French suffered in the whole war'. Wellington's losses were only 1,252, half of them from the Portuguese brigades, but despite inflicting a serious defeat on Masséna, he resisted the temptation to go on the offensive. As his men rested and tended to the wounded, Wellington was left alone with his thoughts in Buçaco convent where he spent the night in one of the simple cells.

The following morning the allied army was once more on the move, heading for winter billets. Wellington could not afford to hold the ridge any longer as Masséna's cavalry had discovered a way to turn his north flank. The Portuguese militia had failed to cover the road and there were too few British cavalry to keep them at bay. It was a bitter disappointment for many soldiers who knew that they had won the battle and resented falling back like a defeated army. Wellington himself later expressed his desire to withdraw with honour: 'When we do go, I feel a little anxiety to go like gentlemen out of the hall door and not out of the back door.'

Wellington's men made a slow withdrawal through southern Portugal, finding towns and villages deserted, while the Portuguese militia and home guard patrolled the roads. Masséna's army followed but the French troops had to rely on foraging to feed themselves and their horses and they found little to eat in the devastated countryside. The majority of the population had fled towards Lisbon, taking with them everything of value and destroying or hiding anything they could not carry; this was a deliberate policy, designed to stop the French living off the land.

As the allied army passed the village of Torres Vedras, some 110 kilometres to the south, on 10 October and moved into new billets, Masséna faced a serious dilemma. Winter was approaching and his logistical problems were increasing; ammunition was in short supply while food was almost impossible to find in the deserted towns. The cold, damp weather would only increase their problems and hungry soldiers often went on the rampage as they searched for food, burning villages and killing anyone who stood in their way.

TOURING THE BATTLEFIELD AT BUÇACO

Leave the A1-EP1 at junction 14, 18 kilometres north of Coimbra, and head along the N234 for Mealhada; Buçaco Ridge rises high in front, filling the horizon. Follow signs for Luso and continue straight on through the traffic lights along the N234, climbing the slopes to the top until you reach Buçaco, 3 kilometres to the east. Note the sign to the right for the military museum at the crest of the steep hill, but continue straight on, heading down the slope into Moura.

There is a large pull-in area on the left of the road beyond Moura village, opposite the side road to Amial. Looking back up the hill it is easy to see how strong Wellington's Buçaco position was. The lower slopes are exceptionally steep and General Masséna's men had to march up the road before deploying on to the hillside in front of the British position. A white obelisk, the battlefield monument, can be seen near the summit, standing to the west of the road; it is positioned where Pack's troops stood, in front of the convent and high above Sula village. The Light Division was deployed on either side of the road, General Spencer's 1st Division held the summit of the ridge to the left, and Cole's 4th Division held the ridge to the right.

Drive back up the hill through Moura, taking the left turn for Moinho de Moura at the far end of the village. The narrow lane turns sharp left to a reconstructed mill. Masséna used the original mill as a command post while he watched Ney's troops attack the Light Division and Pack's brigade.

Return to the main road and turn left, continuing up the hill. Turn right

Masséna's view of Wellington's position.

at the summit for Moinho de Sula and park in the turning area next to the main road. A second mill marks the stand of the Light Division on the crest, and Craufurd's men were lined out along the slopes to the left and right of the road. A plaque remembers their courage.

Go back on to the main road and turn right, driving west down the slope, taking the left turn signposted for the military museum after 500 metres. The building is on the right and contains uniforms, weapons, maps, engravings and a Portuguese artillery team complete with gun as a centrepiece.

Follow signs for the monument from the museum; it is to the right after 500 metres. The white stone pillar is crowned with a star and it stands at the point where Wellington watched the attack on Pack's brigade.

Now take the left-hand fork and follow the road along the steep wooded slope to visit the scene of Reynier's attack. After 5.5 kilometres take the road to the left, running back down the hill and San Antonio de Cantara is at the bottom of the slope. Park at the far end of the hamlet and look back up the seemingly impassable ridge; we can only wonder why Masséna thought it was feasible to send Reynier's men up the hillside unless he thought the summit was deserted; he was wrong. While Foy's and Heudelet's men advanced up the road, Merle's brigade followed a spur to the north to reach the summit.

Now retrace your route up the hillside, turning right at the fork, and head back towards the monument. To visit Wellington's command post during the attack on Picton's division, take the right-hand fork for Cruz Alta 500 metres before the monument. Take the next left fork, leaving the tarmac road, and follow the gravel track. After 700 metres take the right-hand fork. (To help you, there are weather-beaten stone signs for the command post, or 'Posto de Comando', at each fork.) Follow the track for 150 metres and then park your car, walking the last 150 metres down the

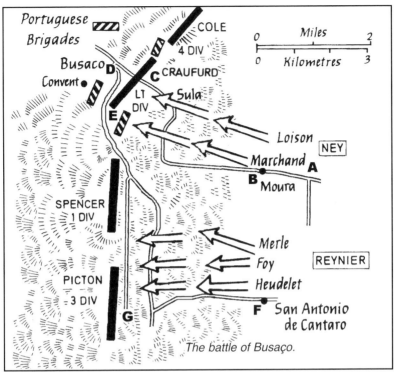

The battle of Busaço.

Craufurd's mill on the summit of Busaço ridge.

Wellington's Army

1st Division, General Brent Spencer, 7,053

Stopford's Brigade	1/Coldstream, 1/3rd Guards, 1 Coy 5/60th
Blantyre's Brigade	2/24th, 42nd, 1/61st, 1 Coy 5/60th
Von Lowe's Brigade	1st, 2nd, 5th and 7th Line KGL, det. Light KGL
Pakenham's Brigade	1/7th, 1/79th

2nd Division, General Rowland Hill, 10,777

Stewart's Brigade	1/3rd, 2/31st, 2/48th, 2/66th, 1 Coy 5/60th
Inglis's Brigade	29th, 1/48th, 1/57th, 1 Coy 5/60th
C. Craufurd's Brigade	2/28th, 2/34th, 2/39th, 1 Coy 5/60th

Portuguese Division, General Hamilton, 5,040

Campbell's Brigade	4th Line (2 Bttns), 10th Line (2 Bttns)
Fonseca's Brigade	2nd Line (2 Bttns), 14th Line (2 Bttns)

3rd Division, General Thomas Picton, 4,143

Mackinnon's Brigade	1/45th, 1/74th, 1/88th
Lightburne's Brigade	2/5th, 2/83rd, 3 Coys 5/60th
Champlemond's Portuguese Brigade	9th Line (2 Bttns), 21st Line (1 Bttn)

4th Division, General Lowry Cole, 7,400

Campbell's Brigade	2/7th, 1/11th, 2/53rd, 1 Coy 5/60th
Kemmis's Brigade	3/27th, 1/40th, 97th, 1 Coy 5/60th
Collins's Portuguese Brigade	11th Line (2 Bttns), 23rd Line (2 Bttns)

5th Division, General James Leith, 7,322

Barnes's Brigade:	3/1st, 1/9th, 2/38th
Spry's Portuguese Brigade	3rd Line (2 Bttns), 15th Line (2 Btts), Tomar Militia Bttn
Baron Enden's Brigade	Lusitanian Legion (3 Bttns), 8th Line (2 Bttns)

Light Division, General Robert Craufurd, 3,787

Beckwith's Brigade	1/43rd, 4 Coys 1/95th, 3rd Caçadores
Barclay's Brigade	1/52nd, 4 Coys 1/95th, 1st Caçadores

Three Independent Portuguese Brigades, 8,363

Pack's Brigade	1st Line (2 Bttns), 16th Line (2 Bttns), 4th Caçadores
Campbell's Brigade	6th Line (2 Bttns), 18th Line (2 Bttns), 6th Caçadores
Coleman's Brigade	7th Line (2 Bttns), 19th Line (2 Bttns), 2nd Caçadores

Cavalry 250	2 Sqns 4th Dragoons
Artillery	60 guns

Masséna's Army 58,000	
Reynier's **II Corps**	**16,000**
Merle's Division	6,550
Heudelet's Division	8,050
Soult's Cavalry	1,400
Ney's **VI Corps**	**22,700**
Marchand's Division	6,650
Mermet's Division	7,600
Loison's Division	6,800
Lamotte's Cavalry	1,650
Junot's **VIII Corps**	**15,850**
Clausel's Division	6,800
Solignac's Division	7,200
St Croix's Cavalry	1,850
Montbrun's Cavalry	3,450

track to the left to find the large stone tablet. Although the area is now heavily wooded, glimpses through the trees of the steep slope and the valley below give a good impression of the strength of Picton's position.

Retrace your route to the museum and follow the road past the entrance, heading west to the hotel and the convent. After passing through the ornate gates drive through the wooded grounds to Buçaco Hotel, an extravagantly decorated building. The convent is immediately behind the hotel. Wellington spent the night after the battle in the convent, sleeping in one of the cells. This peaceful sanctuary is open to the public.

THE LINES OF TORRES VEDRAS, WINTER 1810/11

While Masséna's army began a struggle for survival across central Portugal, the British and Portuguese soldiers were safely camped behind the line of fortifications known as the Lines of Torres Vedras to the south. Before considering the winter of 1810/11, it is necessary to turn the clock back two years to understand how the Lines were conceived, designed and eventually built.

Not long after arriving in Portugal in the summer of 1808, Wellington had realised that he needed both a fortified area where he could gather his troops and a safe harbour for unloading supplies. The British commander also had to consider protecting Lisbon, to encourage support from the Portuguese, and to this end, following the battle of Vimiero, he had studied closely the area north of the capital. On his return to the peninsula in April 1809 he was anxious to develop a secure port so that his troops could be evacuated by ship if the French pushed them back to the sea. He did not want a repeat of General Moore's situation, fighting a desperate rearguard action on the hills surrounding Coruña, while transport ships lay anchored in the nearby harbour, waiting to take his men to safety.

Following the Talavera campaign in the summer of 1809, Wellington turned his attentions once more to the area north of Lisbon. After studying a report by the Portuguese surveyor Neves Costa, and notes captured from Marshal Junot's engineer Vincent, Wellington chose to survey an extensive area of hills and river valleys, stretching from Lisbon to Torres Vedras, 40 kilometres to the north. A series of ridges and isolated hills covered the entire area between the Atlantic Ocean and the river

The Busaço memorial.

Tagus, stretching over 40 kilometres wide at Torres Vedras, narrowing down to 25 kilometres near Lisbon. After riding across the area in the autumn of 1809, Wellington outlined his plans and sent them in a twenty-one page memo to his Chief Engineer, Lieutenant-Colonel Richard Fletcher, on 20 October 1809. He wanted to build dozens of observation posts, gun batteries and earthworks for infantry on the hill tops. The memo outlined three lines of fortifications: an outpost line centred on Torres Vedras, a main line between Mafra and Bucellas and a series of forts protecting a sheltered harbour west of Lisbon.

Construction work started immediately. Over the next twelve months 108 redoubts were built along the three lines under the supervision of Colonel Richard Fletcher and his team of seventeen British engineering officers. Another 150 British non-commissioned officers controlled work on site. The

Lisbon militia regiments provided the backbone of the labour, but more than 6,000 civilians worked alongside them.

Along the first two lines, existing medieval castles were reinforced with earthworks while redoubts and observation posts were constructed on top of every hill and ridge. Where possible, the fortifications were built on natural features and the labourers cleared trees and undergrowth around the earthworks to give the guns extensive fields of fire. Rivers were blocked to flood valleys while thick stone walls were built across roads and ravines to impede movement.

The fortifications varied in size, and while larger forts were typically manned by 300 men and a battery of 6 guns, smaller redoubts usually had a garrison of 200 men and 3 guns. The largest redoubt, manned by 1,600 men and 25 guns, was south of Sobral, while a group of seven redoubts grouped around Monte Agraco had 3,000 men and 55 guns. Ditches were dug around the perimeter and the earth embankments were reinforced with stone and timber. Each fort had many embrasures and stone roads allowed the limbers to move the guns between them while the infantry fired from behind the earth parapets. Billet areas were also protected by earth embankments while the gunpowder was stored in circular stone buildings.

The outpost line ran from the mouth of the river Zizandre on the Atlantic coast and followed the river as far as Torres Vedras before

The site of Wellington's command post during Reynier's attack.

Busaço convent where Wellington spent the night after the battle.

heading south-east to Alhandra on the river Tagus. The line was 45 kilometres long, centred on Monte Agraco, and the thirty-two redoubts were garrisoned by 158 guns; fortresses at Torres Vedras and Sobral covered the two main roads. Towards the end of 1810 it was clear that there was enough time to strengthen the outpost line further, turning it into a another defensive barrier, and another forty-two forts were added. This increased the total number of guns deployed in the Lines of Torres Vedras to over 600.

The main line of forts ran parallel to the outpost line, around 11 kilometres to the south. It was centred on Cabego de Montachique and the sixty-five forts guarded the four roads through Mafra, Montachique, Bucellas and Alhandra, all of which led to Lisbon. This line was 35 kilometres long and 206 guns were deployed in the redoubts.

A short defensive line of eleven forts was built on the coast west of Lisbon, providing a fortified landing area next to Fort St Julian where Wellington's army could assemble in safety. Two battalions of marines and 83 guns would be able to keep the French at bay while the troops embarked on the waiting ships.

One of Wellington's concerns was that Masséna would ferry troops along the Tagus, outflanking the fortifications, and attack his depots. A flotilla of navy gunboats thus patrolled the river around Alhandra, their captains coordinating their movements with the units stationed along the shore.

Wellington arranged for his experienced troops, numbering some 34,000 British and 16,000 Portuguese troops, to rest in billets behind the lines. Meanwhile 25,000 Portuguese and 8,000 Spanish troops were ordered to garrison the fortifications, supported by 2,500 British artillery men and marines manning the guns. A communication system had been established so that all the forts were in contact with one another. Signal stations were built on several hill tops and manned by navy personnel who could rapidly transmit semaphore messages, taking only a few minutes to pass a message all along the line. Wellington's plan was that the outposts would be able to raise the alarm if a threat developed and then keep the French at bay while his reserve assembled and moved to the danger area along one of the many new military roads he had had built.

Nothing had been left to chance. The whole system of fortifications had cost £100,000 and was a tribute to the combination of British military engineering, Portuguese loyalty and allied cooperation. The troops were

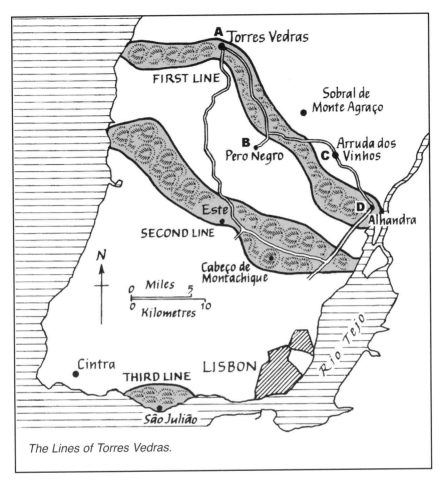

The Lines of Torres Vedras.

safely in position by 10 October 1810 and Wellington based his headquarters at the tiny village of Pero Negro, behind the centre of the first line. His daily routine usually started with a visit to the nearby summit of Monte Socorro so that he could observe the countryside around Sobral.

The French army continued to advance towards Lisbon, and Reynier's II Corps encountered the lines near Alhandra, on the banks of the river Tagus, while Junot's VIII Corps encountered them at Arruda and Sobral to the west. Masséna saw the fortifications at Sobral for the first time on

10 October and was disgusted that his staff had failed to warn him about them, especially when they tried to explain that they had been built in secret. Masséna's furious reply left them in no doubt what his feelings were: 'To the devil with it. He never built those mountains.'

Four days later VIII Corps attacked the fortress at Sobral, one of the strongest in the first line, to test the resolve of the garrison defences; they were quickly driven back. Masséna resigned himself to the fact that he could not penetrate the fortifications with the troops he had available and in a letter to Napoleon outlined his predicament: 'The Marshal Prince of Essling [Masséna's title] has come to the conclusion that he would compromise the Army of His Majesty if he were to attack in force lines so formidable, defended by 30,000 English and 30,000 Portuguese, aided by 50,000 armed peasants.'

As his men settled in for a prolonged siege, Masséna began studying the extent of the allied fortifications. On 16 October he visited the Arruda area, where a line of hills overlooks the village, and strayed too close to Redoubt 120. One of the artillery crews on top of the hill spotted Masséna and fired a warning shot, hitting a wall close to him; he cocked his hat in acknowledgement and withdrew to a safe distance.

Masséna's army camped in front of the Lines for a month, hoping that Wellington would be tempted to deploy and fight, but as the weather grew colder and supplies ran low, morale among the French troops plummeted. The French logistics system could not provide enough food for everyone and the foraging parties struggled to find resources as they searched the same ravaged areas time after time, repeatedly fighting off roaming partisans. In contrast, the allied troops were well fed and warm in their forts and camps to the south.

Masséna came to the conclusion that he had to withdraw to a safe distance and on 15 November his divisions marched north, hidden by thick mist, leaving straw dummies in their outposts to fool the allied sentries. The three corps eventually assembled between Santarém and Rio Maior and settled down for a long and miserable winter. Even though General Drouet brought 9,000 reinforcements to Masséna, sickness was rife and the number of French soldiers occupying northern Portugal had fallen to 47,000 by March 1811.

The situation south of the Lines, where thousands of refugees had fled ahead of the French army, was also becoming critical. The majority were forced to live out in the open at the mercy of the elements, and many succumbed to the cold conditions, weakened by disease and starvation:

Moats and ramparts surrounded many of the hill-top positions.

Thousands of the unfortunate inhabitants of the provinces through which our army had recently retreated were endeavouring to exist between Lisbon and the Lines. There was, therefore, an immense population hemmed up in a small space of country, hundreds of them without a house to cover them or food to eat. In the course of the winter the number of Portuguese who actually died of want was quite dreadful.

By the beginning of March it was clear that Marshal Soult was fully engaged at Badajoz and would not be able to enter Portugal; Masséna's only option now was to withdraw into Spain. Cold, exhausted and hungry, his forces trudged across the border having lost some 25,000 men, the majority due to sickness and malnutrition.

When men became so fatigued with marching and want of food that they could not go further, they were left to perish on the roadside. Disease raged freely in their ranks, but the men would not even lift their comrades to the side of a wall to die in peace, but allowed them to be trodden to death under the feet of the baggage mules. Those French soldiers who were lying on the roads in a still sensible state soon suffered retribution at the hands of the

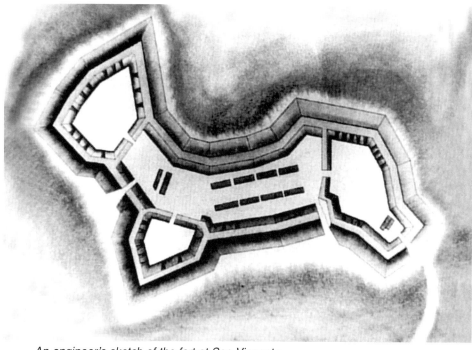

An engineer's sketch of the fort at Sao Vincente.

Portuguese peasantry.

To the south, menawhile, Wellington had at long last been promised reinforcements from London and he could begin to plan for a return to Spain.

VISITING THE LINES OF TORRES VEDRAS

Torres Vedras is 40 kilometres north of Lisbon (Lisboa), alongside the A8 motorway (exit via junction 7 or 8). The town itself stands at the centre of the first line of fortifications, and a monument to the Portuguese soldiers who fought to liberate their country stands in the centre of Parca 25 de Abril, the main square in the centre of the town. The tourist information office is nearby.

Starting from the northern outskirts, drive north along the N8, signposted for Lourinha, and turn left at the first roundabout in the outskirts of the town. Continue straight on at a second roundabout after 400 metres, then take the first right after 100 metres, signposted for Sao

Vincente Fort. Forts 20—23 of the first line are at the top of the hill and all have been reconstructed. The fortifications offer commanding views of the area north of Torres Vedras and are surrounded by earth ramparts and a shallow moat. There are three circular stone-built powder houses, while the earth ramparts running across the interior of the forts were designed to protect the infantry garrison from shell fragments. The forts are simple in design and required the minimum of supervision and expenditure to build; all they needed was a large labour force.

Retrace your route back to the roundabout on the N8 and head east out of the town, following signs for the N248 and Sobral, crossing under a large ancient aqueduct. Turn right after 3 kilometres for Sobral and follow the road through Runa. The whole area is dotted with hills and valleys but the first line of fortifications was built on the line of hills to the left of the road. Continue through several villages, turning right for Lisbon after Dois Portos, and the road follows the valley behind the hill known as Monte Agraco. After 6 kilometres turn right in Perna de Pau for Pero Negro. After crossing the railway lines, head into the village where Wellington based his headquarters while his troops rested behind the Lines. Take the narrow lane to the right at the village square, by a large ancient tree. The large house and surrounding farm buildings stand at the top of a gentle slope. Note on the wall the plaque commemorating his stay. From here Wellington made daily visits to the summit of Monte Socorro, one of the highest hills in the area, to check the Sobral area for signs of French activity.

Retrace your route across the railway lines into Perna de Pau and turn left. After 2.5 kilometres turn right and drive up the steep slopes to the top of Monte Agraco; Sobral is far below in the valley. There is a pull-in area at the top, near a sanctuary, where it is possible to stop. A brief glance is all you need to appreciate the suitability of the terrain for Wellington's needs. This area was in the centre of the first line and the strongest redoubt of all was built on this high plateau; it was the site of one of the few French attacks.

Continue to drive on and turn right, following signs for Fort de Alcuido just after the sanctuary; the turning for the fort is after another 4 kilometres, next to a group of wind turbines. The whole hillside was fortified and assorted overgrown trenches, walls and stone tracks still overlook the valley below. Continue along the N115, past the fort, and the road drops down into Arranho, in the valley behind the first line of forts. Turn left in the village for Arruda, 9 kilometres distant.

Wellington's headquarters in Pero Negro.

Sao Vincente's artillery embrasures look out over the countryside north of Torres Vedras.

The road climbs over the ridge occupied by the line of forts and then drops down into Arruda. Turn right at the roundabout in the village, signposted for Villefranque, and right again at a second roundabout heading for the A10. Stop in the cemetery car park after 1 kilometre to look back across Arruda and the range of hills which Masséna observed on 16 October 1810.

Follow the N248 into Alhandra, heading towards the A10. There is a large tiled fresco on the right-hand abutment of the motorway bridge showing the easterly section of the outpost line; it also details the Portuguese units holding the forts and the French attacks they repulsed.

Turn right at the roundabout under the motorway bridge and head south. After passing under two overhead industrial cable gantries, turn right at the traffic lights, signposted for Sobralinho, and follow the road to the top of

The Portuguese Memorial in Torres Vedras.

the hill and Colonel Fletcher's monument. This stone column, with its statue of Hercules, stands on the site of Redoubt 2 and is inscribed with the words 'Non Ultra — Lines of Torres Vedras'. There are extensive views across the river Tagus, and the first line of redoubts was situated on the ridge to the west.

Return to the main road and turn right at the traffic lights, heading south, and after 7 kilometres take the right slip road for Buscalles. The road runs west along the foot of the Serra de Serves ridge, along the summit of which was built the second line of redoubts. Take the right fork in front of the church in the centre of Buscalles and after 500 metres turn left at the crossroads, signposted for the N8 motorway. Cabeco de

Montachique, the highest hill in the area, is to the left; a signalling station on the summit here could quickly relay messages along the second line. Continue to the N8 motorway and either head north back to Torres Vedras or south towards Lisbon.

Colonel Fletcher's memorial overlooks the Tagus estuary.

Chapter 5

SALLYING FORTH
FROM PORTUGAL

SALLYING FORTH FROM CADIZ, 21 FEBRUARY—4 MARCH 1811

THE FORTIFIED CITY OF CADIZ on the south coast of Spain was an important allied base, its mighty walls protecting both the Spanish Junta and the harbour used by the Royal Navy. The garrison of 20,000 Spanish troops had been reinforced by 5,300 British troops, 180 German cavalry and 10 guns under the command of Major-General Sir Thomas Graham. Although the city had been under siege since January 1810 by Marshal Victor's 25,000-strong French army, the defences were strong and regular supply ships brought the garrison plenty of food, water and ammunition. In January 1811, however, Victor was ordered to send over 9,000 of his troops north, to support Soult's siege of Badajoz, and the reduction of French troops in front of Cadiz's walls tempted the allied commanders into planning how to break the siege.

The plan involved transporting a large expeditionary force by sea to Tarifa, 80 kilometres to the south-east, so they could attack the French siege lines from the rear while the garrison sallied forth. Wellington instructed Graham to command the expeditionary force but the Cadiz Junta insisted that their own commander should take the lead because over 10,000 Spanish troops would be involved. Their choice was the arrogant General Manuela La Peña, an incompetent officer nicknamed 'La Dona Manuela' or 'Madam Manuela' by his own men. Graham eventually agreed to serve under La Peña to pacify the Spanish, but it placed him in a difficult position, particularly for a man described as 'a daring old man, and of ready temper for battle' by the historian Napier.

On 21 February the 14,000-strong task force sailed from Cadiz and headed south past Cap Trafalgar, where Admiral Lord Nelson's ships had defeated the French and Spanish navies in 1805, and three days later La Peña's contingent disembarked at Tarifa. It consisted of two Spanish divisions led by General Lardizábal and the Prince of Anglona, supported by four cavalry squadrons commanded by Colonel Samuel Ford Whittingham, an English officer serving with the Spanish army, plus 1,000 men from the Gibraltar garrison and 1,600 Spaniards irregulars.

Poor weather forced the ships to leave Tarifa and they took the British contingent north-east to Algeciras, a sheltered landing place near Gibraltar. Graham's men eventually marched west on 1 March, heading for Chiclana where Marshal Victor was based.

General La Peña anticipated that the 80-kilometre march would take only two days and he had arranged for General Zayas to sortie out of Cadiz with 4,000 Spanish troops and engage Victor's men as his own force stealthily approached the French from the rear. However, the plan was compromised at an early stage by the Spanish general's clumsy attempt to keep his movements secret. He insisted that his troops had to move at night. The march was a fiasco as units lost their way in the darkness and the poor weather only added to the men's difficulties. The allied force was soon running behind schedule and by 3 March, the date La Peña had set for the attack on the French, had only reached Casas Viejas, 50 kilometres from Cadiz.

La Peña tried to contact the Cadiz garrison but the messenger did not reach the city in time and General Zayas sortied from Cadiz as planned. After bridging the Santi Petri river between the island of Leon and the mainland, the Spanish force advanced south towards the French lines near Torre Bermeja. The attack was a disaster as General Villatte's division stopped Zayas's men in their tracks and they were forced to fall back to a small bridgehead, leaving over 300 dead and injured behind.

After learning that the Cadiz garrison's attack had been repulsed, La Peña abandoned his plan to attack Victor's siege lines and ordered his men to move to the coast road. His objective was simple. He wanted to get his troops back into Cadiz as soon as possible and he aimed to use Zayas's bridgehead over the Santi Petri river to do so. The change in plan did, however, limit La Peña's tactical options, and it was easy for Victor's scouts to guess what his movements were. Instead of taking Marshal Victor by surprise, La Peña was the one who was about to get a shock.

As La Peña's and Graham's tired men marched through Vejer and headed north along the coast, two French divisions, led by General Ruffin and General Leval, were already moving from Chiclana to intercept them at Barrosa Hill. Meanwhile, General Villatte had been ordered to hold Bermeja Ridge, and his division was blocking the shortest route to Cadiz.

THE BATTLE OF BARROSA, 5 MARCH 1811

On the morning of 5 March La Peña ordered Lardizábal's division forward along the coast to attack Villatte's rear. Although the first assault failed, the second succeeded when General Zayas sallied forward once more to make a frontal attack on the French siege lines and Villatte's men fell back across the Almanza salt flats heading for Chiclana. This success opened the road to Cadiz and La Peña ordered the British to leave the summit of Barrosa ridge and head into the Chiclana forest, an order that was challenged by General Graham, who was concerned that his rear would be left exposed if all his troops moved at once, especially now that the French knew of their whereabouts. La Peña agreed to a compromise and arranged to deploy a rearguard of five Spanish battalions and a single composite British battalion, led by Lieutenant-Colonel Frederick Browne, on the summit of the ridge.

As the British troops marched down the slopes into the pine woods, two Spanish guerrillas galloped up to General Graham's aides with alarming news. They had spotted two large French columns approaching from the north, heading towards the summit of Barrosa ridge. Graham's worst fears had been realised and he knew that the small Spanish rearguard would probably run at the first sight of the large French force. He had to do something to save his force from destruction and he would have to do it quickly. While Graham issued orders to prepare for the impending attack, General Leval's division was already marching along the perimeter of Chiclana forest, heading towards the British flank. At the same time General Ruffin's division, supported by 500 dragoons, was heading for Barrosa Tower, where he would cut the coast road.

General Graham ordered his battalions to turn around and head back through the woods in order to confront the French on the slopes of Barrosa Ridge. General Wheatley's brigade, with the 1/28th, the 2/67th, the 2/87th and two companies of the 20th Portuguese, advanced out of the east side of the woods to confront Leval's division. General Dilke's Guards brigade, with the 2/1st Guards, the 2/Coldstream Guards, the 2/3rd Guards and a detachment of the 2/95th, advanced on Graham's right, on to Barrosa Ridge to meet Ruffin's division. Meanwhile, Major Duncan deployed his ten guns at the foot of the slopes in Graham's centre so they could support the attack. Whittingham's small force of cavalry joined the remains of the Spanish rearguard near Barrosa Tower, to try to hold the coast road.

After giving his orders, Graham galloped ahead of his troops to warn his rearguard of the impending attack and found that the situation on Barrosa Ridge was worse than he had anticipated. As expected, the sight of large columns of enemy troops approaching had been too much for the Spanish battalions and some were falling back without a firing a shot. The only troops left on the ridge belonged to the single British battalion, comprising two companies each of the 1/9th, 1/28th and the 2/82nd. Graham was made painfully aware of the proximity of the advancing French when their artillery began shelling Browne's position, and he knew that it was going to be a race against time to stop the ridge being taken.

It would take time for the two brigades to deploy on the edge of the woods so they could meet the French advance, and General Graham would have to rely on Browne's battalion and his rearguard, Colonel Barnard's composite battalion, consisting of two companies of the 2/47th, four rifle companies of the 3/95th and two companies of 20th Portuguese, to delay the two French divisions. It would no doubt result in the loss of the two battalions.

Barnard's battalion advanced out of the woods ahead of General Wheatley's brigade in skirmishing order, and managed to take General Leval's troops by surprise. He immediately ordered his companies to deploy and open fire on the advancing columns. As the air was filled with the sound of muskets, cheers and the cries of the wounded, Colonels Barnard and Bushe of the Portuguese 10th Regiment rode backwards and forwards through the intense fire, shouting 'Que bella musica' ('What beautiful music') to encourage their men. The fight was brief and bloody: the French had overwhelming superiority of numbers and over 250 of Barnard's men were killed or wounded; Colonel Barnard himself was also wounded. But their sacrifice had delayed Leval's division, giving Wheatley's brigade time to form up. As the survivors of Barnard's force fell back, the French troops found four fresh battalions, the Coldstream Guards (from Dilke's brigade), the 1/28th, the 2/67th and the 2/87th, waiting for them.

Wheatley's men did not hesitate and a loud cheer signalled the start of their charge. The French troops reeled as the 87th shouted their battle cry 'Faugh-au-Ballagh' and Colonel Belson of the 28th ordered his men to 'fire at their legs, and spoil their dancing'. Hand-to-hand fighting ensued and for over an hour the battle swayed to and fro but the 1/54th and 2/54th Lignes began to falter under the 1/28th's repeated charges.

General Graham's men counter-attack the French lines on Barrosa Hill.

Meanwhile, Ensign Edward Keogh of the 2/87th was killed as he grabbed the Eagle of the 8th Ligne Regiment, which fell into the hands of Sergeant Patrick Masterman; a lieutenant was severely wounded and seven soldiers died trying to prevent the French soldiers taking it back. (Subsequently the battalion was given the title 'The Prince of Wales's Own Irish' to commemorate the event, and an eagle was added to the battalion's Colours. It was the first time an eagle had been captured in the peninsula and it was later delivered to Whitehall in London, where it was laid up amidst great pomp and ceremony.) When the 2nd Coldstreams joined the fight the 8th and 54th Regiments began to fall back, taking the 45th Regiment and a battalion of grenadiers with them. The men of Wheatley's brigade had defeated a force of more than twice their number.

On Graham's right, Colonel Browne's battalion had the unenviable task of delaying Ruffin's division until Dilke's brigade deployed. This solitary battalion had deployed at the foot of Barrosa Hill, and despite facing grim odds of nearly four-to-one, the men courageously advanced up the slopes. One member of the battalion later recalled in his memoirs how Browne led his men up the steep slopes singing 'Hearts of Oak':

> Colonel Browne rode to the front of the battalion, and said in a voice to be heard by all, 'Gentlemen, General Graham has done you the honour of being the first to attack those fellows. Now follow me, you rascals!' He pointed to the enemy, and gave the order to advance. As soon as we crossed the ravine close to the base of the hill a most tremendous roar of cannon and musketry was all at once opened. Nearly 200 of our men and more than half the officers went down by this first volley. In closing on the centre and endeavouring to form a second line, upwards of fifty more men were levelled with the earth; and the remainder of the battalion now scattered. The men commenced firing from behind trees, mounds or any cover which presented, and could not be got together.

The 200 survivors returned fire from their hiding places, stopping the French from advancing, while Dilke's brigade deployed and advanced past Browne's right flank straight towards Ruffin's division. The sacrifice of Browne's battalion had disrupted the French advance and Graham cheered his men forward with a wave of his hat, shouting 'now my lads, there they are, spare your powder, but give them steel enough', joining them on foot when his horse was injured.

The 1st Foot Guards led the advance in line, supported by the 3rd Foot Guards, and the two battalions charged towards the French at the top of the ridge. A bitter fight followed in which nearly 1,500 men were killed or injured by musket fire and bayonets (Ruffin was wounded and one of his brigadiers, Rousseau, died of wounds) but the British Guards soon had the upper hand as the French began to fall back.

By mid-afternoon the battle was over. Some 5,000 British infantrymen had defeated 9,000 French due to Graham's bold (some might say reckless) attack; the French divisional commander Ruffin later commented on 'the incredibility of so rash an attack'. Although casualty numbers vary according to source, the British certainly lost over 1,200 men while the French suffered over 2,000 losses and Leval's division had to abandon 4 guns.

Even as the two French divisions withdrew from the battlefield, La Peña refused to send any of his own battalions forward to support the British troops on Barrosa Ridge. As Graham's forces were too small to turn the French retreat into a rout, he ordered a general withdrawal and marched his troops across a pontoon bridge on to the Isla de Léon so they could return to Cadiz. La Peña's conduct during the battle soured relations between the British and the Spanish and Lieutenant-Colonel (later Sir General) Andrew Barnard wrote the following words in support of his commander:

> Nothing but the extraordinary coolness and quickness of arrangement which General Graham showed on that day could have extricated us out of the scrape which our allies had drawn us into. Although we occupied the whole force of the enemy, the Spanish general not only did not show a single battalion to save us, but he did not profit by the moment and get possession of the French lines, which were then deserted. He either wanted curiosity or nerves to come himself to see how the affair was going on with us [and] he did not send any of his staff to enquire.

Although Graham had saved his men from destruction, La Peña had one final insult to throw, accusing him of withdrawing without orders and losing the battle for the allies. The Spanish general's ridiculous allegations were ignored and although he was later court-martialled for his conduct during the campaign, he was eventually acquitted.

Graham's Army 5,217 all ranks

Dilkes's Brigade   2/1st Guards, 2/Coldstream (2 Bttns), 2/3rd
Guards   (2 Bttns), 2 Coys 2/95th
Wheatley's Brigade 8 Coys 1/28th, 2/67th, 2/87th
Browne's Battalion 2 Coys each of 1/9th, 1/28th, 2/82nd
Barnard's Battalion 4 Coys 3/95th, 2 Coys 2/47th
Flank Companies   Supplied by 1/20th and 2/20th Portuguese Line Regiment

Cavalry 2 Sqns 2nd Hussars KGL

TOURING BARROSA

If time permits, it is well worth starting your journey from the Rock of
Gibraltar and its port, the Royal Navy's gateway to the Mediterranean.
The mountains of Morocco fill the horizon just 15 kilometres away across
the straits of Gibraltar. Follow the N340 through Algeciras, the landing
area for General Graham's army, and follow the coast road as it winds
over the hills towards the port of Tarifa, 20 kilometres to the west, where
the Spanish troops disembarked.

The N340 then heads north along the coast through Vejer de la Frontera
towards Chiclana, 65 kilometres distant. Graham's troops followed the
road as far as Vejer before veering off towards the coast and heading
north towards Barrosa. The headland of Cap Trafalgar, the site of Nelson's
defeat of the French and Spanish navies in 1805, is to the west of Vejer.

Continue along the A48-E5 north of Vejer, and the turning for Barrosa
is to the left after 25 kilometres. Follow the Carretera de las Lagunes west,
driving through various villages, and turn left at the roundabout after 5
kilometres on to the CA2134, Carretera de la Barrosa. The beach and
Barossa Tower are 3 kilometres to the south-west. The road runs over the
summit of Barrosa Hill as it approaches the beach, and the French troops
advanced on to the summit while Graham's men were camped on the
lower slopes to the right (west). The entire area is covered with extensive
villas and there is little to see apart from the lie of the land.

Heading back from the beach, take the first left and follow the road
down the gentle slope that Graham's men charged up to attack the French
at the summit. Turn left at the T-junction at the end of Calle de Hercules
and head north towards the Santi Petri river where the bridge of boats

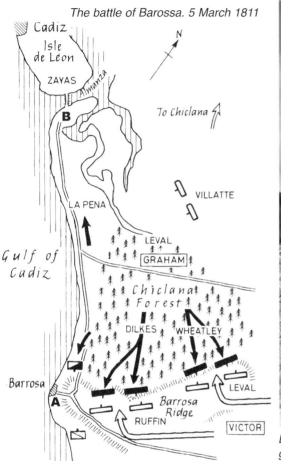

The battle of Barossa. 5 March 1811

Barrosa's watchtower stands guard over the beach.

was. Villatte's division had built siegeworks across the neck of land between the mudflats to the right of the road and the sea to the left. Zayas's troops unsuccessfully attacked them but Graham and La Peña forced the French to withdraw, leaving open the escape route to Cadiz. Chiclana is to the east, and French troops marched from left to right across the horizon before turning towards Barrosa to catch the allies as they marched along the coast. Looking south-east, it is possible to make out the wooded slopes and the summit of Barrosa Hill.

Continue straight on to the Santi Petri river; the road loops around the

The bridge of boats provided an escape route across the Santi Petri river.

end of the isthmus and what remains of the harbour buildings. The bridge of boats crossed the river at its narrowest point and it is possible to see Graham's goal, the city of Cadiz, in the distance. Follow the one-way system around the harbour and then head back through the suburbs to Carretera de la Barrosa, turning on to the Carretera de las Lagunes, heading for the A48-E5.

Cadiz, home of the Spanish government for several years, is worth a visit. The remaining sections of the huge city walls and the wide range of buildings bear testimony to its importance in the history of southern Spain. There is a large monument to the Peninsular War in the Plaza de Espana.

THE BATTLE OF FUENTES DE OÑORO, 3—5 MAY 1811

By the spring of 1811 the French could muster over 70,000 men compared to Wellington's 58,000 but disagreements between the French generals meant that they would not concentrate their armies to confront the British commander. In March Marshal Masséna was withdrawing his exhausted army from Portugal, towards the safety of Ciudad Rodrigo and Almeida on the Spanish border, while Wellington's troops followed close behind. After a few isolated engagements with the French rearguards, the allied army was deployed along the Portuguese border and by 7 April the British troops had isolated the French garrison at Almeida, and plans to besiege the fortress were under way.

On 11 March Wellington heard the news that Soult's Army of the South had taken Badajoz, 240 kilometres to the south in Extremadura, leaving the road to Lisbon open. Against his wishes, he was forced to split his army to counter Soult's success and he sent General Beresford south with the 2nd and 4th Divisions to besiege the border fortress. This move weakened his force in the north by 20,000 men at a time when Masséna was bringing his army back up to strength. By the end of April the French commander was ready to leave Ciudad Rodrigo and once again his men marched towards the Portuguese border.

Masséna's army had 42,000 infantry organised into four corps, supported by 4,500 cavalry and 38 guns. Meanwhile, Wellington had 34,000 infantry (a third of them Portuguese) organised into six divisions, supported by 1,850 cavalry and 48 guns. The allied army was working on the siege lines around Almeida when news that the French were moving to attack arrived at Wellington's headquarters on 2 May. The imminent threat left him with no choice: he had to abandon the siege and meet Masséna.

The position he chose to defend was on the border where the village of Fuentes de Oñoro sat on the slopes of a low ridge astride the main road to Coimbra. The ridge was an ideal defensive position, with the Don Casas stream further hindering any attempts to attack. The stream ran through an impassable ravine north of the road and the French troops would have to wade through the swampy watercourse before they could enter the sprawling village to the south.

Over the next twenty-four hours Wellington's advance units deployed along the west bank of the Don Casas stream and waited for the attack to begin. The majority of his troops were deployed either in or behind Fuentes de Oñoro itself. In total, some 2,260 men, comprising the 2/84th and twenty-eight light companies drawn from the 5/60th, the 42nd, the 2/83rd, the 92nd Regiment and the 5th Line Battalion KGL, held the labyrinth of single-storey stone houses, enclosed gardens and narrow alleys. Command of the mixed force fell to Lieutenant-Colonel William Williams of the 5/60th and he was in no doubt that his men would have to fend off the main French attacks.

Wellington had also deployed a strong reserve on the ridge behind Fuentes de Oñoro, ready to support the troops in the village. Spencer's 1st Division was south-west of the village with Houston's 7th Division in support. Picton's 3rd Division was north-west of the village with Craufurd's Light Division behind; Ashworth's Portuguese brigade was also close by.

Wellington expected Masséna to try to outflank his position and so had deployed troops covering both flanks. On the left flank William Erskine's

5th Division and Alexander Campbell's 6th Division were deployed along the west bank of the Don Casas stream, where it ran through a ravine past the ruins of Fort Conception. The open country to the south of the village was ideal for cavalry but Wellington had only 2,000 horsemen compared to the 4,500 French, and his plan was to tempt Masséna into making a frontal attack against the strongest part of his line. Two battalions, the 85th and the 2nd Portuguese Caçadores, held a small group of dwellings called Poço Velho while Julian Sanchez's guerrilla cavalry held a second hamlet called Nave de Haver.

Masséna's army started to arrive in front of Wellington's position on the morning of 3 May. General Reynier's II Corps deployed his two divisions, led by Merle and Heudelet, north of the Coimbra road, facing Campbell's 6th Division. In the centre General Loison's VI Corps deployed in front of Fuentes de Oñoro, and while Ferey's division prepared to launch a frontal attack on the village, Marchand's and Mermet's waited in support.

Junot's VIII Corps and D'Erlon's IX Corps were still moving towards the battlefield, but General Loison decided to attack Fuentes de Oñoro in the afternoon, in the hope of scoring an early success before Masséna arrived. It was exactly the move that Wellington had hoped for. Ten battalions from General Ferey's division marched over the summit of the ridge and advanced in three columns down the slopes towards the Don Casas stream under fire from the British guns on the opposite hillside. After wading the marshy stream the French columns charged into the village and hand-to-hand fighting erupted in the narrow alleyways and courtyards. The weight of numbers soon began to tell and Williams' men were slowly pushed back up the hill towards the church. Wellington was watching the action from the top of the hill and recognised that reinforcements were needed to stop his light infantry routing. Three of the 1st Division's battalions, the 1/71st, 1/79th and 2/24th, were ordered down the hill to reinforce the light companies.

The arrival of fresh troops turned the tide of battle in the allies' favour and Lieutenant-Colonel the Hon H. Cadogan led the 71st Regiment's charge as his men drove the French from the village. Casualties were heavy and Lieutenant-Colonel Cameron of the 79th had to take command of the light companies when Colonel Williams was seriously wounded. General Loison had also ordered reserves forward but as the two fresh French battalions joined the fray, disaster struck. Through the clouds of musket smoke filling the streets, there was confusion in the French ranks

Fuentes de Oñoro is still a maze of lanes, houses and enclosures.

when the new arrivals mistook the red tunics of the Légion Hanovérienne for British redcoats. One of the new battalions fired a volley at their comrades, while the second battalion fell back in confusion, believing that they had been outflanked.

While Ferey's men rallied along the stream, four battalions of General Marchand's division moved forward to reinforce a second attempt to capture the village of Fuentes de Oñoro. However, this time the British had superior numbers and they were waiting behind the walls and enclosures for the attack to begin. Devastating volley fire stopped the French in their tracks along the Don Casas stream and the water ran red with blood as General Loison recalled his men. By nightfall the first battle for the village was over for the day, but as more French troops arrived on the battlefield, Wellington knew that the fight for Fuentes de Oñoro was far from over. Meanwhile, in Marshal Masséna's headquarters an embarrassed General Loison was explaining why he had made the premature attack and lost over 650 men for no gain; the allies in contrast had lost just 259.

An unofficial truce followed on 4 May and while the generals considered their next move, the men cleaned their weapons and waited for the forthcoming battle. Along the stream the picquets exchanged greetings as men collected water from the stream to quench their thirst, ignoring the bodies from the previous day's fighting. It was the calm before the storm.

Wellington was concerned that the French would try to outflank the village to the south and he spent the day reorganising his line. He could not shift many troops from his north flank because to do so would allow Masséna to reach Almeida; Fuentes de Oñoro was still the key to his position. The only option left to him was to deploy the weak 7th Division, which had only just landed in Portugal, to Poço Velho, and send four regiments of cavalry to reinforce Julian Sanchez.

Masséna spent the day studying the British dispositions and decided to attack Wellington's right flank. Three divisions — 17,000 infantry — led by Marchand, Mermet and Solignac would cross the Don Casas stream near Poço Velho while 3,500 cavalry under General Louis-Pierre Montbrun would cover their flank. Meanwhile, Reynier's II Corps would march against Wellington's left flank to pin down his reserves north of the road. Masséna had seen large numbers of British troops deploying south of Fuentes de Oñoro and he believed that Wellington had weakened the centre of his line. If more reserves were moved south, General Loison's men would be able to renew the attack on the village. As the sun went down over Fuentes de Oñoro, Masséna proudly watched as his troops marched past with drums and bugles, hoping to alarm Wellington's soldiers on the far bank. Few were impressed, however, their thoughts fixed on the forthcoming battle.

Marchand's and Mermet's divisions of VI Corps advanced at first light, supported by Solignac's division from Junot's VIII Corps, towards the British 7th Division. Although Wellington had anticipated a move against his southern flank, it was clear that this attack was much stronger than he had expected. Montbrun's cavalry scattered Julian Sanchez's guerrillas out of Nave de Haver village while the columns of French infantry quickly took Poço Velho hamlet from the 85th and the 2nd Portuguese Caçadores.

Marchand's and Mermet's divisions seemed to be unstoppable and Houston's men were in danger of being overrun as they fought three times their number. Time after time they rallied back, forming ragged but steady squares. Step by step they made a fighting withdrawal in the face of superior numbers, keeping the infantry at bay with their rifles and musket fire, forming squares when the cavalry appeared. Cotton's two brigades of cavalry repeatedly charged and reformed to keep the French at bay, harrying their infantry and artillery while engaging Montbrun's four cavalry brigades.

Although it meant seriously weakening his centre, Wellington sent the Light Division and Bull's battery of Horse Artillery to reinforce the endangered flank. He also ordered Spencer's 1st Division, Picton's 3rd Division and his Portuguese brigade to redeploy on the reverse slopes west of Fuentes de Oñoro, forming a defensive line around the south side of the village. These moves would take time to complete and the British commander was relying on Craufurd's Light Division to stall the French long enough so the new line could be formed.

Eventually the French rallied back to reform and let fresh troops continue the battle and the Light Division took the place of the 7th Division during the lull in the fighting. By the time the French were ready to renew their attack Craufurd's men were ready. Private Wheeler later recounted his experiences during 7th Division's withdrawal:

> We retired through the broken ground in our rear and were pretty safe from their cavalry, but they had brought up their guns and were serving out the shot with a liberal hand. We continued retiring and soon came to a rapid stream. This we waded up to our armpits, and from the steepness of the opposite bank we found much difficulty in getting out. This caused some delay but the regiment waited until all had crossed, then formed line and continued its retreat in quick time.

While the 7th Division marched north, using a shallow valley as cover to withdraw into reserve behind the 1st Division, Craufurd's division carried out a fighting withdrawal for over 3 kilometres, skilfully gaining the time needed for Wellington's plans to be completed. The infantry fell back in square formation while the horse artillery crews repeatedly fired at the advancing French columns, falling back each time they came close. It was a model tactical withdrawal, although when Captain Norman Ramsay's two gun crews refused to limber until it was too late they were briefly cut off by French cavalry; they only just managed to fight their way out and gallop to safety. The only disaster occurred when three companies of the 3rd Guards failed to form square in time when the French cavalry charged; they lost half their number, including their commander. Nevertheless, a catastrophe had been averted and casualties were light (the Light Division only lost 67 men). The historian William Napier later wrote that 'there was not during the war a more dangerous hour for England', while Wellington admitted that Craufurd's withdrawal was 'a near-run thing'.

Masséna waited for two hours, hoping that Wellington would send more troops to his endangered flank, before launching his main attack against his centre. Loison's corps, some 5,000 French infantry, including three battalions of grenadiers, advanced once more down the slope and crossed the Don Casas stream to where the battered 1/71st and 1/79th were waiting in Fuentes de Oñoro with the 2/24th in support. To begin with the fighting went in Loison's favour due to sheer weight of numbers, and the two Scottish regiments suffered heavy casualties. The 79th lost their colonel as they fell back up the slopes to the church on the western edge of the village, where they rallied. Confusion reigned in the narrow streets and once they had reorganised, the Scots counter-attacked, driving the French back into the lower parts of the village.

By midday it was clear that the French would not be able to roll up Wellington's right flank and the feint attacks against his left had failed to entice him to draw fresh reserves from his centre. However, Masséna was determined to take Fuentes de Oñoro by force and he ordered his reserve, General D'Erlon's IX Corps, forward. Conroux's and Claparéde's divisions stormed into the blood-soaked streets, driving the tired British and Portuguese soldiers before them, but once again Wellington was on hand to order the rest of Mackinnon's brigade forward to retake the village. Cheers resounded around Fuentes de Oñoro as the 1/74th and the 1/88th charged down the alleyways, killing and wounding many with their bayonets. Ensign William Grattan of the 1/88th later described what he saw in the village's narrow streets:

> The town presented a shocking sight: our Highlanders lay dead in heaps, while the other regiments, though less remarkable in dress, were scarcely so in the number of their slain. The French grenadiers, with their immense caps and gaudy plumes, lay in piles of ten and twenty together; some dead, others wounded, with barely strength sufficient to move, their exhausted state and the weight of their cumbrous accoutrements making it impossible for them to crawl out of the dreadful fire of grape and round shot which the enemy poured into the town. The Highlanders had been driven to the churchyard at the very top of the village, and were fighting with the French grenadiers across the graves and tombstones.

Fuentes de Oñoro was once again in British hands but Masséna was determined to make one final attempt to take it in the early afternoon; this attack was stopped in its tracks on the outskirts by relentless artillery and musket fire. By mid-afternoon the battle was over, apart from an extended artillery duel and a reckless charge against a French gun battery by the 14th Light Dragoons. The fruitless attacks against Fuentes de Oñoro had exhausted Masséna's reserves, while Wellington still had Spencer's and Picton's divisions hidden behind the ridge south-west of the village.

Although the French had been beaten Wellington knew it would be foolish to advance from the ridge against their superior numbers. He ordered his men to prepare for another day's fighting, making it clear that they had to stop the French ouflanking the village from the south. However, Masséna knew it was over, and while his cavalry spent 6 May probing the allied line north of Fuentes de Oñoro in the hope of finding a way to bypass the village, his infantry prepared to withdraw, having suffered over 2,000 casualties. Two days later they left and Wellington let them go, aware that his cavalry was too weak to threaten them; meanwhile his own infantry units were still suffering, having lost over 1,500 men. It had been a difficult battle, one in which Masséna had nearly outwitted Wellington. Only the tenacity of his infantry and the unbridled bravery of cavalry and artillery alike had saved the British line on several occasions. Wellington later acknowledged how close he had come to defeat, saying 'If Boney had been there, we should have been beaten.'

TOURING FUENTES DE OÑORO

Fuentes de Oñoro is alongside the N620 in Spain or the A25 in Portugal, the main road between Salamanca and Guarda, on the border of the two countries. Approaching from Ciudad Rodrigo, the turning for the village is signposted at the bottom of a long slope, just to the east of the border crossing. Take care turning off the fast road. Continue south through the village for 800 metres and turn left at the small square, by the water fountain with the umbrella-shaped top. Cross Don Casas stream via the concrete culvert and drive up the hill, parking in front of the village cemetery, in the centre of the VI Corps, and later IX Corps, position.

As you look back across the village, it is clear how strong Wellington's position was. The ridge that he had chosen to hold fills the horizon across the valley, while the slopes below are covered by the random network of narrow streets, small houses and enclosures. The track running past the walled cemetery was the old road that was at the centre of General Loison's attack on 3 May and General D'Erlon's final attempt on 5 May. The French battalions had to cross the Don Casas, now a narrow stream flanked by marshy ground, to reach the British. The high water mark of

Fuentes de Oñoro Total 37,614

1st Division General Brent Spencer **7,565**

Stopford's Brigade	1/Coldstream, 1/3rd Guards, 1 Coy 5/60th
Von Lowe's Brigade	1st, 2nd, 5th and 7th Line Bttns KGL, 2 Coys Light Infantry KGL
Nightingall's Brigade	2/24th, 2/42nd, 1/79th, 1 Coy 5/60th
Howard's Brigade	1/50th, 1/71st, 1/92nd, 1 Coy 3/95th

3rd Division General Thomas Picton **5,480**

Mackinnon's Brigade	1/45th, 74th, 1/88th, 3 Coys 5/60th
Colville's Brigade	2/5th, 2/83rd, 2/88th, 94th
Power's Brigade	9th Portuguese Line (2 Bttns), 21st Portuguese Line (2 Bttns)

5th Division General William Erskine **5,158**

Hay's Brigade	3/1st, 1/9th, 2/38th, 1 Coy Brunswick Oels
Dunlop's Brigade	1/4th, 2/30th, 3/44th, 1 Coy Brunswick Oels
Spry's Portuguese Brigade	3rd Line (2 Bttns), 15th Line (2 Bttns), 8th Caçadores

6th Division General Alexander Campbell **5,250**

Hulse's Brigade	1/11th, 2/53rd, 1/61st, 1 Coy 5/60th
Burne's Brigade	2nd, 1/36th
Madden's Portuguese Brigade	8th Line (2 Bttns), 12th Line (2 Bttns)

7th Division General William Houston **4,590**

Sontag's Brigade	2/51st, 85th, Chasseurs Brittaniques, 8 Coys Brunswick Oels
Doyle's Portuguese Brigade	7th Line (2 Bttns), 19th Line (2 Bttns), 2nd Caçadores

the attacks was the church, half-way up the slope.

Drive back across the stream, passing through the small square, and climb up the hill to the church where there is a memorial remembering all the men who fought in and around the village. Continue past the church and follow the road for 400 metres, up to the top of the ridge, where there is a small pull-in to the right. From here it is possible to look back across the village to the French positions. This part of the ridge is also where Wellington deployed Picton's and Spencer's divisions to prevent Marchand's outflanking manoeuvre after Houston's division and Craufurd's Light Division had fallen back from Poço Velho.

Masséna's Army   48,250

Reynier's **II Corps 11,050**
Merle's Division and Heudelet's Division

Loison's **VI Corps 17,100**
Marchand's Division, Mermet's Division and Ferey's Division

Junot's **VIII Corps 4,700**
Solignac's Division

D'Erlon's **IX Corps 11,100**
Claparede's Division and Conroux's Division

Montbrun's Cavalry **2,500**
Bessieres's Cavalry **1,700**

Artillery **38 guns**

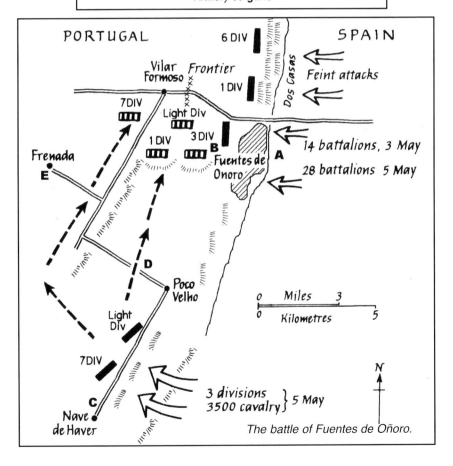

The battle of Fuentes de Oñoro.

Fuentes de Oñoro church and the memorial to those who fought in the battle.

Walk south for 100 metres to view the wooded gulley where the French advance was brought to a standstill. Again it is clear that although Marchand's men very nearly turned Wellington's flank, the British position on the ridge was very strong. Turn around in the pull-in (or continue into Villa Formoso to find an easier turning area) and drive back past the church, turning left by the Don Casas stream to return to the main road.

The rest of the battlefield is in Portugal and it is necessary to cross the border at the checkpoint. Turn left at the first roundabout 300 metres beyond the checkpoint, signposted for Sabugal, and after 200 metres turn left in front of the railway station. The road makes a U-turn over the railway tracks and then heads out of Villa Formoso. Follow it south, turning left after 5 kilometres for Poço Velho. Take the turning to the right signposted for Nave de Haver, bearing right at the T-junction at the far end of the small village after 2 kilometres. Continue south for another 3.5 kilometres and park alongside the walled cemetery on the northern outskirts of Nave de Haver.

Look back towards Poço Velho. Houston's division held the low ridge immediately north of the village while the French cavalry charged over the far end of the ridge to fight their British counterparts. On the way back to Poço Velho it is possible to view the route of the British withdrawal to Fuentes de Oñoro from their perspective. It must have taken a great deal of skill, discipline and nerve to manoeuvre thousands

Poço
Velho

British

French
cavalry

The view from Nave de Haver towards Poço Velho; the French cavalry charged over the crest to the right.

of men through the open woods while French cavalry milled around, looking for an opportunity to strike. Meanwhile, Houston's division followed the crest of the ridge to the left (west) of the road.

Retrace your route through Poço Velho, where it is possible to see the ground where Craufurd's Light Division fought a running battle with the French cavalry during the withdrawal towards Fuentes de Oñoro. Turn right at the crossroads on to the N332 road and follow the ridge north; this was used by Houston's division during the withdrawal.

Some 2.5 kilometres north of the crossroads take the narrow road to the left and head west for 4 kilometres to Freineda, the small village where

Wellington's winter headquarters in Freineda.

Wellington lived during the winter of 1812/13. Turn right in the centre of the village and you will see his house standing next to the church; a plaque remembers his stay. Return to the N332 and head north back into Villa Formoso to complete your tour.

THE BATTLE OF ALBUERA, 16 MAY 1811

General Beresford's siege of Badajoz, the fortress astride the southern road into Portugal, had started on 5 May 1811 but a week later bad news arrived at his headquarters. It was clear that Marshal Soult had left Seville (Sevilla) and was heading north to attack him. The British commander had no choice but to lift the siege immediately and the following day his troops marched away from the city. At Albuera, a small village 20 kilometres to the south-east, they deployed on a low ridge behind the village, a position that Wellington and Beresford had previously selected. On 15 May the British troops there were joined by Generals Joaquin Blake and Francisco Castaños and their 14,000 Spanish troops, increasing Beresford's numbers to 32,000 men supported by 50 guns.

The rolling countryside around Albuera consisted of low hills, shallow valleys and scattered woods, and Beresford used a low ridge running north to south behind the village as the basis of his defence. Although the Albuera stream ran in front of the allied position, its two tributaries, the Chiçaspiernas and the Nogales, were fordable by infantry and artillery to the south. Woods to the east concealed Marshal Soult's approach until his men were dangerously close to Beresford's positions, while olive groves lining the banks of the streams made it difficult to see the French deploying.

Beresford had made Albuera the centre of his position, expecting Soult to advance from the east, and he placed Hamilton's Portuguese division on his left flank supported by Collin's brigade; Otway's Portuguese cavalry brigade was stationed along the stream to stop anyone crossing. Stewart's 2nd Division occupied the centre of the allied line overlooking Albuera, while Alten's King's German Legion brigade was holding the village in front of the main position. General Blake's three Spanish divisions, led by Lardizábal, Ballasteros and Zayas, were deployed along the ridge south-east of Albuera. Beresford only had three regiments of British cavalry: the 13th Light Dragoons held the riverbank immediately south of Albuera, while the 3rd Dragoon Guards and the 4th Dragoons had been placed behind Stewart. The Spanish cavalry covered the right flank.

General Beresford's men had faced a long march and the head of his army only started to arrive on the battlefield late on 15 May. Troops continued to reach the deployment area during the night but some units were still not in position by the time the sun rose the next morning. When Soult began his attack, General Stewart's 5,500 British infantry were in position but General Lowry Cole's 4th Division, which had a similar number of men, had still not arrived.

Marshal Soult had 24,000 men, including 4,000 cavalry, and 60 guns but he was unaware that Blake's Spanish contingent had joined Beresford and he assumed that his army outnumbered the British by two-to-one. He deployed Godinot's and Werle's brigades with Briche's cavalry in front of Albuera, with orders to make feint attacks while V Corps made a large sweep around the allied right (south) flank.

The first French attack began at dawn on 16 May when six battalions of Godinot's brigade crossed the bridge south of Albuera supported by cavalry and artillery. It was a bold move towards the centre of the British line but it was only a feint designed to prevent Beresford moving troops to where the main assault against his right flank was imminent. Werle's brigade of nine infantry battalions was also deploying along the stream in front of Blake's position, again hoping to draw the British general's attention away from the troops moving to the south.

Meanwhile, General Jean-Baptiste Girard's and General Honoré Theodore Gazan's divisions, comprising over 8,400 men, were taking advantage of the woods and rolling

General William Beresford.

countryside to stay hidden as long as possible. They had left the Sevilla road and turned south along the Nogales stream before heading west across the Chiçaspiernas stream. As the two divisions moved ever closer, General Zayas eventually spotted them approaching from the south in march column. It appeared that General Beresford's position was in peril, as the nineteen battalions of V Corps deployed into lines and columns, an organisation known as *ordre mixte*, while three batteries of artillery opened fire on the Spanish positions. On hearing the news of the French advance, General Beresford rode across to Blake to assess the situation and anxiously watched as Latour-Maubourg's cavalry scattered the Spanish cavalry.

It was time to act, and act fast. Beresford ordered General Blake to redeploy his division so it was facing south ready to meet the French attack. He then rode back to the centre of his line and ordered General Stewart to send reinforcements to the threatened flank. Blake, however, was not yet convinced that Girard's division was making Soult's main attack and he still believed that the troops to his front were waiting to advance. As soon as Beresford left, he overruled his commander and ordered just a single brigade from Zayas's division to move. Thus only four Spanish battalions and a battery of guns, little more than 1,000 men, faced an entire French corps. To make matters worse, Soult had also started to withdraw Werle's brigade and a large part of his heavy cavalry so they could move around to join the flank attack. Although he did not realise it yet, Beresford's flank was in danger of being overwhelmed.

As Girard's division approached the top of the hill, Zayas's men opened fire in their three-deep lines and the French returned fire. Although they had overwhelming numerical superiority, the French officers chose to engage in a lengthy fire-fight rather than charging. The Spanish were falling all around, but despite losing one-third of their strength, they stood their ground.

While Zayas's men were keeping the French at bay, Beresford was busy bringing up reinforcements, knowing that he faced a race against time to save his flank. Wellington later explained how the Spanish refused to move either forwards or backwards:

> The Spanish troops, I understand, behaved admirably. They stood like stocks, both parties at times firing upon them, but they were quite immovable, and this is the great cause of all our losses. After they had lost their position, the natural thing to do would have been to attack it with the nearest Spanish troops, but they could not be moved. The British troops were brought up, and must always in these cases be brought up, and they suffered accordingly.

Meanwhile, Beresford had been busy reorganising his line. General William Stewart was ordered to move his 2nd Division up in support of

Polish lancers charge the 3rd Foot as they form square.

the Spaniards and to deploy his brigades in a second line so the Spanish forces could rally behind them. Two regiments of heavy dragoons and a brigade of Spanish cavalry were also moved to the endangered right flank. General Hamilton's Portuguese Division also moved south, taking the 2nd Division's place behind Albuera, while the King's German Legion brigade continued to hold the village.

As soon as the 2nd Division had formed behind the Spanish, Zayas ordered his battered brigade to withdraw through Hogton's and Abercrombie's brigades, revealing a line of fresh battalions in front of Girard's division. So far Beresford's plan to reinforce his flank was working. Although Stewart had been instructed to hold his position and engage the French with volley fire to buy more time, he decided instead to counter-attack. Sir John Colborne was ordered to wheel his brigade forward and drive V Corps back. It was a bold move and the sight of 1,600 men advancing in lines over the summit of the ridge towards their flank caused consternation in the French ranks.

While Girard's battalions tried to counter the threat nature intervened.

Dark clouds had been threatening a thunderstorm all morning and a sudden downpour over the battlefield reduced visibility and soaked the men. Neither Colborne nor Lumley's cavalry saw Latour-Maubourg's cavalry assembling behind a low ridge due to the rain and smoke but Latour-Maubourg had coolly watched the brigade deploy into line, exposing its flank a short distance in front of his 3,000 hidden horsemen. This opportunity was too good to miss and the 1st Polish Lancers immediately levelled their deadly lances and cantered over the summit of the low ridge. Suddenly the four regiments of British infantry realised they were in deadly peril. For many it was too late. As the regiments desperately tried to form square, many men discovered that their rain-soaked muskets would not fire. The 1/3rd, 2/48th and 2/66th regiments did not have time to protect themselves and the French lancers carved their way through the unfortunate brigade, riding down anyone who got in their way; only the 2/31st was able to form square. The 2/66th lost both of its colours, and while only 85 men out of the 728-strong 1/3rd Regiment survived unscathed, the severely wounded Lieutenant Latham was later found protecting the regiment's King's Colour inside his blood-soaked tunic.

Some lancers attacked Beresford's staff and the general himself was obliged to parry one lance thrust before dragging the trooper to the ground. Many rode on behind Zayas's line, veering off when they encountered Hoghton's brigade and the British dragoons. When Latour-Maubourg's men finally returned to their lines to rally, they left behind a trail of destruction, including at least 1,300 dead and injured British soldiers, the majority of them from Colborne's brigade; six guns had also been abandoned.

As Beresford tried urgently to regain control of the situation, Stewart's two remaining brigades, led by Hoghton and Abercrombie, had finally formed up behind Zayas's division and as they opened their ranks, the Spanish infantry withdrew to rally behind them. Girard's exhausted division now faced seven fresh British battalions deployed in two deep lines. As the redcoats opened a devastating volley fire, the French infantry reeled back; some tried to rally while others simply ran, causing confusion in Gazan's division, which was so close behind that it did not have room to deploy. What followed was a ferocious fire-fight at point-blank range and dozens fell with every volley as both sides fired blindly into the smoke. Colonel Inglis was heard to shout 'Die hard 57th, Die hard!' before being wounded, and his battle cry became the 57th's motto.

One soldier serving with the battalion later described the slaughter:

> This murderous contest of musketry lasted long. We were the whole time progressively advancing upon the enemy. The slaughter was now dreadful: every shot told. To describe this wild scene with fidelity would be impossible. At intervals, a shriek or a groan told that men were falling around me, but it was not always that the tumult suffered me to catch these sounds. A constant feeling [closing ranks towards the centre of the battalion] more truly bespoke the havoc of death.

The engagement continued for nearly an hour but neither side would give ground despite the mounting casualties; the 57th and the 48th both lost over 400 men, while the 29th lost over 300. Eventually, numbers began to tell and as Hoghton's and Abercrombie's battered brigades began to waver, Beresford tried to get assistance from General Blake but Carlos de España's brigade refused to move forward. It was a desperate situation but help was at hand.

The 4th Division had been marching towards Albuera all morning, guided by the sound of the guns. General Sir Lowry Cole spurred forward when Major Henry Hardinge, the deputy quartermaster-general of the Portuguese army, told him of the dangerous situation Beresford faced. There was a strong possibility that Stewart's division would be beaten by Soult's V Corps if the 4th Division did not reach the battlefield in time. Lowry Cole's troops advanced rapidly astride a stream bed towards Beresford's stricken flank, out of sight of the French beyond the ridge where Stewart's men were fighting for their lives. The subtle contours allowed his battalions to deploy into lines unmolested while the Lusitanian Legion formed squares on the left flank and light companies did the same on the right for protection against cavalry. As Lowry Cole's battalions advanced over the summit of the ridge Girard's and Gazan's troops were shocked to see another wave of fresh troops appear on their right flank. The French artillery rapidly switched targets but the roundshot had little effect on the thin lines. Meanwhile, Latour-Maubourg's dragoons took up the challenge and charged. They were stopped by an impenetrable wall of bayonets and disciplined volley fire.

Soult was determined to break Beresford's lines and he ordered his reserve, the 6,000 men of Werlé's brigade, forward. Although they were still outnumbered, General William Myers' brigade advanced forward to link up with the survivors of the 2nd Division. The three battalions of fusiliers, the 1/7th, 2/7th and 1/23rd, deployed alongside Stewart's men, edged forward, wrapping around the French left flank. Abercrombie's brigade did the same, closing in on the opposite French flank and completing a large semi-circle around V Corps. As 2,000 muskets fired repeatedly, the French columns started to fall back, but as Myers gave the order to charge, the French artillery fired a devastating round of grapeshot. Napier described the carnage:

> The Fusilier battalions, struck by the iron tempest, reeled and staggered like sinking ships; but suddenly and sternly recovering they closed on their terrible enemies, and then was seen with what a strength and majesty the British soldier fights. No one could stop that astonishing infantry.

Over a thousand fusiliers were killed and injured during the fighting but Soult's men were at last beaten. They had fought long and hard to break Beresford's army but now they were falling back down the slopes, heading for the safety of the woods where they had started earlier that morning.

Losses had been high on both sides. The allies had suffered nearly 6,000 casualties, the majority of them infantry, while the French had lost over 7,000. Stewart's division had been devastated and the following list of casualties demonstrates how bloody the fighting had been:

Colborne's Brigade:	1,413 casualties out of 2,066 or **68** per cent
Hoghton's Brigade:	1,044 from 1,651 or **63** per cent
Myer's Brigade:	1,045 from 2,015 or **52** per cent

When Wellington visited Albuera on 21 May the course of the battle could be followed by the hundreds of corpses 'literally lying dead in their ranks as they stood'. Torrential rain soaked the battlefield later that night as Soult's army retired towards Sevilla, but Beresford did not go in pursuit; instead he returned to Badajoz to resume the siege.

Both commanders were disappointed by their performance and Wellington criticised Beresford's dispatch for its despondent tone, responding crisply: 'This won't do. It will drive the people in England mad. Write me down a victory.' But he also offered Beresford some reassurance: 'You could not be successful in such an action without a large loss and we must make up our minds to affairs of this kind sometimes, or give up the game.' Meanwhile, Soult felt that he had been

The 1/7th and 2/7th Fusiliers stop Soult's final attack.

Beresford's Army at Albuera 20,300 men

2nd Division General William Stewart **5,450**

Colborne's Brigade	1/3rd, 2/31st, 2/48th, 2/66th
Hoghton's Brigade	29th, 1/48th, 1/57th
Abercrombie's Brigade	2/28th, 2/34th, 2/39th
Divisional Light Troops	3 Coys 5/60th

4th Division General Lowry Cole **5,000**

Myers's Brigade	1/7th, 2/7th, 1/23rd
Kemmis's Brigade	1 Coy each of 2/27th, 1/40th, 97th
Harvey's Portuguese Brigade	11th Line (2 Bttns), 23rd Line (2 Bttns), 1st Bttn Lusitanian Legion

Portuguese Division General Hamilton **4,800**

Fonseca's Brigade	2nd Line (2 Bttns), 14th Line (2 Bttns)
Campbell's Brigade	4th Line (2 Bttns), 10th Line (2 Bttns)
Alten's Independent Brigade	1st Light and 2nd Light Bttns KGL
Collins's Independent Brigade	5th Line Portuguese (2 Bttns), 5th Caçadores

British Cavalry **1,995**
3rd Dragoon Guards, 4th Dragoons, 13th Light Dragoons
Portuguese Cavalry1st, 5th, 7th, 8th Line

Artillery
24 British guns and 12 Portuguese guns

Soult's Army 24,250 men

V Corps 8,400
Girard's Division 4,250
Gazan's Division 4,150
Werle's Brigade 5,600
Godinot's Brigade 3,900
Grenadier Brigade 1,000
Cavalry 4,000
Artillery 60 guns and 1,350 men

---

cheated. Although he had achieved important tactical successes, outmanoeuvring Beresford at the beginning of the battle, the resolve of the British and Spanish troops had prevented his victory: 'They could not be persuaded they were beaten. They were completely beaten, the day was mine, and they did not know it, and would not run.'

The Spanish infantry had fought well for the most part but Wellington's despatch cast them in a bad light and it soured relations between the two armies; biased Spanish reports only increased the bitterness. However, Wellington did not have time to worry about his allies' feelings; he had to surround Almeida and Ciudad Rodrigo.

TOURING ALBUERA

Leave Badajoz along the N432, signposted for Sevilla; Albuera is 25 kilometres to the south-east. Leave the bypass at the slip road signposted for Albuera, turn left at the T-junction at the end and head south-east towards the village. As the road begins to drop down towards the houses and past the cemetery on the right, slow down and turn on to the narrow track leading back to the walled enclosure. There are extensive views across the village and the surrounding countryside from the car park in front of the entrance.

The cemetery stands north-west of Albuera in the centre of Beresford's first position, which ran along the ridge west of the village. He placed his British troops behind the village and while the Portuguese held the area north of the cemetery, the Spanish troops held his right flank. It is clear why he chose this ridge in the open rolling country because Marshal Soult's men would have to cross the Albuera stream before they could deploy. However, as his men marched up from the south-east, the French commander decided against a frontal attack. An advanced guard moved straight towards the bridges in front of Beresford's position, but the rest of his force turned to the south and crossed the stream 4 kilometres south of Albuera. From here, they could turn north towards the Spanish troops holding Beresford's flank.

Return to the main road and drive into Albuera. Take the first left and then the first right, joining the old road through the centre of the village. There is a monument in the main square next to the church. A bust of General Castaños sits in the centre, between two pillars, with the names of the British and Spanish generals engraved alongside. There is a small

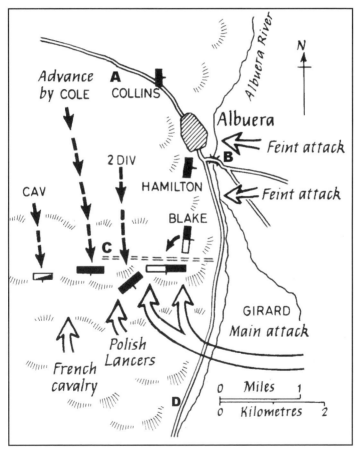

The battle of Albuera.

British line

Spanish f

Initially General Beresford deployed on this high ground west of Albuera.

The memorial to General Castaños in Albuera's square.

museum behind the church (the opening hours are limited).

Continue along the main street, turning left on to the N432 at the south end of the village. At the junction stands one of a pair of identical tiled monuments; the other is at the north end of the village. The road crosses Albuera stream after 500 metres, with the original stone bridge to the left. Take the narrow turning on to the old road after 500 metres and drive back towards the bridge where Goudinot's men made a diversionary attack to try to draw Beresford's attention away from the main attack to the south.

Cross the old bridge and rejoin the main road, heading back towards Albuera. Turn left by the garage before entering the village, and head south along the N435, signposted Almendral. The road runs along the foot of the slope on which General Blake's Spanish troops were initially deployed before moving south to counter Marshal Soult's outflanking manoeuvre. Stop in the pull-in on the left-hand side of the road in front of the first house after 1 kilometre. Cross the busy road and walk up the track to the top of the slope to visit the centre of the battlefield.

Blake's troops were deployed along the crest of the low ridge, facing the French advance from the south (left of the track). At the top of the first small summit it is possible to see a second one another 500 metres further on (just beyond a junction of farm tracks); continue to it to obtain the best all-round view of the battlefield. A study of this area answers many of the questions posed about the battle as the subtleties in the terrain become clear. At first glance the ground seems to be almost flat but a closer look

One of the two tiled memorials on the outskirts of Albuera. 'In rows, just like they fought, they lay like the hay in the open countryside when the night falls and the mower falls silent. That is how they were slain.'

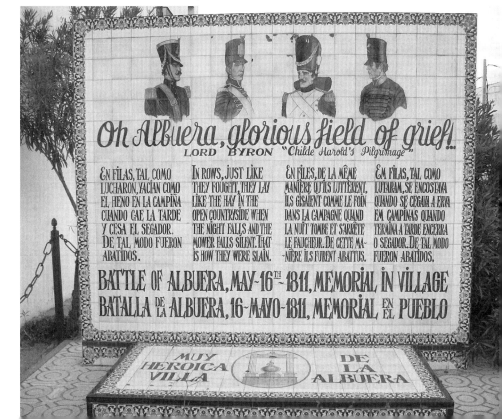

Godinot's attack was held at bay at this bridge over the river Albuera.

reveals how units could move about unseen, particularly when the smoke and noise of battle dulled the senses.

The first attacks eventually drove the Spanish back off the crest of the ridge but their resolute defence had given General Stewart enough time to line out along the dead ground behind, creating a new line. The dip in the ground to the left (south) of the ridge is where Colborne's brigade deployed, and it is possible to see how the French lancers could approach the British flank unnoticed. To the west, where a solitary farm stands, is where the British cavalry deployed. Look north to the shallow valley along which General Cole's men approached, and you can see how his troops were hidden from view until the last minute.

Cole's brigade was decimated in this area of low ground when French lancers charged from hidden ground to the right.

French lancers

Colborne's brigade

Colborne's brigade

Return to your car and drive another 3 kilometres south to a pull-in area on the right, where it is possible to turn round. The French army moved south behind the low wooded ridge to the west (left of the road) before swinging round to head back north towards Beresford's flank. Driving back towards Albuera, it is possible to see how well hidden their approach was as they climbed the slopes to the left of the road.

THE BATTLE OF ARROYO DOS MOLINOS, 28 OCTOBER 1811

The 2nd Division had suffered appalling casualties at the battle of Albuera but after several reorganisations it was back at full strength under General Hill and he had three new brigades led by Howard, Byng and Wilson. Many of the men were new drafts from England who had arrived as replacements and had had little time to acclimatise to campaign life before being called upon to take part in a hazardous operation.

In October 1811 General Girard's division of General Drouet's corps, numbering 5,500 infantry and cavalry, crossed the river Guadiana at Mérida and marched north-east, heading for Talavera de la Reina. General Hill was ordered to follow the French across the rugged hills and valleys of Extremadura, assisted by General Pablo Morillo's Spanish brigade, a total of over 10,000 men. After several arduous days on the road, Girard's division was finally spotted on 27 October, camped at Arroyo dos Molinos, a small village at the foot of the steep, rocky hills of the Sierra de Montanches. Hill realised that if he could get his men close to the French camp before dawn and ready to attack at first light, he could surprise Girard's men. His plan was to cut the three roads out of the village and trap Girard's men at the foot of the rocky slopes before they could organise themselves, forcing them to surrender or escape into the mountains.

By nightfall Hill's troops had assembled at Alcuescar, only 6 kilometres west of the French camp, and they spent a miserable night there, lashed by heavy rain and hail. As dawn broke on 28 October the storm relented, only to be replaced by a thick mist, which was ideal for concealing Hill's men as they approached Arroyo dos Molinos. A low hill on the west side of the village hid the allied troops from view as they split into two columns and prepared to attack the French camp. Stewart's brigade prepared to attack the village from the west, supported by Howard's brigade and Morillo's Spanish brigade while Wilson's brigade and three Portuguese battalions marched south to cut the roads to Medellín and

Mérida. Erskine's British and Penne Villemur's Spanish cavalry brigades waited in support, ready to charge through the camp when the alarm was raised.

Stewart's brigade surprised the first French picquet covering the road west to Alcuescar, and although most of the guards were captured, a few managed to escape and raised the alarm. A short distance away in Arroyo dos Molinos General Girard's troops had also made an early start. The 64th and 88th infantry regiments and a cavalry regiment had already left, but over 4,000 troops were still waiting their turn to strike camp and join the march east.

The picquet's alarm sent a shockwave through the camp, and while the infantry packed their equipment and formed up ready to leave as quickly as they could, the cavalry mounted up and moved out piecemeal. A single infantry battalion stayed behind as a rearguard and its men opened fire as the 71st and 92nd entered the village led by their pipers. A volley was followed by a cheer and a charge as the Scots swept the French aside and rampaged through the village. Hundreds were taken prisoner in the confusion and General Girard's baggage train was captured.

The 71st pushed on and, with the help of three guns, engaged the French troops still in the village as they tried to escape. They headed south only to find Hill's cavalry waiting to cut them off. As Girard's infantry headed east along the foot of the Sierra de Montanchez mountains, his chasseurs and dragoons formed up to engage their opposite numbers. The 9th Light Dragoons and 2nd King's German Legion Hussars took up the challenge and in the ensuing mêlée many French horsemen were taken prisoner, including General Brun, who was pulled off his horse by Trumpeter Martin of the 9th Light Dragoons.

While the fighting in and around the village raged on, Howard's and Wilson's brigades had been marching across country, south of Arroyo dos Molinos, hoping to catch the French infantry. The light companies of the 28th, 34th and 39th led the advance and opened fire on escaping columns of men in the hope of drawing them into a firefight. The opening volleys did not entice the French to stop and return fire but they did cause Girard to panic and he ordered his officers to run for the safety of the mountains, before the allied cavalry arrived. The order caused panic. Officers abandoned their horses and men discarded anything they could not carry easily, before scrambling up the rocky slopes. Many thought it was hopeless to try to escape and simply laid down their arms as Howard's brigade approached; over 1,300 French troops were taken prisoner.

General Girard's men tried to escape up these rocky slopes but many were hunted down by General Morillo's Spanish soldiers

A deadly scramble up the mountainside followed as Morillo's Spanish brigade chased the French troops to the top, killing anyone who tried to hide. Around 500 reached the top of the mountain and escaped to safety, including General Girard, but his division had been destroyed. Hill's troops had suffered around 100 casualties.

This battle brought a difficult campaigning season to an end and news of the success at Arroyo dos Molinos was welcomed at Wellington's headquarters. As his troops withdrew back into Portugal, Wellington was already planning how he could take the fighting deep into Spain while the French controlled the two main roads across the border. He had no option. His men would have to assault two large fortresses, Ciudad Rodrigo in the north and Badajoz to the south.

Touring Arroyo Dos Molinos

Head north along the A66 from Mérida heading for Cáceres and turn right on to the EX381 after 30 kilometres, signposted for Alcuésar. Pass through Alcuésar and turn right for Arroyomolinos after 5 kilometres. Take the right fork just before the village and turn right on to Calle San Martin at the crossroads on the outskirts. Head west along the road for 2 kilometres and it passes over the hill that General Hill used to conceal his troops. Cross the stream and turn around on the far side of the culvert, heading back towards the village, and it is possible to appreciate how the dead ground hid several thousand troops.

The centre of Arroyomolinos is a maze of narrow streets that have changed little over the last 200 years. Continue straight on to the church and follow the road around the ancient building, passing under the unusual archway beneath the tower (car access only). Retrace your route back to the crossroads and turn left.

Turn left after 900 metres and head into the centre of the village (cars only), turning right on to Calle Cervantes at a small square after 700 metres. Follow the narrow street, passing the small chapel with its cylindrical tower, out of the village. Girard's troops fled along this street and along the foot of the steep rocky slopes. Many were trapped by the British and surrendered but several hundred clambered up the mountain to escape. Morillo's Spanish guerrillas followed, killing anyone they caught.

Larger vehicles can continue past the outskirts of the village to a large pull-in area on the left. Both stops give good views of the Sierra de Montanches.

Chapter 6

OPENING THE ROADS INTO SPAIN

THE BALANCE OF POWER CHANGES

THE THIRD YEAR of Napoleon's attempt to conquer the Iberian peninsula was a year of major changes for the French army. Napoleon decided to change command of the armies operating in Spain following the battle of Fuentes de Oñoro in May 1811. Marshal

Marshal Auguste Marmont.

Masséna was recalled to France after frequently quarrelling with his army commanders, losing their respect and support after the retreat from Portugal at the end of 1810. His replacement, Marshal Auguste Marmont, was the youngest marshal in the peninsula and although he had only just taken over Ney's VI Corps his promotion was an inspired choice. His initial grasp of strategy and outstanding organisational talents impressed his subordinate officers while his flamboyant style proved to be popular with the men.

Despite his warm welcome, the new French commander faced a difficult problem, caused by the impending French invasion of Russia. Napoleon had withdrawn a number of divisions to join the army gathering in Prussia, and the number of replacements available to Marmont would steadily decrease as the importance of conquering Spain and Portugal reduced. As Marmont came to grips with the situation on the Iberian peninsula, his army dwindled to such a level that he was forced on to the defensive along the border with Portugal, relying on the fortresses at Ciudad Rodrigo and Badajoz to block the main roads into Spain. The Army of Portugal based at Almaraz, west of Madrid, had sent many units to other parts of the country, and 10,000 troops had reinforced General Louis-Gabriel Suchet's assault against Valencia on the east coast. The reduction in numbers meant that Marmont could only deploy two divisions to oppose the allied armies, since the rest of his forces were needed to protect supply bases and lines of communication.

The reduction of troops across Spain was noticeable everywhere and the news soon reached Wellington. At the end of the year he decided it was time to cross the border, taking advantage of the fact that the French armies would be spread far and wide in their winter billets, and try to force open the two main roads into Spain. His plan was to take the two Spanish border fortresses early in the new year before the French commanders could concentrate their troops. His first target was the medieval fortress of Ciudad Rodrigo, to the north, astride the road to Salamanca and the plains of Castilla, north of Madrid. Once the northern road was open, he could turn his attentions to supporting General Beresford's force, which had made several fruitless attempts to take Badajoz, a larger fortress sitting astride the road between Lisbon and Madrid.

Wellington's first step was to mislead Marmont into believing that the allied army was going to rest until the spring. While agents and guerrillas spread false rumours across Spain, fake orders and falsified reports fell into French hands and quickly found their way to the marshal's headquarters. Marmont's staff eagerly read extensive lists of officers who had been sent home on leave and exaggerated reports detailing the numbers of sick and wounded in the hospitals. Deployment orders also reported that the British divisions were scattered across Portugal in winter billets. All this false information led the French to believe that Wellington's army was at rest and likely to stay that way. In fact as 1811 came to an end, Wellington's troops were secretly gathering along the Portuguese border, while the French were concentrating on operations along the opposite coast.

On 25 December Suchet advanced towards Valencia and encountered the Spanish army along the river Guadalaviar. There was little resistance to the French attack and General Blake's men were soon falling back into the city, swelling the garrison inside the fortress to an unmanageable number. Although the port was protected by strong fortifications, it was isolated from the rest of the Spanish army and the limited stocks of food would not last long. An early attempt to break the siege on 29 December failed and a week later the French siege artillery opened fire on the crowded city. As the guns battered the walls, feelings began to run high inside the fortress and after only three days Blake surrendered the city and the garrison, handing over large stocks of guns, ammunition and food to General Suchet's troops. The fall of the city left an important port in French hands but it had seriously overstretched Marmont's armies just as Wellington prepared to advance across the border.

THE SIEGE OF CIUDAD RODRIGO, 8–20 JANUARY 1812

The fortress of Ciudad Rodrigo stands close to the Spanish border, astride the main northern route into Spain, and had been blockaded as early as February 1810 by Marshal Ney, as Wellington withdrew into Portugal. On 16 June French troops invested the town and began their siege while the 6,500-strong Spanish garrison led by General Andrés Herrasti watched helplessly from the walls. Before long the French had dug entrenchments and four battery positions on the high ground north of the town and after three weeks of bombardment the siege train had blown a large breach in the northern wall. The attack began on 9 July and despite heavy losses in front of the walls, Ney's men were soon rampaging through the crowded streets.

When Wellington's army crossed the frontier in snow and heavy rain on 4 January 1812, Ciudad Rodrigo had already been surrounded for some time by Julian Sanchez and his guerrillas. The Spanish irregulars had been able to stop the garrison foraging for food while supply trains could not get through. They also captured the governor, a Swiss gentleman named Reynaud (some believed he allowed himself to be captured so he could join his brother in England), leaving the 2,000-strong garrison under the command of General Barrié.

By 8 January Wellington's troops had reached Sanchez and his engineers set to work preparing the siege lines north of the fortress. The small oval fortress stands on a low hill on the north bank of the Agueda river; to the north-east there were suburbs surrounded by a secondary wall. Santa Cruz Convent stood beneath the western wall and San Francisco Convent stood to the north.

A series of ramparts topped by a 10-metre high wall surrounded the

The artillery crews' view of the town and the Greater Breach

town but although the fortifications were strong there was a serious weakness in the defence: two ridges ran close to the north wall. The northern one, the Greater Teson, posed the greatest threat because it was higher than the fortress walls, giving the allied gunners a perfect view of their target, and many used the cathedral tower as their aiming point. The lower ridge, the Lesser Teson, ran close to the north-west corner of the fortress and assault columns could use it to assemble close to the wall without being seen.

Wellington knew that he had to work quickly. Spies had noted that Marmont and Dorsenne were on the move and there was a strong possibility that both of them were marching towards the town in the hope of relieving General Barrié. He planned to attack Ciudad Rodrigo from several directions at once. His guns would target the north-west corner where the French had first breached and then repaired the wall, expecting it to be the weakest point. The main assault parties could use the Lesser Teson as an assembly point. A secondary assault would be made against the southern wall, and once into the moat, all the assault parties would converge on the breach at the north-west corner.

The allies' first objective was to take Reynaud Redoubt, an earthwork fortification on the summit of the Greater Teson, and 300 men of the Light Division were chosen to attack it. On the night of 8 January Colonel John Colborne of the 52nd led two companies from the 43rd, 52nd and 95th

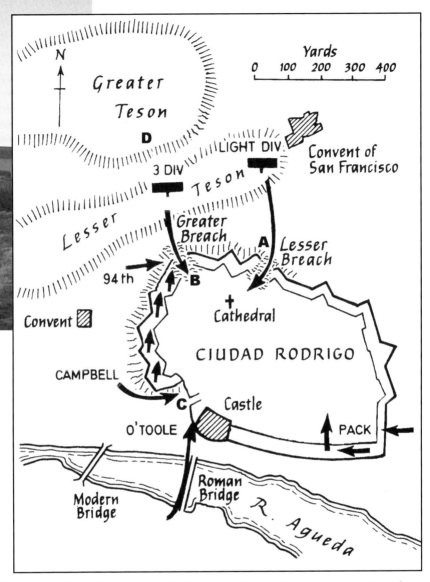

Rifles forward in silence towards the redoubt while two companies of Portuguese Caçadores followed. They crept close to the fortification before the alarm sounded and while half the men opened fire, the rest charged and scaled the ramparts. Within minutes the redoubt's 60-strong garrison had been overwhelmed and the fort was in British hands; only 26 men had been killed or injured in the assault.

This gateway was quickly reduced to ruins, forming the Lesser Breach

Work could now begin in earnest and Colonel Fletcher decided to dig the first siege-trench (known as the First Parallel) along the forward slopes of the Greater Teson. The French guns on the walls of Ciudad Rodrigo targeted the infantry as they dug and work progressed slowly under heavy fire. The work was dirty, dangerous and tiring, and the cold weather chilled the men to the bone, so Wellington made sure that each division took its turn. Work continued around the clock and over the next five days the first battery positions and a connecting trench were completed.

As the guns rolled into position and began hammering the north-west corner of the fortress, excavation work began on the Second Parallel on the northern slope of the Lesser Teson. Work was easier here because the trench was out of sight of the French guns but General Barrié was determined not to let Wellington's men dig right up to the walls without a fight. Just before midday on 14 January a large French force emerged from the safety of the fortress and advanced towards the freshly dug trenches on Lesser Teson. The poorly armed British working parties were quickly driven back and Barrié's men caused a great deal of damage to the trenches, filling in a number of sections, before returning to the fortress, taking as many entrenching tools as they could carry with them.

Undeterred, the British returned to work, and within a few hours all the damage had been repaired.

No fewer than twenty-seven guns were soon battering the north-west corner of the fortress and huge plumes of dust and debris flew into the air as Ciudad Rodrigo's walls crumbled. Wellington's assessment had been correct: the French repairs were poor and the weak mortar soon gave way as the stonework of the main wall and the outer ramparts crumbled, filling the moat with heaps of smashed masonry. This gap would soon become known as the Greater Breach, and Picton's 3rd Division was detailed to attack it.

Wellington was concerned that French troops had been using the San Francisco Convent at the eastern end of the Lesser Teson as an observation post and took steps to stop them. On the night of 14 January three companies from the 40th Regiment crept towards the convent, overwhelming the French observers hidden in the building. For the first time the French gunners did not have observers directing their fire against the British entrenchments. It also meant that a fourth battery could be built alongside Reynaud Redoubt and on 18 January it was ready to accept guns; they were soon targeting the tower standing over a gate in the centre of the northern wall. By nightfall the top of the tower lay in ruins, leaving huge piles of broken masonry on either side of the wall. This new gap was known as the Lesser Breach and the Light Division would attack it.

By the following evening the two breaches had been opened but Wellington could see through his telescope that both of them were smaller than he wanted; the slopes of rubble leading up to the top of the Greater Breach were also steeper than desired. Work had progressed on the assembly trenches across the Lesser Teson at a steady rate but they were still not complete. He could also see that there was a large drop into the moat and hay sacks would have to be made for the Forlorn Hopes, so they could throw them down into the ditch to break their fall.

Although preparations for the siege were far from ready, bad news reached Wellington's headquarters on the evening of the 19th. Marmont was only 80 kilometres, or three days' march, away: Wellington had run out of time. Although his plans were incomplete he either had to issue orders to attack immediately or call off the siege. He chose to take the chance and attack, and even as he wrote his orders in the trenches on Greater Teson, the French guns continued to fire unabated from the walls of the town. Wellington was well aware that a premature assault could

General Robert Craufurd.

fail but he was in no mood for discussion; he had already lost over 500 men in the preparations for the assault and he did not want to abandon the siege. His orders were brief and to the point and concluded with the words 'Ciudad Rodrigo must be stormed tonight'.

A sombre air fell over the camps when the men heard that they were to attack that night. Some wrote letters to loved ones in case they did not survive, while others prepared their equipment. The majority exchanged final words with friends or, as Grattan of the Connaught Rangers noted, went through a final ritual in preparation for the assault:

Each arranged himself for the combat in such manner as his fancy would admit of. Some by lowering their cartridge-boxes, others by turning them to the front for more convenient use; others unclasped their stocks or opened their shirt collars; others oiled their bayonets. Those who had them took leave of their wives and children, an affecting sight, but not so much so as might have been expected, because the women, from long habit, were accustomed to such scenes of danger.

The plan involved two diversionary assaults, which would start as darkness fell, to draw the garrison's attention away from the main attacks on the north and west walls. Colonel O'Toole would lead a detachment across the Roman bridge over the river Agueda, south of the town, a few minutes earlier, aiming to take the guns guarding the southern gate before the troops assembling behind Santa Cruz Convent reached the walls. General Pack's Portuguese brigade would attack the San Pelayo Gate on the eastern wall at the same time as the main assault went in, hoping to reach the inner Santiago Gate overlooking the river.

The two main attacks would be made by the Light Division and General Picton's 3rd Division. The latter would approach the Greater Breach in the north-west corner from two directions, one brigade advancing from behind the Lesser Teson while the second assembled at Santa Cruz Convent to the west. General Craufurd's Light Division would advance from the Convent of San Francisco and cross over the Lesser Teson, heading towards the Lesser Breach.

As the light began to fade over Ciudad Rodrigo the two generals toured the camps, checking plans with their officers and giving encouraging talks to the men; Picton addressed the 1/88th with the following rousing words: 'Rangers of Connaught. It is not my intention to expend any powder this evening. We'll do this business with a cauld iron.' Loud cheers met the challenge. Meanwhile, Craufurd, or 'Black Bob', addressed his men with the following advice: 'Soldiers, the eyes of your country are upon you. Be steady, be cool, be firm in the assault. The town must be yours this night . . . Now lads, for the breach!'

As darkness fell Colonel O'Toole led the 2/83rd light company and the 2nd Caçadores across the Roman bridge and climbed the slopes towards the fortification covering the approaches to the southern gate, the Puerta de la Colada. After scaling the walls, O'Toole's men captured two artillery pieces covering the gate and the adjacent ramparts that the 2/5th Regiment was due to attack a few minutes later. The second diversion also went to plan and after forcing their way through the San Pelayo Gate, Pack's Portuguese soldiers advanced along the foot of the wall and attacked Santiago Gate at the south-east corner of the town. The diversions drew the garrison's attention, masking the noise made while the two assaulting divisions assembled to the north and west. Then precisely at 19:00 a signal rocket burst high in the sky: the main assault had begun.

Wellington aimed to get as many men as possible to the Greater Breach and his plan had men approaching from three directions. The Forlorn Hope, comprising 500 volunteers from the 88th, advanced over the summit of the Lesser Teson, leading Mackinnon's brigade straight for the breach. To the west, Campbell's brigade emerged from woods behind Santa Cruz Convent and climbed the slopes to the foot of the western wall, before turning north towards the breach. Meanwhile, the 2/5th used ladders to climb a low section of the outer ramparts next to the southern gate, where O'Toole's detachment had captured the guns. Once inside the ditch, the regiment headed north along the foot of the wall towards the breach.

Hundreds of men were converging on the Greater Breach but the Forlorn Hope had to clear the way forward and after throwing their hay sacks into the ditch, they jumped down and began climbing the rubble slope. Braving shot, shell, muskets and grenades, the Connaughts

The 1/88th swarm across the debris of the Greater Breach

clambered towards the top of Greater Breach, hacking a way through the maze of deadly obstacles laid by the French. Casualties were high but the seething mass of men was unstoppable.

Everything was going to plan when two 24-pounder guns, one hidden on each side of the breach, opened fire with grapeshot, killing and wounding many men. Ditches had been dug in front of the guns as protection but the 1/45th used abandoned planks to get at one gun crew, while the 88th dropped their muskets and clambered across the trench, attacking the second gun crew with their bayonets. The guns only fired twice before their crews were killed.

As the Forlorn Hope clambered up the final stretch of the breach, it seemed that the walls had been taken but as the first group of men stepped on to the ramparts, the French revealed their final terrifying secret. Their engineers had dug a large cavity into the rubble and filled it with explosives. The fuse was lit as the Forlorn Hope climbed the final few metres and the top of the breach erupted in a mass of smoke, flame and debris, sending burning bodies into the air, just when victory seemed inevitable. The explosion killed virtually everyone on the wall, including General Henry Mackinnon and many of the Frenchmen guarding the breach.

The explosion should have brought the attack to a halt but the rest of the 3rd Division pushed forward undeterred, seeking revenge for their lost comrades. Before long, hundreds of men were clambering up the rubble slope and on to the ramparts; Joseph Donaldson of the 94th advanced up the slope with Campbell's brigade:

> Some time after it was dark, we advanced rank entire under a heavy fire to the brink of the ditch. After descending, we moved along towards the breach. Our orders were to remain there and protect the right brigade, but, our colonel finding no obstacles in

The Light Division's Forlorn Hope assaults the Lesser Breach as a mine explodes under the Greater Breach.

the way, pushed up the breach. In mounting the breach, we found great difficulty in ascending from the loose earth slipping under our feet at every step, the enemy at the same time pouring their shot amongst us from above.

While the 3rd Division stormed the Greater Breach, the Light Division advanced from its assembly positions behind San Francisco Convent led by the Forlorn Hope, volunteers from the 52nd commanded by Lieutenant Gurwood. As Craufurd's men raced along the road towards the collapsed tower, the French gunners along the north wall fired canister until the mine was detonated under the Greater Breach. Some of the Light Division men were killed or injured by flying debris when the mine exploded, and Gurwood himself was temporarily knocked unconscious leading his men across the ditch, but the rest of the Forlorn Hope clambered up the rubble slope to the top of the breach. Rifleman George Simmons later recorded how the explosion threw the French garrison into confusion:

The Forlorn Hope and storming parties moved on at about seven o'clock, and the head of the column followed close behind. A tremendous fire was opened upon us, and, as our column was entering the ditch, an expense magazine on the ramparts blew up. The night was brilliantly illuminated for some moments, and everything was made visible. Then as suddenly came utter darkness, except for the flashes from cannon and muskets, which threw a momentary glare around.

Canister and musket fire greeted the troops of the Light Division as they clambered over the mound of rubble, but they continue to advance, entering the streets beyond the wall. One of the many casualties was Major-General Robert Craufurd, who was mortally wounded by a musket ball. His loss was a serious blow, and he was mourned by all the men of the Light Division; after his death on 24 January he was buried by the Lesser Breach. He was an outstanding commander and was described as a 'soldier's soldier'. Despite the loss of their commander, the men of the Light Division pushed on into the narrow streets in the north-west corner of the town. Lieutenant Gurwood eventually recovered and entered the castle, capturing the governor and taking possession of his sword so he could present it to Wellington.

Both divisions had entered the town and now it was only a matter of time before the town was in British hands. What remained of the garrison surrendered soon after the breaches were taken but in many cases no quarter was given. Many officers had lost their lives in the assault and discipline evaporated as the leaderless men went on the rampage through the dark streets:

> Our troops, as soon as the breach was gained, more eager for plunder than their duty, broke and ran in defiance of their officers and committed shameful excesses disgraceful to the whole army. Not a soul that was not rifled, and the dead were scarcely cold when they were inhumanly stripped. No intentional murders were committed, though some men were so drunk that they fired promiscuously in the streets and killed many of their comrades.

Picton's men went on the rampage through the streets around the cathedral, and alehouses received their special attention. William Grattan of the 1/88th Connaught Rangers watched in disgust as drink fuelled the soldiers' thirst for revenge:

> Scenes of the greatest outrage now took place, and it was pitiable to see groups of the inhabitants half-naked in the streets while

their houses were undergoing the strictest scrutiny. Some of the soldiers turned to the wine and spirit houses, where, having drunk sufficiently, they again sallied out in quest of more plunder; others got so intoxicated that they lay in a helpless state in different parts of the town, and lost what they had previously gained.

The assault on Ciudad Rodrigo had cost both sides dearly. Over 550 men had been killed or injured, the majority in front of the two breaches. The number included 59 officers, including Generals Craufurd and Mackinnon, both mortally wounded, and Vandeleur, who was injured leading his brigade towards the Lesser Breach. A similar number of French soldiers were killed or injured and over 1,350 were later rounded up in the square beneath the castle walls and marched into captivity. They had also lost their siege train and the heavy guns would soon be used to bombard Badajoz to the south.

With Ciudad Rodrigo in British hands, Wellington now had control of the road to northern Extremadura, leaving Marmont in a dilemma. He knew that Wellington could now operate freely towards Salamanca but he was powerless to counter him. Although he would have been able to strike the allied army while it was camped around the town, it was too strong for him now that the fortress had fallen.

The victory was well received in London and the British government's response was to elevate Wellington from viscount to earl. Meanwhile, the news was gratefully received in Cadiz where the Spanish Junta awarded him the title of Duke of Ciudad Rodrigo and made him a Grandee of Spain. Wellington knew none of this as he tried to sleep in the Palace de los Castros, near the Salamanca Gate, contemplating the losses his army

Wellington's Army at Ciudad Rodrigo

3rd Division General Thomas Picton

Mackinnon's Brigade	1/45th, 5/60th, 74th, 1/88th
Campbell's Brigade	2/5th, 77th, 2/83rd, 94th

Light Division General Robert Craufurd

Vandeleur's Brigade	1/52nd, 2/52nd, 3/95th
Barnard's Brigade	1/43rd, 1/95th, 2/95th
O'Toole's Detachment	83rd (Light Coy), 2nd Caçadores

had suffered. Chaos still reigned on the streets and his officers spent the night trying to regain control over their men; many would have to sleep off their hangovers before they were fit for duty again.

VISITING CIUDAD RODRIGO

Ciudad Rodrigo stands on the road from Salamanca heading towards the Portuguese frontier at Fuentes de Oñoro. Leave the motorway on the east side (est) of the town and follow signs for the tourist information office, Officina Touristica; it is just outside the walls in front of the cathedral and Puerta de Amayuelas, the site of the Lesser Breach. There is a large parking area nearby. Obtain a map of the town and details of the Sitios Napoleonicos museum, an interesting display in the centre of the town dedicated to the two sieges.

Walk towards the gate at the top of the slope. The tower was never rebuilt and the wall is quite thin at this point. Turn right in front of the wall, and walk westwards along the ditch at the foot of the wall. The Greater Breach is at the north-west corner after 200 metres; it is easy to locate by the repaired state of the wall where there is no rampart at the top. It is possible to pass through a short tunnel into the outer moat to see what the British troops had to cross before they could scale the inner wall.

Mackinnon's brigade climbed up the glacis to the left, heading for the top of the breach. The French detonated a large mine as they clambered up the rubble, and the majority of the Forlorn Hope were killed in the explosion, including Mackinnon. The 3rd Division's second wave then surged forward, reaching the top of the slope.

Continue past the breach to the car park by the small gate, Puerta de Sancti-Spiritus. Campbell's brigade

The cathedral still bears its scars of the siege; General Herrasti's memorial stands in front.

followed this part of the moat, hugging the foot of the wall to get to the Greater Breach. To see where they entered the moat, follow the road as it snakes down the hill towards the next gate. Many British troops gathered behind the Convent of Santa Cruz which stood on the site of the Bull Ring on the lower slopes to the west. O'Toole's detachment captured two guns to the right (east) of the gate at the beginning of the siege, allowing Campbell's men to get to the foot of the wall safely. Go through the gate and turn left up the slope on to the ramparts. It is possible to get a good view of the castle from the top of the gate.

Follow the ramparts along the top of the west wall back towards the Great Breach. The repaired wall section is easy to locate and an old plaque remembering the first siege marks the site of it. It is possible to look across to the site of the British guns and assembly trenches from the top of the repaired wall. Apartment blocks cover most of the Lesser Teson where the British infantry assembled ready to attack. The Greater Teson, where the British guns were sited during the siege, is the open ridge beyond the railway cutting. Mackinnon's brigade crossed the Lesser Teson to reach the breach and the Forlorn Hope threw sacks into the moat before scrambling up the rubble, hacking their way through the maze of French entanglements.

The walls above the door of the cathedral are pockmarked by shot and shell and steps lead down to the memorial to Julian Sanchez, a local guerrilla leader, at the foot of the ramparts. A memorial garden built in honour of General Herrasti, the Spanish governor who resisted Marshal Ney in 1810, stands in front of the cathedral. Continue around the ramparts alongside the cathedral, taking the flight of wooden steps leading down to the site of the Lesser

Julian Sanchez's memorial.

Breach. A plaque remembering General Craufurd and his men is on the inner wall to the west of the gate.

There is a second tourist office opposite the memorial. Cross the road

and walk down the narrow Carrer de los Cáceres for 150 metres into a small square. Wellington stayed in the Palacio de Los Castro, the medieval building to the left, after the battle; the door is surrounded by distinctive columns and carvings.

The Sitios Napoleonicos museum is situated in the Palacio de Los Aguila, just off the Plaza Major in the centre of the town. It contains J.R. Cid's collection of documents and maps relating to the Napoleonic Wars as well as paintings and relics relating to the two sieges of the town. The exhibition's opening times are:

Tuesday to Friday	12:00 until 14:00
Saturday	12:00 until 14:00 and 17:00 until 19:00
	Closed Sundays and Mondays

Return to your car by the Tourist Information Office outside the Lesser Breach and take the turning immediately left, driving along the foot of the outer earthworks to the Greater Breach. The huge mass of the glacis is to the left. Turn left at the T-junction and immediately right after 50 metres. Follow the road over the low crest of the Lesser Teson and turn right at the T-junction after 200 metres. Park in front of the sports facility area on the left after 300 metres and walk up the track along the left-hand side of a small sports hall. Taking care on the railway level crossing, climb up to the top of the hill, close to the site of Reynaud Redoubt, which was taken by Colonel John Colborne and a picked group of men from the Light Division on the night of 8 January.

Looking back, the low ground between the two Tesons is where the divisions gathered, the Light Division to the left and the 3rd Division to the right. Ciudad Rodrigo sits high on its hill and the two breaches were on either side of the cathedral tower, the Lesser Breach to the left and the Greater Breach to the right. Return to your car and retrace your route back, turning left at the foot of the Greater Breach, heading along Avienda de Portugal. The ruins of the Convent de San Francisco, from where the Light Division started its attack, are to the left of the roundabout after 500 metres.

THE THREE SIEGES OF BADAJOZ

The French Siege, January–March 1810

At the end of 1810, as Masséna withdrew his army from Portugal and Wellington's troops rested behind the Lines of Torres Vedras, Marshal

Soult was making plans to take Badajoz, the Spanish border fortress. Soult had gathered every available man by December 1810 and eventually 20,000 troops headed north from Sevilla towards Badajoz in atrocious weather. After defeating Ballesteros's division and capturing Olivenza on the border, his men reached Badajoz on 26 January 1811. Initially Soult did not have enough troops to surround the city and his army threw a cordon around the south side of the city. A few days later, on 5 February, General Mendizabal's Army of the Left appeared on the north bank of the river Guadiana and a stand-off followed, with neither side wishing to cross the river. The French took the initiative on the night of 18 February, building a pontoon bridge over the river, and 7,000 troops had crossed before dawn before the Spanish noticed.

Mendizabal only realised the danger when French cavalry charged his flank at first light, riding down many units. The rest formed a huge square for safety but as the cavalry hovered nearby, French batteries unlimbered their guns in front of the square and fired canister relentlessly into the Spanish ranks. When the time was right, the cavalry scattered the survivors, killing and injuring some 8,000 men. It was a complete disaster for the Spanish. Only 4,000 of Mendizabal's men escaped, many of them crossing the river and taking refuge behind Badajoz's walls; he had also lost all his guns and baggage.

With Wellington still hiding in Portugal and the Spanish army defeated, Soult could now concentrate on sealing off the fortress. For the next three weeks the French soldiers dug assembly trenches and battery positions but the Spanish garrison showed no signs of wavering. The French siege train battered a hole in the wall, but even as the guns fought to increase the size of the breach, time was running out for Soult. Three of Wellington's divisions led by General Beresford were closing in.

On 4 March the town's commander, General Rafael de Menacho, was killed. His replacement, Jose Imaz, did not have the same resolve as his predecessor and despite having plenty of ammunition and food for his garrison, surrendered the town a week later. This was a disaster for Wellington. It completely changed the situation south of the river Tagus in favour of the French: they now had a powerful new base within striking distance of Lisbon. Thousands of Spanish troops had been captured, while large amounts of guns, ammunition and food had fallen into French hands. Wellington was stunned by the fall of Badajoz and he summed up his disgust at the news in a letter to Lord Liverpool:

Although experience has taught me to place no reliance upon Spanish troops, this recent disaster has disappointed and grieved me much. The loss of this army and its consequence, the fall of Badajoz, have materially altered the situation of the Allies and it will not be an easy task to place them in the situation in which they were, much less in that in which they would have been if this misfortune had not occurred.

The First British Siege, May–June 1811

When Ciudad Rodrigo was once again in British hands, Wellington turned his attentions to Badajoz, aiming to restore his position in southern Extremadura and opening the southern road into Spain. He had sent General Beresford at the head of 18,000 men towards the city and after retaking Olivenza, he drove back the French troops in the area and invested the fortress. A large number of Spanish troops had joined Beresford's army but the British siege train was still to the north and a number of antiquated guns had to be brought up from the nearby town of Elvas.

The siege went badly from the beginning. There was a shortage of engineers and heavy rain hampered the work, flooding the siege works. Beresford had decided against reopening the French breach in the south-east corner and chose instead to attack the curtain wall surrounding the medieval castle in the north-east corner of the town. After capturing San Cristóbel Fort, a fortification on the north bank of the river Guadiana standing high on a promontory overlooking Badajoz Castle, the siege started in earnest on 8 May. The number of suitable siege guns was limited and the artillery crews were often left idle owing to a lack of cannon-balls. As the days passed, it was clear that it would take time to make a practical breach — and time was not on Beresford's side. Soult had already crossed the Sierra Morena with 25,000 troops and the British general was forced to move many of his troops to block his way. The result was the bloody battle of Albuera on 16 May.

Wellington arrived outside Badajoz on 19 May 1811 with 44,000 troops, only to find that the French had destroyed large parts of the siege works. The engineers immediately returned to work and after five days the siege guns were back in position, bombarding the walls. Yet again the antiquated siege guns struggled to demolish the wall and the troops had to endure three long weeks in the shadow of the fortress before the breaches were ready.

The first assault was made on 6 June but the French waited until the British Forlorn Hope had climbed down into the ditch surrounding the fortress before their hidden cannon opened fire with grapeshot, killing and wounding many men. William Wheeler later recalled the shock of the cannon fire:

> We advanced up the glacis . . . Not a head was seen above the walls, and we began to think the enemy had retired . . . when sudden as a flash of lightning the whole place was in a blaze. A deep trench or ditch filled with men who were endeavouring to mount the walls by means of ladders. The top of this wall crowded with men hurling down shells and hand grenades on the heads below, and when all these are expended they each have six or seven loaded firelocks which they discharge as quick as possible. Add to this half a dozen cannon scouring the trench with grape.

The men on top of the walls could not miss as they fired into the crowded trench below but as the survivors raised their ladders, expecting to climb out of the trap, they found, to their horror, that they were too short. There was nothing they could do and they had to withdraw, leaving many dead and wounded behind. A second attempt to enter the fortress, made three days later, also failed.

The French garrison was nearing starvation but on 17 June Wellington heard the news that the new French commander, Marshal Marmont, was heading towards him with 60,000 troops. All he could do was lift the siege and his army withdrew two days later.

The Second British Siege, March–April 1812

Wellington decided to return to Badajoz immediately after Ciudad Rodrigo had been taken and duly headed south at the end of February 1812, leaving the town in Spanish hands. Of the 60,000 troops he had to hand, over half had to be deployed to make sure the siege was allowed to progress unmolested. While General Hill moved north with 14,000 men to watch Marmont's movements, General Graham took 19,000 men south to guard against Soult. This left Wellington with four divisions, some 27,000 troops, and 52 guns to storm Badajoz; this time he also had an adequate siege train and extra engineers.

Badajoz was manned by a 5,000-strong garrison (including over 500 sick), including the elite German Hesse d'Armstadt Regiment. In command was the determined General Armand Phillipon, who had spent the past ten months repairing the damage done by earlier sieges, while

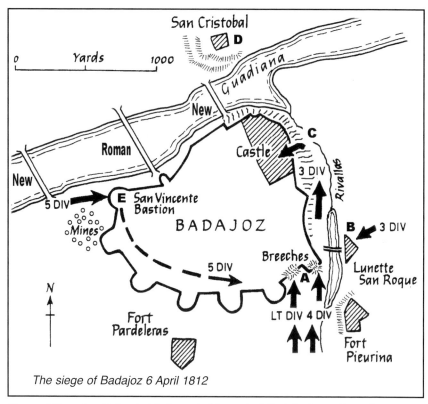

The siege of Badajoz 6 April 1812

General Beresford intended to breach this part of Badajoz's castle walls.

adding new works and improving existing defences. The fortress had nine towers connected by walls varying from 7 to 15 metres high, while the castle acted as the town's citadel. San Cristobal Fort and the Werle Lunette earthworks, which had caused so many difficulties the year before, still covered the high ground on the north bank of the river Guadiana, while the Tete du Pont protected the Roman bridge. The Rivillas stream ran along the foot of the eastern walls and a dam had been built to flood the low ground there, limiting movement in the area. Meanwhile, Fort Picurina had been built on an outcrop to the south-east of the town while the San Roque Lunette earthworks guarded the Mérida road. A third defensive position, Fort Pirdaleras, had been built on a hill covering the southern approaches to the town, and General Phillipon had completed his defensive works by mining the western side of the town.

Wellington had made a detailed reconnaissance of Badajoz and plans of part of the defences had been taken from a French sapper sergeant who had deserted. Although San Cristobel was an obvious target in its isolated position on the north bank (it was taken early on), Wellington decided to breach the walls of the Santa Maria and Trinidad bastions in the south-east corner. But first he had to take Fort Picurina and on 16 March 3,000 British troops began digging trenches a kilometre or so from the outpost. The British faced practical problems as high winds and heavy rain hampered the digging, and the work again suffered from a shortage of engineers. General Phillipon was determined to delay the inevitable and a French sortie on 19 March damaged many entrenchments; the assualt party took a large number of tools with them when they withdrew back into the fortress.

Wellington's bad luck continued when a pontoon bridge across the river Guadiana was swept away on the 22nd, dividing his forces until it was replaced. However, three nights later 500 men of the 3rd and Light Divisions successfully stormed Fort Picurina and work immediately started on building gun positions in and around the earthworks. On 30 March thirty-eight guns began to shell the walls of Badajoz; it was the start of a three-week-long bombardment. Phillipon did not give up, however, and while his guns returned fire his infantry made repeated sorties against the British trenches.

Marmont's operations had been hindered by Napoleon's interference and lack of understanding of the situation across Spain. Although he had appointed his brother as commander-in-chief on 16 March, Joseph was too far away to join the attempt to break the siege of Badajoz. Wellington did not have time to worry about the new appointment either, with Soult on the move in the south and Marmont heading into Portugal in the north: time was running out for the besiegers. The French commanders were only a few days away from interfering in the British plans when the decision was taken to attack on 5 April.

The two breaches had been completed but Wellington's plan was to attack the fortress from four different directions simultaneously in order to divide the garrison's attention. While General Charles Colville's 4th Division assaulted the gap in the Trinidad Bastion, the Light Division would storm the adjacent Santa Maria Bastion; both divisions had to assemble some distance away out of sight of Fort Pardaleras. Meanwhile, the 5th Division would draw attention away from the two attacks, and while one brigade made a diversionary attack against Fort Pardaleras, another would attempt to climb the walls of the San Vincente Bastion in the north-west corner of the fortress.

The 3rd Division would attack the castle in the north-east corner. Attempts to destroy the dam across the Rivillas stream had failed. General Picton had ordered Major Wilson of the 48th to lead an advance party against the San Roque Lunette, a fortification on the east bank, so the rest of the division could use the bridge across the stream. His men could then carry ladders up the hillside and scale the low curtain wall.

As the Forlorn Hopes and assault parties assembled, officers reported that the attack had been delayed by twenty-four hours, to Easter Sunday. Wellington wanted a third breach made in the curtain wall between the two breaches in the south-east bastions, giving his men an extra way into the fortress.

Some believe that this delay gave General Phillipon the opportunity to turn the breaches into death traps; whether this is true or not, the assault parties certainly faced a formidable array of defensive measures before they could enter the fortress. The British had hoped to assemble in a ditch in front of the walls but the French had dug a channel in the bottom beforehand and flooded it. They then had to climb the mountain of rubble which had been covered by chevaux-de-frise made from planks of wood studded with spikes and sword blades. An array of sandbags, fascines of wood and woolpacks then had to be scaled at the top of the breaches. Meanwhile, the men defending the walls were armed with barrels of gunpowder, loaded muskets, grenades and rocks while artillery pieces loaded with grapeshot aimed their barrels at the breaches.

As the final hours ticked by veterans quietly contemplated what lay ahead, saying a few calming words to the new arrivals. Sergeant Donaldson later remembered how a feeling of dread crept over everyone as the moment of the assault drew near:

> We felt a dead weight hanging on our minds; had we been brought hurriedly into action, it would have been quite different, but it is inconsistent with the nature of man not to feel as I have described. The long warning, the dark and silent night, the known strength of the fortress, the imminent danger of the attack, all conspired to produce this feeling. It was not the result of want of courage, as was shown by the calm intrepidity of the advance when we came in range of the French cannon.

The assault had been timed to begin at dusk but some units were delayed and the main attack did not go in until two hours later. The first attack was made by the 3rd Division and Major Wilson and his men captured the San Roque Lunette after a short fight, allowing the rest of the men to cross the Rivillas stream. Some used the bridge while others waded through the flooded stream or queued up to cross the dam in single file. When the French guns opened fire many were killed, while the injured fell into the water and drowned; General Picton was one of those wounded early in the attack and command of the 3rd Division then passed to General Kempt. Joseph Donaldson was with the 94th as he approached the castle walls:

> At last the order was given, and with palpitating hearts we commenced our march. Being apprised of our intentions, they threw out fire balls in every direction. By this means they were enabled to see our columns, and they opened a fire of round and grape shot which raked through them, killing and wounding whole sections. We still advanced as before and got down into the ditch. The ladders were not yet brought up, and the men were huddled on one another in such a manner that we could not move. When we first entered it we considered ourselves comparatively safe, thinking that we were out of range of their shot, but they opened several guns and poured in grape shot upon us from each side. Our situation at this time was truly appalling.

Once at the foot of the walls, the British troops hoisted their ladders up as the French threw rocks, timber and barrels of gunpowder into the crowds of men waiting below. As Kempt's men began to climb, the Frenchmen at the top pushed the ladders away from the walls, sending the climbers

Picton's men storm Badajoz's walls and enter the castle courtyard.

crashing down to their deaths, while those who reached the top faced men armed with bayonets, muskets and pikes. Donaldson summed up the horror of the attack in his account:

> When the ladders were placed, each eager to mount, the men crowded them in such a way that many of them broke, and the poor fellows who had nearly reached the top were precipitated a height of 30 to 40 feet and impaled on the bayonets of their comrades below. Other ladders were pushed aside by the enemy on the walls, and fell with a crash on those in the ditch, while those who got to the top without accident were shot on reaching the parapet, and, tumbling headlong, brought down those beneath them.

After an hour of fierce fighting no one had reached the ramparts and the ground at the foot of the walls was littered with the 3rd Division's dead, dying and injured.

The two main attacks in the south-east corner of Badajoz were not faring any better. The two Forlorn Hopes of the Light Division and the 4th Division led the assault parties towards the breaches and Colonel Andrew Barnard's men cheered as they climbed down their ladders into the ditch. (Barnard had been leading the Light Division since Ciudad

Rodrigo.) Many men fell into the ditch in the darkness as it filled with men, but the whole scene was soon lit up by bonfires on the walls. The French then opened fire with their muskets and cannon, and Rifleman George Simmons described the carnage in front of the Santa Maria Bastion:

> Our columns moved on under a most dreadful fire that mowed down our men like grass. Eight or ten officers and men innumerable fell to rise no more. Ladders were resting against the counter-scarp. Down these we hurried and rushed forward to the breaches, where a most frightful scene of carnage was going on. Fifty times they were stormed, and as often without effect, the French cannon sweeping the breaches with a most destructive fire. Lights were thrown amongst us that burned most brilliantly, and made us easier to be shot at. I had seen some fighting, but nothing like this.

Some of the 4th Division's Forlorn Hope drowned in the flooded ditch in front of the Trinidad Bastion before the alarm could be raised. Those following were compelled to find another way around the obstacle and were soon mingling with the men of the Light Division, adding to the confusion. Sergeant William Lawrence later recalled how he was injured as he scaled the steep slope of broken stones, heading for the top of the breach:

> I was one of the ladder party. On our arriving at the wall a shower of shot, canister and grape, together with fireballs, was hurled amongst us . . . Still, I stuck to my ladder and got into the ditch. Numbers had by this time fallen, but we hastened to the breach. There, to our great discouragement, we found a cheval-de-frise had been fixed. Vain attempts were made to remove this fearful obstacle, during which my left hand was fearfully cut by one of the blades, but, finding no success in that quarter, we were forced to retire for a time.

Just as it looked as if the walls were about to be scaled, the French unleashed their final surprise: mines. Fuses detonated barrels loaded with gunpowder which had been buried in the rubble, killing and maiming the majority of the two Forlorn Hopes. Those men following close behind reeled back at the carnage but they were were pushed forward into the chaos by the relentless advance from behind.

As explosions lit up the smoke billowing around the walls, screams, cheers and gunfire filled the night sky. Time after time the two divisions pushed forward — some accounts say more than forty times — but each time the British fell back, leaving more dead, dying and injured in the ditches and on the rubble slopes; over 2,200 men fell in an hour. At the top of the walls the shouts and jeers of the French could sometimes be heard through the noise as they taunted Wellington's men to 'Come into Badajoz'.

It was beginning to look as though the assault had failed, but then fortunes started to change in the 3rd Division's sector. Some accounts state that Major Ridge of the 5th Regiment was the first to climb on to the ramparts after finding a low section of wall where an embrasure gave some protection. By the time the French realised men were climbing the ladder, it was crowded with men and too heavy to throw back. Ridge climbed with his sword over his head, encouraging the men behind him to thrust their bayonets upwards to keep the French at bay. Unfortunately, he was killed not long after reaching the top of the castle ramparts.

Other accounts say that the first man to scale the walls was Corporal Kelly of the 45th, who killed a French colonel in hand-to-hand combat on the ramparts. Lieutenant Macpherson was close behind and he replaced a French Tricolour with his red jacket so it could be seen by everyone. Men were soon climbing other ladders and as they poured over the wall, panic began to set in among the French.

Meanwhile, in the 5th Division's sector Walker's brigade had braved the minefield at the north-west corner of the fortress and scaled the low walls of San Vincente Bastion. After the 44th Regiment had planted its colours on the parapet, men moved east through the town and Private George Hatton captured the Hesse D'Armstadt's regimental flag during the fighting. As the French sounded the alarm, the 5th Division's bugles were answered by the 3rd Division and French resistance began to collapse as the two divisions headed for the breaches.

Wellington had been about to call off the frontal attacks on the breaches when news of the two successes reached him. With British troops flooding through the narrow streets, it was time for the Light Division and the 4th Division to renew their attacks. Men were soon crawling tentatively up the rubble-strewn slopes in front of the Santa Maria and Trinidad Bastions but although there was some firing, resistance was only light. General Phillipon escaped across the river Guadiana to the Fort San Cristobal with many of his garrison; they surrendered the following morning.

Wellington's Army at Badajoz	
3rd Division General Picton	
Kempt's Brigade	1/45th, 3/60th, 74th, 1/88th
Campbell's Brigade	2/5th, 77th, 2/83rd, 94th
4th Division General Colville	
Kemmis's Brigade	3/27th, 1/40th
Bowes's Brigade	1/7th, 1/23rd, 1/48th
5th Division General Leith	
Hay's Brigade	3/1st, 1/9th, 2/38th
Walker's Brigade	1/4th, 2/30th, 2/44th
Light Division General C. Alten	
Barnard's Brigade	1/43rd, 4 Coys 1/95th, 2 Coys 2/95th, 5 Coys 3/95th, 1st Caçadores
Vandeleur's Brigade	1/52nd, 2/52nd, 4 Coys 1/95th, 3rd Caçadores

By the early hours Badajoz was in British hands and the survivors went on the rampage, the start of a drink-fuelled orgy of destruction that would last two days and nights. Men plundered, robbed and raped as they ran riot through the streets, sometimes shooting officers who stood in their way. Robert Blakeney later recalled the scenes of horror he saw in Badajoz:

Every house presented a scene of plunder, debauchery and bloodshed committed with wanton cruelty by our soldiery . . . Men, women and children were shot for no other reason than pastime; every species of outrage was publicly committed and in a manner so brutal that a faithful recital would be shocking to humanity. Not the slightest shadow of discipline was maintained. The infuriated soldiery resembled rather a pack of hell-hounds vomited up from the infernal regions for the extirpation of mankind than a well-organised, brave, disciplined and obedient British army.

The total cost of the siege had been over 4,900 casualties, including many experienced officers and NCOs, but the majority were killed or injured on the rubble in front of the two breaches. The French had suffered 1,350 casualties and lost many guns and a large quantity of supplies and ammunition. They had also lost control of the main road between Lisbon and Madrid, leaving the way open into southern Extremadura.

Meanwhile, the siege had restored Anglo-Spanish relations.

Many would later comment unfavourably about Wellington's command of the siege, criticising his siege plans, the timing of the attack and the plundering that followed. As he admitted in a private letter to Lord Liverpool written the day after the assault, it could all too easily have been a total failure:

> The capture of Badajoz affords as strong an instance of the gallantry of our troops as has ever been displayed. But I anxiously hope that I shall never again be the instrument of putting them to such a test as that to which they were put last night. I assure your Lordship that it is quite impossible to carry fortified places by 'vive force' without incurring great loss, and being exposed to the chance of failure, unless the army should be provided with a sufficient trained corps of sappers and miners . . .

As Wellington contemplated the forthcoming campaigning season, he could for the first time plan an advance deep into the heart of Spain where he could engage the French armies.

VISITING BADAJOZ

Badajoz has been built up but large parts of the walls, including those parts attacked during the siege, can still be visited. The castle and San Cristobal Fort are both standing and it is possible to find interesting viewpoints of the city and follow the various assaults.

Start at the bull-ring, a large, circular, brick building at the south-east corner of the walled city. Walk to the modern bridge over the Rivillas stream, which now runs in an open concrete culvert to the east. The Light Division and the 4th Division assembled to the south, close to the open high ground, to the west of the channel. The guns were positioned around Fort Picurina on the opposite bank, on the high ground east of the stone bridge.

The road passing north-east of the bull-ring goes through a gap in the city wall where the Light Division attacked the section of curtain wall breached by the guns across the river. Santa Maria Bastion is to the left, Trinidad Bastion to the right. Follow the path along the foot of Trinidad Bastion, which was rebuilt after the siege. The moat area here was a mass of rubble and bodies after the attack. There is a second gap in the east wall of the bastion, made for a road to pass through; cross the pedestrian crossing to get to the bank of the Rivillas stream. Across the stream is the San Roque Lunette, the small fortification that was captured by Major

San Cristóbel's outer defences.

The Light Division's Breach.

The 3rd Light Division scaled these walls and entered the keep.

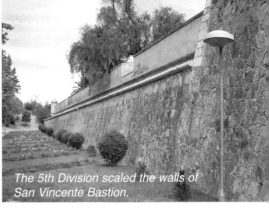

The 5th Division scaled the walls of San Vincente Bastion.

Wilson. The 3rd Division then swarmed across the bridge and entered the moat before turning right (north) to climb the slopes to the wall at the top.

Walk back to your car. Drive through the Breach and immediately turn right. Then drive through the San Vincente Bastion, turning left in front of the San Roque Lunette. Follow the river for 500 metres before parking to the right in the car park area of a petrol station. The perimeter wall of the castle is at the top of the hillside across the road. After crossing the river at the San Roque Lunette, the 3rd Division turned right and entered the moat before scaling the slopes. Once at the top, General Picton's men fought to scale the walls, eventually climbing their ladders to enter the castle grounds.

Turn right back on to the road and continue straight on at the roundabout, as the road follows the foot of the hill and the castle walls. Turn right on to the bridge, signposted for Caceres, and cross the river Guadiana. Drive straight on at the roundabout and up the hill, turning right at the T-junction after 500 metres. Immediately turn right on to a gravel track and park off the road. The ruins of San Cristobal Fort are at the top of the hill. Although the fortress is in a poor state, the walls, artillery emplacements, moats and buildings can be explored and there are extensive views of Badajoz castle and the town walls.

Drive back down to the bottom of the hill and recross the river, turning right (west) on the south bank, heading towards the ancient stone bridge. The San Vincente Bastion, where the 5th Division attacked, is at the north-west corner of the walled town, 300 metres west of the restored gate and the stone bridge. Parking is difficult in this area but after finding your way to the bastion it is easy to work out where Leith's men finallyclambered over the low western section of the wall.

Elvas Cemetery

The walled town of Elvas is 20 kilometres west of Badajoz, inside Portugal. The outstanding feature of the area is the huge ancient aqueduct spanning the valley to the east. There is a small cemetery in the town containing British graves dating from the Peninsular War in São João da Carujeiro Bastion.

Chapter 7

ADVANCING DEEP INTO SPAIN

THE CAPTURE OF SALAMANCA, JUNE 1812

IN MARCH 1812 NAPOLEON took steps to stop his marshals arguing by placing all the French troops across Spain under the command of his brother, Joseph, the King of Spain. Marshal Jean-Baptiste Jourdan was also promoted from commander of the Army of the Centre to Chief of the General Staff. Unfortunately for Joseph, his domineering brother had recalled large numbers of soldiers, including the Imperial Guard, from Spain so they could join the invasion of Russia. The reduction in troops meant that Soult's Army of the South and Marmont's Army of Portugal were operating below their normal strength and the Spanish guerrillas were quick to notice the reduction of French activity in their areas. It all served to make life difficult for the French marshals as the number of attacks against messangers, patrols and supply trains increased.

Marshal Jean-Baptiste Jourdan

Wellington planned to cross the border at Fuentes de Oñoro and advance on Salamanca but he was aware that he was short of troops. He had only 48,500 men and 50 artillery pieces while Marmont's Army of Portugal had 50,000 men and 78 guns. His army also had to advance across the barren lands of Extremadura, relying on extended lines of communication for food and ammunition. While his troops concentrated along the Portuguese border at the beginning of June, the Spanish commanders increased their activity across the country to stop the French marshals moving troops to block his route.

The invasion of Spain began on 13 June as Wellington's men marched across the border, passing the fortress of Ciudad Rodrigo before heading north-east from the river Agueda. Four days later they entered the city of

Salamanca, only to find a small French garrison holding three fortified convents on the western side of the town. Marmont had left behind over 800 men and 36 small artillery pieces to delay Wellington, and while the majority of the men were in Fort San Vincente, the largest fort, the rest held Fort San Gaetano and Fort La Merced. The garrison had also destroyed large areas of housing in front of the convents to make any assault more difficult.

The 6th Division had been chosen to take the city, and after throwing a cordon along the banks of the river Tormes, Clinton's men began digging trenches in the ruins surrounding the forts. Two gun emplacements came next and the artillery crews were soon shelling Fort San Vincente while the infantry extended the trenches. Accurate fire caused many casualties among the gun crews and riflemen had to be called upon to snipe at the French positions so they could continue their work — work that was further delayed when the supply of cannon-balls ran out.

The first attack against Fort San Gaetano, made by 400 men on 23 June, was a total failure and over a quarter of the attacking troops were killed or taken prisoner, including General Bowes. It looked as though Clinton's men were in for a prolonged siege. A new trench was dug overnight, close to the foot of Fort San Vincente, and over the next three days new assembly trenches were completed in front of the two smaller forts. Just as Clinton was preparing to give the order to carry out a second assault, the artillery scored a welcome success on 27 June. The gun crews had been firing red-hot cannon-balls at the tinder-dry timber roofs, in the hope of setting them on fire. As smoke and flames rose over Fort San Vincente, the French garrison knew that they would have to abandon their burning strongholds, and they made it very clear that they wanted to surrender.

The Salamanca Campaign, July 1812

With Salamanca safe, Wellington could turn his attention to Marmont's army. Marmont, having chosen not to interfere with the siege, had spent the last days of June trying to establish the whereabouts of the allied army so he could manoeuvre his troops into a favourable position. It was the start of a long game of cat and mouse. During the first two weeks of July Wellington and Marmont marched their men back and forth around Salamanca, but neither was able to gain an advantage over the other. Each time one thought he had the upper hand, he was either mistaken and had to withdraw, or scouts warned of an approaching trap. At the end of the second week Wellington heard that reinforcements were moving to join Masséna, a move that would increase his army to a dangerous size. Despite his desire to engage the French, he had to consider the safety of his men and so contemplated a withdrawal back into Portugal. He did not contemplate for long. The two armies were very close together and on 18 July they were marching parallel to each other, on either side of the river Tormes, while their bands held an impromptu musical competition.

For the next forty-eight hours Wellington and Marmont considered their diminishing options as their troops marched almost side-by-side towards Salamanca. By the 20th the allies were close to the eastern outskirts of the city, while the French were camped 16 kilometres to the east. The following morning torrential rain soaked the men as both armies crossed the river Tormes and headed south. Wellington's troops used the bridge at Santa Marta and the ford at Cabrerizos, while Marmont crossed the bridge at Huerta-de-Tormes. The heavy rains caused the river levels to rise and the Light Division, the army's rearguard, only just managed to wade through the floodwaters.

Wellington's army pitched camp in a valley to the north of the village of Los Arapiles, out of sight of Marshal Marmont's army, and settled down for the night. When General Foy's outposts advanced from Calvarrasa de Arriba to the east, they found General Alten's riflemen waiting for them and only a prolonged skirmish across a stream and rocky outcrops stopped them discovering the whereabouts of the main army.

Both armies spent a miserable night camped close to each other on the open farmland, the rain intensifying as a thunderstorm rumbled across the skies and the men huddled together for shelter. Several were killed by lightning, and around twenty men of the 5th (Princess Charlotte of Wales's) Dragoon Guards were injured when their horses stampeded. A battle was imminent but neither Wellington nor Marmont knew exactly where the other's army was. All they knew was that they were close, and as dawn broke over Salamanca the two generals both had an idea of what his adversary was going to do: the question was who was going to be proved correct.

The Battle of Salamanca, 22 July 1812

The village of Los Arapiles stands in the centre of an undulating plain, the subtle contours of which meant that it was easy to move large numbers of troops without them being seen. A low ridge runs in an arc to the north-

The British deployment viewed from the summit of the Greater Arapile; the city of Salamanca is in the background.

east of the village and Wellington had deployed his men in the dead ground behind it. A high rocky outcrop, known as the Lesser Arapile, stands to the east of the village and gives commanding views across the battlefield, but it was impossible to deploy troops on it. A second steep outcrop, known as the Greater Arapile, is to the south, and a low ridge known as Monte de Azan runs west of it, south of Los Arapiles.

Wellington knew that 22 July was going to be a decisive day, one on which he would either have to engage Marmont's army or turn for the Portuguese border before the French cut his lines of communication. He had already ordered his hospitals and supply depots in Salamanca to pack up and head west in case he had to take the second option.

As the sun rose, Leith's 5th, Clinton's 6th and Hope's 7th Divisions struck camp and moved south from their hidden positions around Carajosa towards Los Arapiles. Meanwhile, the 3rd Division had finally crossed the swollen Tormes river and Pakenham's men were moving to join the right (west) flank of Wellington's army. To the east the Light Division was still engaged north of the Lesser Arapile, while General Campbell's 1st Division waited in close support behind the ridge, out of sight. As the fighting increased in ferocity General Alten was forced to withdraw, but the riflemen still prevented Foy's division discovering the whereabouts of the rest of the allied army.

As Wellington's troops gathered in the valley north of Los Arapiles, Marmont took the decision to march his men in a huge arc to the south of the allied position, in the hope of outflanking his adversary. He gave the order to march through the woods east of Los Arapiles, heading south before turning west. It was a daring plan, and one based on the assumption that Wellington was a cautious general who preferred to deploy on defined ridges and would not dare to engage the French army in the open rolling countryside around Los Arapiles.

General Jean Thomiére's division led the way south through the woods as advanced guards moved forward to seize the Greater and Lesser Arapiles, to stop British observers using them to spy on the rest of the army. Pack's Portuguese brigade was driven from the summit of the Greater Arapile but Anson's brigade, from the 4th Division, prevented the French troops reaching the Lesser Arapile. Another of General Cole's brigades, led by Ellis, also prevented the French troops from occupying Teso de San Miguel, the ridge overlooking Los Arapiles. The Light Division continued to hold the third area of high ground to the north of the Lesser Arapile. Although Marmont had extensive views of the area from the summit of the Greater Arapile, he could not see the key area north of Los Arapiles, where the bulk of Wellington's troops remained hidden.

Marmont assumed that Wellington did not want to fight, which left the British commander with limited options. He could not reach Salamanca city because the French troops would catch his men along the banks of the river Tormes. He could not move east because three of his divisions were holding Calvarrasa de Arriba and the rest of his army was moving to the south. Wellington had to head west. The only flaw in Marmont's thinking was that he did not know the main army's exact whereabouts.

From his vantage point on top of the Greater Arapile, Marmont scanned the horizon for new signs of movement but Wellington was keeping his men out of sight. The only signs of movement were in the

The Lesser Arapile.

north-west as Pakenham's 3rd Division and D'Urban's cavalry brigade moved south from the river Tormes to join the rest of the army. The clouds of dust thrown up by the infantry and the cavalry was soon spotted by the French marshal and he assumed they indicated the presence of the allied baggage train. The signs of movement on the western horizon confirmed his suspicions: he was convinced that Wellington was heading west.

As the two leading French corps continued their march Wellington was, in fact, doing nothing; he was simply watching and waiting on the low ridge north of Los Arapiles. Three hours passed as the French marched west across the Monte de Azan ridge, but as noon approached Wellington became concerned that Marmont was moving troops forward to capture Los Arapiles, immediately in front of his hidden divisions. The time had come to deploy and he gave the order to move forward into view, exposing his first line of troops while the rest waited behind the crest of the low ridge. He was hoping to tempt the French to turn and attack but Marmont was convinced that the thin line of troops was only a rearguard and the rest of the allied army was escaping westwards.

The Light Division was already deployed north of the Lesser Arapile, holding Wellington's left (east) flank and it had the 1st Division in support. Cole's 4th Division had moved into position west of the hill while Clinton's 6th Division moved up in support and Leith's 5th Division occupied Teso de San Miguel overlooking Los Arapiles village, with Hope's 7th Division in reserve. Le Marchant's cavalry covered the flank, and Pakenham's division was moving up to join the cavalry. As usual, the majority of Wellington's troops were hidden just behind the crest of the ridge, but there were just enough on view to tempt Marmont.

Maucune's division turned to engage Leith's division around Los Arapiles with long-range artillery fire and skirmishing, but the encounter came to nothing. As Wellington joined his staff for lunch on Teso de San Miguel hill to watch for developments, Marmont decided that it was time to put his plan into action. Now that he had forced the British commander to deploy, his own divisions could rapidly head west to cut off the enemy line of retreat across the river Tormes. General Curto's light cavalry brigade would lead Thomiére's and Brennier's divisions as they marched off, hidden behind the crest of the Monte de Azan ridge, to cut off the British.

Marmont ordered a rapid march, but the speed at which his divisions moved off turned out to be the cause of their downfall. As Thomiére's and

Wellington's view of the Greater Arapile.

Brennier's divisions set off, a large gap appeared between them; Maucune's division was still skirmishing while Clausel's, Sarrut's and Bonnet's divisions were deployed west of the Greater Arapile. Foy's and Ferrey's divisions were still facing the Light Division, north of the Lesser Arapile. Marmont's orders had spread his army out across 6 kilometres of open countryside between Miranda de Azan and Calvarrasa de Arriba.

A short distance away Wellington watched the southern horizon closely, noting any movement across the undulating countryside. At first it looked as if the French were marching to a new deployment area, south of Los Arapiles, from where they would turn north to face the Britsh lines. However, by mid-afternoon it was clear that large numbers of troops were heading west and their flank lay in the path of Pakenham's division. The opportunity to strike a decisive blow against Marmont's army had come. With the words 'By God, that will do', he threw the chicken leg he was holding to one side, slammed his telescope shut and mounted his horse. He galloped to the summit of the Lesser Arapile with his Spanish aide, the Duke of Alva, to get a better view of the French movements. When their predicament was clear, he declared, 'Mon cher Alva, Marmont est perdu' ('My dear Alva, Marmont is lost').

Wellington now galloped west along his line and outlined the urgency of the developing situation to Major-General Edward Pakenham. His message was simple and to the point, as he indicated Thomiére's division, saying: 'Ned. Do you see those fellows over there? Throw your division into column, and drive them to the devil.' It was the start of a devastating attack on Marmont's army.

It was late afternoon when Packenham's 3rd Division advanced from its hidden positions towards Thomiére's division as it left the crest of the Monte de Azan ridge. Wallace's brigade led, followed by Power's

Portguese brigade and Campbell's brigade, and although the French columns were taken by surprise by the new threat, they had plenty of time to turn and fire at the advancing troops. Their volleys sent Pakenham's men reeling and Private Stephen Morley later remembered how the general had to rally his shaken men:

> We were going up an ascent on whose crest masses of the enemy were stationed. Their fire seemed capable of sweeping all before it. Truth compels me to say that we retired before this overwhelming fire, but General Pakenham approached and very good naturedly said, 'Reform', and in a moment, 'Advance. There they are, my lads; just let them feel the temper of your bayonets.' We advanced, everyone making up his mind for mischief. At last the bugles along the line sounded the charge. Forward we rushed and awful was the retribution we exacted for our former repulse.

While Arentschildt's light dragoons cantered forward to engage Curto's light cavalry, D'Urban's dragoons joined Pakenham's men and they fell on Thomiére's troops, completing the rout. The hapless French division was virtually destroyed in the fighting that followed, and hundreds fell to the British volleys and charging Portuguese cavalry, including Thomiére himself, who was killed. The leading regiment lost over 1,000 of its 1,449 men, while the second regiment suffered over 850 casualties out of 1,123 men; total casualties were 2,130 out of 4,500. The French artillery crews had tried in vain to deploy their guns but they were carried away in the panicking crowds and every piece of ordnance was captured; the 88th also captured a regimental musical instrument, known as a Jingling Johnny, from the 101st Regiment.

Thomiére's men might have expected support from Maucune's division, but this was facing its own problems as the second stage of Wellington's plan unfolded. While Pakenham moved forward to attack Thomiére's command, the British commander was galloping back to Teso de San Miguel to speak to his subordinates. General Leith was ordered to prepare to attack the flanks of three of Marmont's divisions, led by Maucune, Clausel and Brennier, as they moved across his front. Bradford's Portuguese brigade would advance at the same time, while Le Marchant's brigade of heavy dragoons would move forward in the centre of the infantry formations.

When the moment was right, Wellington gave General Leith the order to advance and the 5th Division headed towards the flank of Clausel's

Wellington issues orders to his staff during the battle of Salamanca.

division. Greville's and Pringle's brigades led the march in two lines, each two deep and over a kilometre wide. When Lieutenant-Colonel Cameron of the 1/9th was given the order to advance by one of Wellington's aides he replied, 'Thank you sir, that is the best news I have heard all day', before turning his horse to face his men, raising his hat and shouting 'Now boys, we'll at them!'

Although the French artillery teams had stopped to deploy their guns, their roundshot had little effect on the thin lines of men; only their final round of grapeshot would be effective. However, Le Marchant's dragoons were the first threat that Maucune had to deal with and he gave the order to form square as they approached the head of his division. It was the correct deployment to meet cavalry but when the 5th Division appeared over the horizon minutes later, the French general knew he had been caught out.

The sight of nine infantry battalions in dense squares was exactly what Leith's men had hoped to see, and as they drew closer over 1,500 muskets fired three volleys in quick succession. The storm of musket balls caused consternation in the French ranks as hundreds fell dying and injured. Le Marchant then ordered his dragoons to charge 'with a terrible roar always remembered by the few who survived'. The sight of three regiments of heavy cavalry bearing down on them was too much for the Frenchmen to bear and the already shattered division fled, joining the general rout into the woods to the south. Five French battalions were totally destroyed and cheers were heard across the battlefield when Lieutenant Pearce of the 44th Regiment raised the 62nd Regiment's eagle above his head on a sergeant's halberd.

General Maucune probably expected assistance from Brennier's division, which had been moving parallel to his own. However, Brennier's men were marching on the reverse slopes of the Monte de Azan ridge and did not see the approaching infantry and cavalry until it was too late. His battalions were stretched out due to the rapid pace of the march and were ridden down by Le Marchant's dragoons as they struggled to form square. Over 2,500 men were taken prisoner, while 12 guns and 2 eagles were captured in the fighting that followed, and a third French division was scattered into the woods to the south.

Rather than rallying, many of Le Marchant's dragoons followed the fleeing French soldiers in a reckless charge, cutting down men as they rode through the panicking crowds. One squadron, headed by Le Marchant himself, chased a group of infantry into the woods, where Le

British infantry clash with Clausel's division near the Lesser Arapile during the final charge.

Marchant was killed by a musket ball; he was one of Wellington's most capable cavalry commanders.

With their work done, the tired but triumphant dragoons cantered back to their own lines, having broken the centre of Marmont's huge column. In less than an hour Marmont's left flank had been routed and over 20,000 French soldiers were running for their lives.

As Marshal Marmont tried to comprehend the extent of the unfolding catastrophe, disaster struck the French high command when he was hit by a cannon-ball and badly injured. General Bonnet was then killed before he could take over command of the disintegrating army, and control eventually fell on to the shoulders of General Bertrand Clausel. The new commander-in-chief had to immediately assert himself in order to stem the rot in the French army. But even as his leading divisions fell back in disorder, Wellington, hoping to completely rout the rest of the army, ordered Cole's 4th Division forward from the ridge north-east of Los Arapiles towards Clausel's division while Pack's Portuguese brigade attacked Bonnet's division. It was an optimistic attempt to destroy Marmont's command once and for all, but was repulsed by the large numbers of French infantry waiting on the low ridge west of the Greater Arapile.

Suddenly the tide of battle began to turn in favour of the French. As Cole's men fell back in disorder, Clausel's and Bonnet's divisions counter-attacked while Boyer's dragoon brigade followed, hoping to exploit the gap appearing between the 4th and 5th Divisions. To the west, Sarrut's division had deployed across the summit of Monte de Azan, protecting Clausel's left flank, and was waiting for Pakenham's rallied 3rd Division to advance. It was beginning to look as if Wellington had overstretched his men and the French counter-attack might break his centre.

Wellington had already joined Beresford at the critical point as the two French divisions marched forward, and between them they hurriedly prepared a defensive line to meet the attack. Clinton's 6th Division formed the backbone of the defence, with Hulse's and Hinde's British brigades deployed in two-deep lines east of Los Arapiles, and Rezende's Portuguese waiting in support. General Leith had also moved Spry's Portuguese brigade forward to hold the village while General Cole had moved Anson's brigade forward to support Clinton's left. Around 9,000 British and Portuguese soldiers waited patiently in line as 13,000 French troops advanced towards them in four huge columns across the open plain.

Although the deployment was the classic column versus line, in which the line traditionally triumphed, for once Wellington's men had to stand in the open while the massed batteries of French artillery around the Grand Arapile bombarded them. Cannon balls tore holes in the waiting line, killing and maiming dozens as the French tirailleurs drove back the thin screen of British skirmishers. Every British gun crew within range turned their weapons to fire on the advancing columns.

Despite heavy casualties, Clinton's division held its ground while Spry's Portuguese brigade manoeuvred forward to engage Clausel's left flank. The smoke-blackened redcoats fired volley after volley but their battalions were decimated where they stood. Colonel Bingham of the 2/53rd led by example, waving the King's Colour in front of his battalion to rally his men. Casualties were horrendous. Colonel Cuyler's 1/11th Regiment suffered 340 casualties (earning themselves the nickname the 'Bloody Eleventh'), while the 1/61st Regiment lost 365 men; only 81 would answer the evening's roll call. Clinton's division would eventually lose 1,800 men in a short time, and General Beresford was among the wounded.

Nevertheless, the solid line of British and Portuguese soldiers stood their ground and the French columns eventually began to waver and then fall back. Neither Clausel nor Bonnet could stop the retreat turning into a rout, as the number of French divisions running for safety rose to five: more than half of Marmont's original command. Clinton's division followed up the retreat, only to find Ferrey's division waiting for them west of the Greater Arapile. Wellington ordered his forward guns to shell the fresh division and it too was soon falling back, forming a rearguard as the rest of the French army headed south. Ferrey deployed his five battalions in a 1.5-kilometre-long three-deep line, with the battalions at each end forming square to guard against cavalry attack. Although his men held Clinton's 6th Division at bay until nightfall, allowing Sarrut's and Foy's divisions to escape, Ferrey did not live to see it through; he was killed by a cannon-ball.

By late afternoon the battle was over. Wellington wanted to order a general advance to complete the victory, but all his men bar the Light Division were too exhausted. As the sun set across Los Arapiles and the survivors looked forward to the cool night air, fires spread quickly through the long, dry grass, indiscriminately burning to death the wounded from both sides.

General Foy's division took over as rearguard and kept the British cavalry at bay. Wellington believed that Carlos de Espana's Spanish troops were holding the bridge at Alba de Tormes to the south, but in fact they had left before the French army arrived. Any chance of trapping Marmont's shattered troops on the north bank of the river Tormes had evaporated. Even so, the battle of Salamanca was an important victory for the allies. Marmont's Army of Portugal had been shattered. The exact numbers of French casualties are hard to determine but around 6,000 were killed or injured and a similar number were taken prisoner. Three generals were killed and another four wounded, while more than 130 officers were casualties. A large number of trophies were seized by the British, including 2 eagles, 6 colours and 20 guns. Allied casualties were over 5,200, of which 3,176 were British. Two generals had been killed and another six wounded. Wellington himself had a lucky escape: a spent bullet had pierced his holster and cloak, but did not injure him.

The battle of Salamanca (known to the Spanish as the battle of Los Arapiles) was an opportunist encounter, in which Wellington had used the terrain to his advantage. Marmont had assumed that the British would withdraw to fight another day but his estimation of the British commander was inaccurate. As a result, he committed the serious tactical error of marching his army across his enemy's front. Meanwhile, Wellington timed his first attack to perfection and boldly, sometimes too boldly perhaps, followed it with further attacks to roll up the French line. General Foy lavished praise on his adversary a few days after the battle:

> It raises Lord Wellington's reputation almost to the level of Marlborough. Hitherto we had been aware of his prudence, his eye for choosing a position, and his skill in utilising it. At Salamanca he has shown himself a great and able master of manoeuvres. He kept his dispositions concealed for almost the whole day; he waited till we were committed to our movements before he developed his own; he played a safe game; he fought in the oblique order — it was a battle in the style of Frederick the Great.

The battle of Salamanca was a turning point, the beginning of the end of French domination in Spain, and on 12 August Wellington's victorious army was greeted by jubilant crowds when it entered Madrid. The citizens were free once more after three-and-a-half years under French rule.

Wellington's Army 48,569

1st Division General H. Campbell **6,423**

Fermor's Brigade	1/Coldstreamers, 1/3rd Guards, 1 Coy 5/60th
Von Lowe's Brigade	1st, 2nd and 5th Line Bttns KGL
Wheatley's Brigade	2/24th, 1/42nd, 2/58th, 1/79th and 1 Coy 5/60th

3rd Division General Sir Edward Pakenham **5,877**

Wallace's Brigade	1/45th, 74th, 1/88th, 3 Coys 5/60th
Campbell's Brigade	1/5th, 2/5th, 2/83rd and 94th
Power's Portuguese Brigade	9th Line (2 Bttns), 21st Line (2 Bttns) and 12th Caçadores

4th Division General Sir Galbraith Lowry Cole **5,236**

Anson's Brigade	3/27th, 1/40th and 1 Coy 5/60th
Ellis's Brigade	1/7th, 1/23rd, 1/48th and 1 Coy Brunswick Oels
Stubb's Portuguese Brigade	11th Line (2 Bttns), 23rd Line (2 Bttns) and 7th Caçadores

5th Division General Sir James Leith **6,691**

Greville's Brigade	3/1st, 1/9th, 1/38th, 2/38th, 1 Coy Brunswick Oels
Pringle's Brigade	1/4th, 2/4th, 2/30th, 2/44th, 1 Coy Brunswick Oels
Spry's Portuguese Brigade	3rd Line (2 Bttns), 15th Line (2 Bttns) 8th Caçadores

6th Division General Sir Henry Clinton **5,541**

Hulse's Brigade	1/11th, 2/53rd, 1/61st, 1 Coy 5/60th
Hinde's Brigade	2nd, 1/32nd, 1/36th
Rezende's Portuguese Brigade	8th Line (2 Bttns), 12th Line (2 Bttns) 9th Caçadores

7th Division General Sir John Hope **5,183**

Halkett's Brigade	1st Light KGL, 2nd Light KGL, remainder Brunswick Oels
De Bernewitz's Brigade	51st, 68th, Chasseurs Britanniques
Collins's Portuguese Brigade	7th Line (2 Bttns), 19th Line (2 Bttns) 2nd Caçadores

Light Division General C. Alten **3,548**

Barnard's Brigade	1/43rd, 4 Coys of 2/95th, 3/95th and 1st Caçadores
Vandeleur's Brigade	1/52nd, 1/95th and 3rd Caçadores

Independent Portuguese Brigades **4,499**

Pack's Brigade	1st Line (2 Bttns), 16th Line (2 Bttns)
	4th Caçadores
Bradford's Brigade	13th Line (2 Bttns), 14th Line (2 Bttns),
	5th Caçadores

Cavalry **4,025**

Le Marchant's Brigade	3rd Dragoons, 4th Dragoons, 5th Dragoon Guards
Anson's Brigade	11th Light Dragoons, 12th Light Dragoons,
	16th Light Dragoons
V. Alten's Brigade	14th Light Dragoons, 1st Hussars KGL
Bock's Brigade	1st and 2nd Dragoons KGL
D'Urban's Brigade	1st and 11th Portuguese Dragoons

Artillery 1,186 British (**54 guns**) and 114 Portuguese (**6 guns**)

Marmont's Army 46,550

Left Flank on Monte de Azan Ridge

Thomiére's Division	4,550
Maucune's Division	5,250
Brennier's Division	4,550

Centre facing Los Arapiles

Clausel's Division	6,550
Bonnet's Division	6,500
Sarrut's Division	5,000

Right Flank at Calvarrasa de Arriba

Foy's Division	5,150
Ferey's Division	5,650
Curto's Light Cavalry	1,850
Boyer's Dragoons	1,500
Artillery 78 guns	

TOURING SALAMANCA

Head south from Salamanca along the E70 motorway, noting the Lesser and Greater Arapile hills to the left as the road enters open countryside. Take the slip road signposted for Arapiles after 8 kilometres and turn right at the roundabout under the motorway; continue straight on at the second roundabout and head straight into the village. Drive through the village, where there is an interesting museum, 'Le Interpretation Los Arapiles', on the right near the end of the village. It is worth a visit but is only open from 10:30 to 13:30 on Thursdays and 10:30 to 14:00 on Saturdays.

Continue straight on out of the village and head between the two Arapile hills, the Greater to the right and the Lesser to the left. Follow the road for 3 kilometres into the village of Calvassa (Calvarrasa de Arriba) and turn left on to the main road at the traffic lights. Turn left after 600 metres by the pedestrian crossing and follow the road out of the village, continuing along a rough track for 800 metres. There is an open turning area just before a rocky outcrop where an old stone building stands above a small stream.

The area in front is where General Foy's division first encountered Wellington's troops. The British had crossed the river Tormes to the north and collected behind the Lesser Arapile to the west. Wellington was anxious to keep his dispositions a secret until he was ready to attack and he called upon the Light Division to stop the French taking the hill in front. After heavy fighting on the slopes beyond the stream, Foy's men withdrew, leaving General Marmont in the dark about Wellington's intentions. While the battle raged across this shallow stream, the bulk of the French army headed west, moving behind the Greater Arapile.

Return to your car and head back into Calvassa, where you turn right at the traffic lights, retracing the route towards the two Arapile hills. The Lesser Arapile is now private property but just beyond the railway crossing at the foot of the rocky slopes, you can take the rough track to the right to visit San Miguel Hill, the rocky outcrop some 300 metres north of Arapiles from where Wellington watched the French. During good weather it is possible to follow the track a little way, parallel to the railway, before turning left along a second track after 400 metres to reach Wellington's position.

Salamanca can be seen to the north but the delights of that town were far from the men fighting on the fields around here in July 1812. The

General Foy's division tried in vain to capture this hill from the Light Division.

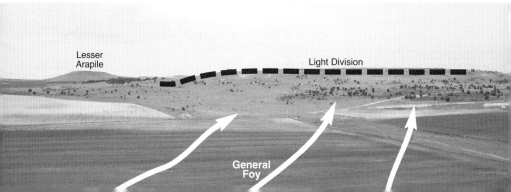

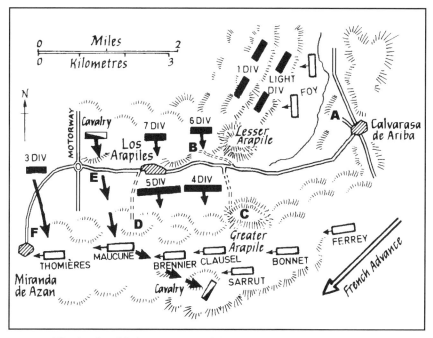

The battle of Salamanca., 22 July 1812

British general waited on this rocky outcrop as Marmont's men marched behind the Greater Arapile, heading directly west (to the right) behind a series of low hills. The French general, assuming that Wellington had decided to make a run for it to the west, had ordered his divisions to march quickly westwards in the hope of cutting off his enemy's retreat. Wellington watched closely, looking for signs of movement along the horizon, while his own troops lay hidden behind San Miguel Hill and the Lesser Arapile. Wellington moved quickly when it was clear that Marmont was marching across his front, and galloped 3 kilometres to the west to find Pakenham's 3rd Division so the British attack could begin.

The area between the viewpoint and the Greater Arapile is where the final counter-attack organised by Clausel was made against Clinton's 6th Division and Cole's 4th Division. Leith's 5th Division advanced to the south-east, beyond the village, catching Clausel's division in the flank to the right of the Greater Arapile.

Return to the tarmac road and head west towards Arapiles village; the

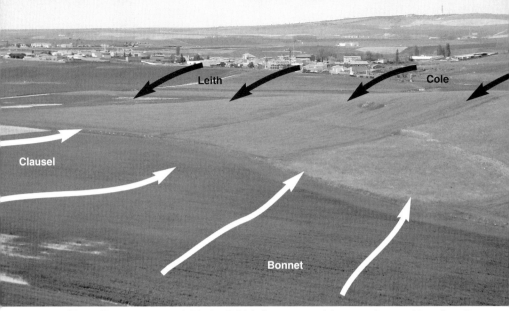

Clausel's counter-attack hit the British line across this ground east of Los Arapiles

turning for the track to the Greater Arapile is on the left after 200 metres. The rough narrow track leads to the foot of the steep-sided ridge where there is restricted parking for cars. Climb the steep slopes to the monument.

The battlefield should be viewed from the west end of the hill. Starting from the north-east, you can see Calvassa and the hill held by the Light Division, as well as the route Wellington's men followed from the river Tormes to the north. Many of Wellington's troops were hidden in the dip to the west (left) of the Lesser Arapile when General Marmont took the decision to take up the imaginary chase to the west. The rocky outcrop where Wellington waited for events to unfold can be seen to the right of Arapiles village.

Return to the tarmac road and turn left, continuing into the village; passing the museum on the left, head through the houses. After 300 metres turn left at a crossroads at a sharp right bend, and follow the road as it turns into a rough track and head south until the track forks some 400 metres further on across the low ridge to the south. Brennier's division was marching from east to west (with the Greater Arapile behind it) when Le Marchant's dragoons charged over the crest of the summit and slammed into its flank. The French division scattered. Turn around and return to the village, turning left to head out of the houses.

It is worth stopping at the garage on the left just before the motorway. Le Marchant's dragoons started their charge from this area, catching

Maucune's division in the flank on the high ground to the south of the large car park before turning east (or left) to attack Brennier's division. The garage is also a good place to stop for refreshments and fuel.

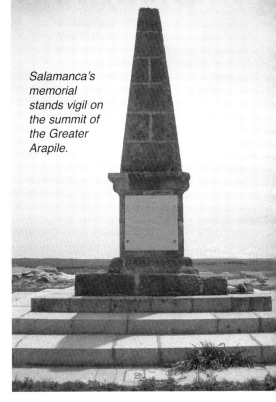

Salamanca's memorial stands vigil on the summit of the Greater Arapile.

To visit the western end of the battlefield, head west, driving straight on at the two roundabouts, and pass under the motorway. Continue straight on across the N630, signposted for Miranda de Azan. The road swings to the left after 1.5 kilometres and drops down between two small hills into the village; this is where Pakenham's 3rd Division caught Thomiére's division in the flank as it moved behind the low Monte de Azan ridge to the left of the road. The French were marching west behind the ridge hoping to catch the British retreating towards Portugal but instead they were caught in the flank as the British attacked from the north.

Immediately after crossing the stream into the village turn left and drive through the houses for 400 metres to the end of the village. Turn around at the end of the tarmac road, noting the Monte de Azan ridge to

Le Marchant's cavalry galloped up this slope to charge General Maucune's division in the flank.

Clausel   Brennier   Maucune

the north. Head back into Miranda de Azan, retracing your route, and turn right across the stream. Head back to the E70 motorway to complete your tour.

The Siege of Burgos, 19 September—22 October 1812

Burgos, the capital of Old Castile, had served as a key communications centre for the north of Spain throughout the French occupation. Although Wellington had considered besieging the fortress immediately after the battle of Salamanca, he had chosen instead to head east to free Madrid from French rule. As the allied army approached, thousands of refugees, including French soldiers and their supporters, fled from the Spanish capital carrying their belongings on hundreds of wagons. At their head was King Joseph of Spain and his extensive entourage. The declaration of the 1812 Constitution was a sign that Spain was regaining its confidence but, for the time being, the country was financially destitute. It would be a long time before the politicians and generals would be able to fulfil their grandiose promises, and many of them would never be fulfilled at all.

Wellington's march across central Spain and the French withdrawal from Madrid left Marshal Soult's Army of the South in an exposed position and it too was soon falling back, abandoning Cadiz and Sevilla. Although the battle of Salamanca had given the allies the upper hand, Wellington still had only 60,000 British troops to hand, while there were 200,000 French troops operating across the peninsula. Wellington had been promised over 100,000 Spanish soldiers but many of these units existed only in the minds of the Spanish generals, while others were unreliable conscripts or militia.

Despite his doubts, Wellington had no choice but to continue the campaign against the French and on 31 August his army headed towards his original objective, Burgos fortress. The need to garrison Madrid reduced the number of men marching north-east to just 24,000 British troops followed by 11,000 Spanish. A similar number had to remain behind to protect the capital. It was a case of too much area to cover and too few troops.

Upon hearing the news that the allies were advancing, the French withdrew from the Castile area towards the Pyrenees, leaving behind a garrison of 2,000 veteran troops under the command of General Jean-Louis Dubreton in Burgos castle. The withdrawal left Wellington with only two options: to withdraw to Madrid or besiege the fortress. He chose the latter.

Burgos castle stands on a steep ridge north of the cathedral and it guards all the approaches to the city. The medieval fortress had two enclosures. The keep stood in the upper courtyard on the summit of the hill while a curtain wall had been built along the north-west slopes. A redoubt, known as the Hornwork, had been recently added on San Miguel Heights to the north-east.

Wellington's troops reached Burgos on 19 September and proceeded to surround the fortress while plans were made to begin the siege. Although his men were rather over-confident following the capture of Madrid, there was a serious shortage of engineers to supervise the digging of the siege works. Suitable artillery pieces were also in short supply and ammunition was low. The crews of the three 18-pounder guns, nicknamed 'Thunder', 'Lightning' and 'Nelson' (because it had only one trunnion), would eventually have to hunt for French cannon-balls to use in their bombardment of the castle.

The first part of Wellington's plan was to capture the Hornwork so that battery positions could be dug for his artillery on the San Miguel heights. General H. Campbell's 1st Division was chosen to make the attack and on the night of 19 September the 1/42nd Regiment silently moved off from its assembly positions. The British artillery remained silent but the element of surprise was lost when French outposts spotted the assault parties creeping towards the Hornwork in the bright moonlight. John Mills, a Guards officer, also blamed the Portuguese for alerting the French guards:

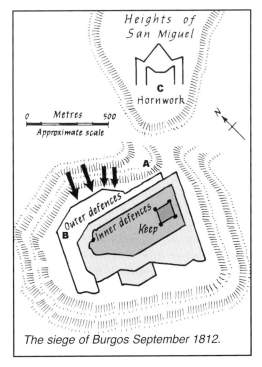

The siege of Burgos September 1812.

The 42nd, as the strongest regiment in the division, was selected for the purpose, supported by the light companies of the Highland Brigade and General Pack's Portuguese Brigade. At eight o'clock they advanced but the

Portuguese, who thought to raise their spirits by it, began to shout and thereby drew the enemy's fire upon them. The 42nd advanced gallantly and planted their ladders which proved to be too short, and after persisting for some time they were beat back. They returned again, and with Major Cocks and his light companies got in scrambling over without ladders.

While the French fought off the main assault, a smaller party scaled the rear wall of the redoubt and took the garrison by surprise, allowing the 42nd to renew its attacks. Over 400 allied soldiers were killed in the fighting, twice the number of the French casualties. However, with the San Miguel heights now in British hands, Wellington could turn his attentions to Burgos castle, although he was concerned that he did not have adequate resources to take the fortification. A note in his Despatches says: 'I doubt, however, that I have the means to take the castle, which is very strong.'

As the engineers organised the siege works, the infantry dug trenches across the steep-sided valley separating the San Miguel heights from the west wall of the castle. The wall stood at the top of a steep slope and as heavy rain repeatedly flooded the trenches at the bottom, Wellington's infantry dug into the side of the hillside. Although there was a shortage of siege artillery and the French interfered with the British plans at every opportunity, a breach had been opened in the north-west wall by 23 September.

An assault was made but it was poorly planned and was a failure; over 150 men were killed or injured. John Mills, with the Guards, later condemned the attack as foolish:

During the whole of this time they [the French] kept up a constant fire from the top of the wall and threw down bags of gunpowder and large stones. At last, having been 25 minutes in the ditch and not seeing anything of the other parties, they retired, having lost half their numbers in killed and wounded. Thus ended the attack, which was almost madness to attempt.

While the infantry reorganised, the engineers resorted to mining and began tunnelling into the hillside under the walls of the lower enclosure. The plan was to detonate a 1,000lb mine beneath the breach, obliterating the French garrison and clearing the way for the Forlorn Hope. When the mine was set on 29 September, the explosives detonated harmlessly in front of the breach. The engineers had mistaken the remains of an ancient foundation for the base of the wall and the tunnel had been too short. The Forlorn Hope found the French waiting for them and the attack failed.

Wellington's situation deteriorated over the days that followed. On 1 October two of his heavy guns were knocked out by French artillery. A second mine was successfully detonated beneath the breach three days later and although the assault troops entered the castle's lower enclosure, they found themselves in a trap. The garrison had already withdrawn to the main castle walls from where they were able to fire down on the British. It was pointless to try to hold the courtyard and the attackers withdrew to safety before nightfall, having suffered nearly 250 casualties. The British siege plans were subsequently found on the body of an officer and were taken to General Dubreton. The garrison's commander was thus able to study Wellington's strategy in detail and plan his defence accordingly.

Dubreton's first action was to send sorties out of the castle to destroy the entrenchments. Two were made on the 5th and the 8th, and both inflicted heavy casualties. Ensign Thompson was one of the few to survive one attack:

> Aided by the most tremendous fire which I ever saw of cannon, they succeeded in driving us out but a small party of about thirty of our men maintained themselves behind a breastwork, the enemy being on the near-side and stabbing with bayonets, and from their spirited conduct the work was regained.

Over the days that followed Wellington's one remaining heavy gun demolished a sector of the south-west corner of the fortress and on 18 October two simultaneous attacks were launched against the lower compound. As mines detonated under the breaches, two assault parties, each 300-strong, were launched by the Guards and the King's German Legion. For the second time the assault parties came under heavy fire from the walls as they entered the lower enclosure. Private Fletcher's account graphically illustrates the difficulties faced by the men of the 1st Division:

> A most tremendous fire opened upon us from every part which took us in front and rear. They poured down fresh men, and ours kept falling down into the ditch, dragging and knocking down others. We were so close that they fairly put their muskets into our faces, and we pulled one of their men through an embrasure . . . We had hardly any men left on the top, and at last we gave way.

Shells and shot batter Burgos during the unsuccessful siege.

How we got over the palisades I know not — the fire was tremendous: shot, shell, grape, musketry, large stones, hand grenades and every missile weapon were used against us.

The attack gained some degree of success. Campbell's men had taken the lower courtyard but it had cost over 200 casualties and they were unable to go further. They would have to repeat the process to take the upper enclosure but the French could monitor their movements from the walls and the keep. The rocky ground made it impossible to tunnel and so conventional storming methods would have to be used.

Over the next three days new trenches were dug at the foot of the curtain wall so the infantry could assembly. The plan was to use ladders to scale the wall while the artillery opened a breach in the northern wall so the keep could be attacked from two directions. Before the attack could be launched, however, Wellington learned on the 21st that the French armies of Soult, Joseph and Suchet were converging on Madrid. It was time to take stock and consider the strategic situation across the whole of Spain. Over 50,000 French troops were heading for General Hill's garrison in the capital, while the siege of Burgos was sapping the morale of his men as casualties rose to over 2,000.

Wellington realised it was time to fall back to the Portuguese border and on the night of 21/22 October his troops slipped away under cover of darkness. The wagons and guns silently left San Miguel Heights with straw wrapped around the wheels so the castle guards would not hear them. Wellington's army had to march fast because the French had a three-to-one superiority in cavalry and they were already moving towards Burgos. The British forces covered more than 40 kilometres on the 23rd, and the first skirmish occurred at Venta del Pozo, where Anson's and Bock's brigades failed to stop Faverot's cavalry brigade forcing its way across the bridge. Although Wellington had planned to make a stand behind the river Carrion at Torquemada, the capture of the Palencia Bridge meant he had to prepare to move at once. The retreat was delayed when his men found the town's wine cellars and went on a drunken rampage.

Despite this momentary lapse in discipline, the British and Portuguese soldiers were on the road again the following morning and heading for Valladolid, where Wellington wanted to make a stand behind the river Duero. His plans to allow his men to rest were frustrated when a group of over fifty French soldiers swam across the flooded river at Tordesillas on 29 October and drove back the German troops guarding the west bank. French engineers soon built a pontoon bridge allowing more Frenchmen to cross, but the small bridgehead was quickly contained when British troops arrived in the area.

There were some 50,000 veteran French soldiers deployed along the Duero but Wellington now had 80,000 men (including 25,000 new Spanish recruits) holding the west bank of the river. By 6 November the French realised that Wellington would not be drawn into battle and they called off the pursuit and turned their attentions to Madrid, where General Hill faced odds of over two-to-one, with more French troops on their way. He abandoned the Spanish capital on 31 October and headed west, aiming to join Wellington at Salamanca.

As over 100,000 French troops converged on the scattered allied forces, Wellington and Hill had only one option left: they had to cross the Portuguese border as quickly as possible so that the French would need to rely on extended lines of communication. As both armies trudged along, the autumn rains turned the already muddy roads into quagmires, causing the men's hearts to sink as they once more left Spain. Joseph Donaldson of the 94th was with General Pakenham's 3rd Division during the retreat:

> The rain pouring down in torrents drenched us to the skin, the road, composed of clay soil, stuck to our shoes so fast that they were torn off our feet. The nights were dismally dark, the cold winds blew in heavy gusts, and the roads became gradually worse. After marching in this state for hours, we halted in a field by the roadside, piled our arms, and were allowed to dispose of ourselves as we best could. The moon, wading through dense masses of clouds, sometimes threw a momentary gleam on the miserable beings huddled together in every variety of posture, and trying to rest or to screen themselves from the cold. Some were lying on the wet ground rolled in wetter blankets; some placed their knapsack on a stone, and sat on it, with their blankets wrapped about them, their heads resting on their knees, their teeth chattering with cold. Long before daylight we were again ordered to fall in, and proceeded on our retreat.

Their misery increased when the new Quartermaster-General, Colonel James Gordon, mistakenly ordered the supply trains to move on ahead of the men, leaving them without food for four days. The starving men killed a few oxen with the column for food, but they struggled to light fires in the wet conditions.

Despite the hardships, the men continued to head west towards Ciudad Rodrigo during what Wellington later described as 'the most agonising retreat of his career'. Over 5,000 men fell ill, putting a tremendous strain on the limited medical services, and 2,000 of them died of sickness; another 1,000 fell by the wayside and were taken prisoner. Donaldson never forgot the faces of the men they had to leave behind at the mercy of the French cavalry:

> It was piteous to see the men, who had long dragged their limbs after them with a determined spirit, finally fall down in the mud

unable to proceed further. The despairing looks that they gave us, when they saw us pass on, would have pierced the heart at any other time; but our feelings were steeled, and we had no power to assist, even had we felt the inclination.

By 9 November Hill had joined Wellington at Salamanca but the misery continued for another nine days, during which General Sir Edward Paget, the new commander of the 1st Division (who had just returned to Spain after recovering from losing an arm in the fighting in Oporto in 1809), was captured on the 17th. Once the armies reached the fortress of Ciudad Rodrigo they were safe, and the exhausted survivors went gratefully into billets and settled down for the winter in eastern Beira.

Wellington's only consolation was that the Spanish government had asked him to take overall command of the Spanish armies on 22 September. He had referred the request to senior officers in London and accepted the command on 21 November when they gave a favourable response. For the first time all the allied armies would be acting under a single commander, bringing an end to over four years of divisive command.

VISITING BURGOS CASTLE

Burgos Castle stands on a high ridge on the north-west outskirts of the town. Head towards the cathedral and the Parc que de Castillo, drive through the outer gate and up the winding road. Continue straight on past the inner gate and stop in the car park to the left after 300 metres.

The Hornwork was on San Miguel Heights across the steep-sided valley to the north of the car park, which itself is in the outer courtyard of the castle, the area where the siege works were. The walls that the British guns battered and the engineers mined were demolished after the siege. The infantry never managed to reach the inner wall, which still stands at the top of the slopes.

After capturing the Hornwork, the first stage of Wellington's plan involved digging trenches across the valley and digging tunnels under the outer wall on the north side of the car park. Once the wall had been breached and troops entered the outer courtyard they found the French garrison waiting for them, looking down on them from the parapet of the next wall. Heavy casualties were suffered as the infantry tried to dig their way across the courtyard and attempts to scale the inner wall failed.

There is a footpath across the courtyard and steps at the end lead to the castle gates. The opening hours of the inner courtyard are limited to weekends and bank holidays between 11:00 and 14:00 hours. Visits have to be booked by ringing (0034) 947-288874 at other times.

Return to your car and turn left out of the car park through the gap in the wall to visit the Hornwork. The road goes through the centre of the extensive fortifications, and turning right at the far side of the earthworks leads you back down the hill, past the castle walls, to the town.

The castle's medieval walls.

Chapter 8

DRIVING THE FRENCH FROM SPAIN

THE ADVANCE TO VITORIA, 22 MAY–20 JUNE 1813

B Y THE END OF 1812 the Russian campaign was over and Napoleon was short of troops, having lost thousands of men to enemy action, starvation, disease and the cold on the frozen steppes. Although Joseph did not have enough troops to garrison the areas of Spain under his control, the Emperor now ordered him to send 20,000 reinforcements. The order had serious repercussions across the peninsula, as French control was limited to town garrisons and isolated outposts in many areas. This meant that Spanish guerrillas could operate virtually freely, without fear of reprisal, attacking French supply trains, couriers and patrols.

Napoleon's actions severely limited effective operations in Spain and Joseph's generals often had no idea about allied movements, while Wellington was kept up to date with French activities. Despite the cutback in numbers, the Emperor was adamant that his brother should continue military operations across the country and ordered new actions, even though they stretched the French troops to their limits and beyond.

The northern part of Spain, particularly the Pyrenees Mountains, was one of the areas most at risk and Napoleon wanted the Army of Portugal to search out the brigands operating there under the command of the guerrilla fighter Francisco Espoz y Mina. All supplies and reinforcements had to pass through these mountainous areas, particularly in the San Sebastián and Barcelona areas, and General Clausel was given the task of keeping the guerrillas under control. However, he had only been allocated 40,000 troops and this was insufficient. The guerrillas simply scattered and hid in the mountains every time the French approached, often torturing and killing the cavalry patrols sent out to find them and then leaving their mutilated bodies behind as a gruesome warning. Espoz y Mina's men then reassembled as soon as the French patrols had gone and resumed their reign of terror. Clausel asked for another 20,000 men to control the problem but Joseph was unable to spare any.

The sensible answer to Joseph's problems would have been to withdraw troops from the desolate areas of western Spain and reorganise his armies so that troops could be sent north to regain control. But Napoleon refused to sanction any withdrawal, believing that Wellington's army was in a poor state after the retreat from Burgos. He was also concerned about the deteriorating situation across Prussia and needed his armies to maintain a show of strength across the peninsula. In reality, only the Army of the Centre and the Army of the South were in a position to face Wellington. But Suchet was fully engaged in the Alicante area on the east coast while the insubordinate Soult refused to follow Joseph's orders and Napoleon finally had to intervene, recalling the obstinate marshal to France.

By the spring of 1813 Wellington's army had fully recovered from the Burgos débâcle and his situation was improving daily. Reinforcements had been shipped from England, bringing his existing units back up to strength, and new units of cavalry and artillery had also been sent to the peninsula. His army had been able to spend the winter recovering and training in Portugal, where the Lines of Torres Vedras had once again kept his men safe. Improvements in medical services had also reduced sickness to a manageable level, helping to reduce the strain on the logistics chain. Many local improvements to equipment and clothing, all tried and tested on campaign, had been adopted with the approval of the officers and men. Wellington had also taken steps to improve the standard of leadership across his army. When incompetent officers returned to England on leave or through sickness, he promoted experienced rankers to replace them, bypassing the usual system of men having to purchase a rank. It meant that for the first time many of his senior officers were hand-picked seasoned campaigners.

The improvements were felt across the whole army but Wellington still faced a range of strategic difficulties, many of them long-standing problems that had troubled the allies since the peninsular campaign had begun. The Spanish army still needed a great deal of work before he would look on it as a reliable and competent force, and there were still issues with the government. Meanwhile, the guerrilla bands across Spain were getting out of hand in many areas and some had turned to terrorising the local population after the French had withdrawn. While the Portuguese troops had proved themselves to be worthy allies, the country had been left devastated and the people destitute, and the effects of this were now spilling over into the army.

Despite the problems that Wellington faced, he was ready to advance into Spain by the spring of 1813. His army left Portugal on 22 May 1813, heading for the open plains and mountains of north-east Spain. As the troops marched across the Spanish border Wellington reportedly turned and waved his hat in the air, saying: 'Farewell, Portugal, for I shall never see you again.' The army marched in two columns, with General Sir Thomas Graham leading the northern one, numbering 40,000 troops, as it headed for Valladolid. He would continue to advance north of Burgos, outflanking any potential defensive lines along the Duero and Esla rivers. A second column of 30,000 men led by General Sir Rowland Hill marched through Extramadura towards Salamanca, heading along the well-trodden route towards Burgos. Wellington was hoping to fool Joseph into thinking that this southern column was his main advance, and he accompanied it during the early stages of the advance.

The French believed that Wellington would have to rely on his supply base in Lisbon, limiting him to a campaign in central Spain. In earlier campaigns this was the case but during the winter months the navy had shipped large quantities of stores to Corunna on the north-west coast of Spain. The plan was to establish a new, shorter logistics chain, widening Wellington's strategic options. As Graham's troops moved beyond Burgos, the navy would transport food and ammunition to Santander, considerably shortening the overland lines of communication.

The advance went according to plan and the French fell back to Burgos as Graham's force headed north before turning east, crossing sparsely populated areas where a foraging French army could not survive for long. On 10 June the British reached Burgos, the scene of the disastrous siege the previous autumn. This time the garrison surrendered after only two days, when Joseph's lines of communication were threatened. They destroyed the fortress before retiring across the river Ebro at Miranda de Ebro. Graham continued his relentless advance and his men crossed the river downstream of the French on 15 June. As they headed into the Cantabrian mountains, Joseph realised that his position had been compromised and he was forced to order his armies to withdraw to the north-east and concentrate at Vitoria, where he had decided to make a stand in front of the town.

THE BATTLE OF VITORIA, 21 JUNE 1813

Joseph had chosen a strong defensive position to the west of the town. Mountain ranges to the north and south protected the French flanks, and the allies had to either cross, or deploy astride, the winding Zadorra stream which crossed the northern side of the plain before turning west in front of Arinez Hill. The stream was impassable to artillery but several bridges crossed it to the west while others bridged it to the north of Vitoria. There was ample space to deploy his three armies of 66,000 men on the open fields west of the town and the undulating terrain offered perfect fields of fire for his 138 guns.

Joseph assumed that Wellington would advance from the west, passing through the Puebla Gorge, and had ordered his three generals to deploy one in front of the other astride the main road into Vitoria. General Theodore Gazan deployed his Army of the South and its 26,000 infantry in the front line. Conroux, Daricau and Leval deployed their divisions side by side at the foot of the Puebla Heights with Maransin's division in reserve, while Villatte's division was holding Arinez Hill behind his right flank. General D'Erlon's two infantry divisions, 9,500 men led by D'Armagnac and Cassagne from the Army of the Centre, were deployed behind Gazan near Arinez village, from where they could either reinforce Gazan or extend his line to north or south. General Charles Reille's Army of Portugal was held in reserve, and Sarrut and Lamartiniére had placed their two divisions, totalling 11,500 infantry, in front of Vitoria. Joseph knew that General Clausel's troops had recently left Pamplona and were on their way to join him.

The French position was a strong one but it had two flaws. All the French infantry were positioned to face an attack from the west, illustrating that Joseph did not appreciate that Graham's troops could reach his right flank. The French right (north) flank was covered by over 11,000 cavalry deployed along the banks of the Zadorra stream between Tres Puentes and Durana, a distance of over 10 kilometres. Joseph also did not expect the allies to attempt an advance over the Puebla Heights to the south.

After making his deployments Joseph began to have second thoughts. He did not know that Wellington was planning to attack his flanks in strength but he was worried about overextending his deployment and briefly considered withdrawing his men to a shorter line nearer Vitoria. Illness prevented him from pursuing the idea and new deployment

Hill

Marasin

Hill's troops advanced over the Puebla Heights to attack Gazan's right flank.

orders were never given. It did not stop him, however, from ordering a division to escort the royal baggage train to the French border.

Wellington spent 20 June studying the French positions and eventually decided to use all his troops to attack them from several directions. His plan was to deploy a small part of his force in front of the French positions around Arinez. The majority of his troops would attack both of Joseph's flanks and threaten his rear. By dividing his army into four separate columns, including 27,500 Portuguese and 7,000 Spanish troops, and sending them against different parts of the French line, he hoped to distract Joseph's attention and encourage him to divide his reserves. His plan would also allow him to deploy the maximum number of troops at the same time and make the most of his superiority in numbers.

The first attack would be made by Hill's 2nd Division and Morillo's Spanish division. Some 20,000 men would climb the Heights of Puebla, south of the gorge, and advance through the Puebla pass. They would then threaten Gazan's left flank and, he hoped, make Joseph deploy some of his reserves. The second stage of the plan involved Picton's 3rd Division and Dalhousie's 7th Division advancing through the valley of the Bayas to the north. They would appear on the French right flank, and attempt to cross the river Zadorra near Mendoza. Wellington was hoping that the appearance of troops behind his right flank would make Joseph commit even more of his reserves to help Gazan's men. The third attack would be made by 20,000 men, including Howard's 1st Division, Oswald's 5th Division, two Portuguese brigades and a Spanish brigade, which were marching through the mountains south of Bilbao. Wellington wanted General Graham to cross the river Zadorra north-east of Vitoria, cutting the Bayonne road at Durana and Gamarra Mayor, and threaten the French rear.

As Joseph deployed his reserves and concentrated on countering the threats to his flanks and rear, Wellington could launch the final stage of his plan, a frontal attack on Gazan's corps. Lowry Cole's 4th Division and

Alten's Light Division would advance from Nanclares, where Wellington would be waiting to watch his plan unfold. The final stage of the plan meant that a total of 50,000 allied troops would be engaging Gazan's 35,000 from four directions at different times.

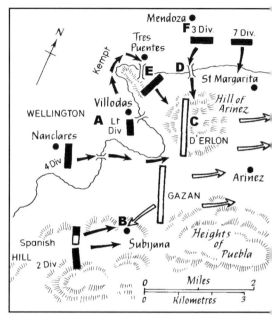

The battle of Vitoria. – Wellington's attack.

On the morning of 21 June 1813 the mist and light rain soon cleared, but the gloomy conditions on the top of Arinez Hill meant that although Joseph, Marshal Jourdan and General Gazan could see the French corps arrayed in front of them, the majority of Wellington's troops remained hidden. Wellington was out of contact with his subordinates and would have to rely on them to carry out his orders accurately or his plan would fail.

General Hill and General Morillo duly crossed the river Zadorra west of the Puebla Gorge early in the morning, as planned, and started the long climb to the top of the Puebla Heights. When General Gazan spotted British, Portuguese and Spanish troops marching over the summit of the pass, he was, as Wellington hoped, forced to reconsider his deployment. Maransin's brigade moved to Subijana de Alvana and met the attack on a ridge west of the village, stopping Hill's advance in its tracks. Disaster struck the French when the 71st Regiment, mistaking a French battalion moving up in support for Spanish troops, attacked them in the flank; over 300 men were killed or injured and for a time chaos reigned in the French ranks.

Hill's men seized the advantage and began advancing down the slopes towards Subijana de Alava village but casualties were heavy; General Cadogan was killed leading his brigade while General Morillo was wounded. When it was clear that the British attack was threatening to take Zumelza village, Gazan was forced to redeploy Conroux's and

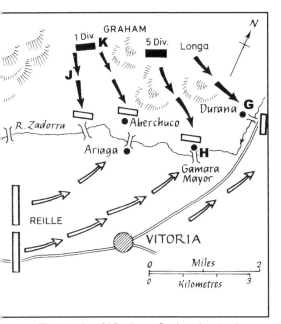

The battle of Vitoria. – Graham's attack.

Daricau's divisions and counter-attack. George Bell later recalled how Conroux's attack was stopped in front of the village:

We were gaining ground along the side of the mountain when we were met with a biting fire, and the battle here remained stationary for some time. Then, passing the Zadorra we won the village of Subijana de Alava and maintained our ground in spite of all opposition. There was a good deal of fighting in the church-yard, and some open graves were soon filled up with double numbers. As Colonel Brown said, 'If you don't kill them, boys, they'll kill you: fire away.'

Although Hill was making slow progress, the movement of two divisions to Joseph's left flank was exactly what Wellington had hoped for: Gazan's central position had been weakened.

The first stage was going according to plan but as noon approached problems began to emerge on the opposite side of the battlefield. By this time the 7th Division was supposed to have reached Mendoza and should have been deploying south of the village, ready to cross the Zadorra stream. But unknown to Wellington, General Dalhousie had been delayed in crossing the mountain passes and the British commander eventually decided that he needed to take action. If he waited any longer to make a second attack, the advantage gained by Hill's assault could be lost. Thus he took the decision to let the 4th Division and the Light Division begin their frontal assault at the first opportunity.

The Light Division was deployed at Villodas, and its men were preparing to clear the French outposts covering the village bridge before advancing on to Arinez Hill. However, just as they were about to make their attack, a Spanish peasant brought important news to General Alten's headquarters. The bridge at Tres Puentes, a short distance downstream, was still intact; better still, it was unguarded and hidden from the French by a rocky outcrop. It appeared that the Light Division could have an easy way across the Zadorra stream. While General Kempt's brigade was ordered to march along the riverbank to investigate, Vandeleur's brigade kept the French guarding Villodas bridge occupied.

General Kempt was delighted to discover that the information was true (although sadly the peasant never received his reward, for he was killed en route to the bridge). It was the break that Wellington had been looking for; he now had a new way to threaten Gazan's right flank. The 1/43rd and two battalions of the 95th Regiment assembled in the trees before rushing the narrow bridge and they were followed by the 15th Hussars. Wellington now had a foothold on the east bank of the Zadorra, one which would make it easier to cross at Mendoza bridge.

On Wellington's left flank the 7th Division had still not reached Mendoza but the 3rd Division had. General Picton's impatience was notorious, but he also had enough experience to understand that it was important to capitalise on the advantage created by Kempt's advance. As the riflemen established themselves on the south bank of the Zadorra, he became increasingly concerned that his late appearance was going to have an adverse effect on the tactical situation. After angrily questioning one of Wellington's aides who was searching in vain for General Dalhousie, he realised that the 7th Division must have been seriously delayed. Picton decided it was time to take matters into his own hands and hastily dismissed the bewildered aide with a typically fiery outburst, saying: 'You may tell Lord Wellington from me, sir, that the 3rd Division under my command shall in less than ten minutes attack the bridge and carry it, and the 4th and 6th Divisions may support if they choose.' He then returned to the head of his men and gave the order to advance in his own unique manner: 'Come on, ye rascals! Come on, ye fighting villains!'

As the 1/45th Regiment stormed Puentes Mendoza bridge at the head of Brisbane's brigade, Colville's brigade waded the Zadorra 800 metres to the east, forming a second bridgehead on the south bank. General D'Erlon had spotted the threat to his flank at an early stage and had moved D'Armagnac's division and Cassagne's division from Arinez Hill ready to meet the 3rd Division's attack. A fierce battle unfolded, and although they were outnumbered with their backs to a river, Picton's men fought courageously to retain their slender bridgehead.

The 7th Division eventually reached Mendoza. General Dalhousie waited at a distance ready to reinforce Picton and as soon as the bridgehead looked to be in danger he sent Grant's brigade across. The 3rd Division rallied on the fresh brigade and as the advantage passed to the British, D'Erlon's men were pushed back. One soldier with the 82nd Regiment later recalled how his comrades drove the French back:

> Our front was exposed to a French regiment on the right of the battery, but, after politely receiving us with a few sharp volleys, which we as politely returned, they retreated into a thicket. Towards this we advanced firing, and drove them furiously before us till they were completely routed.

This counter-attack created enough room to deploy the rest of the 7th Division on the south bank and as Barnes' brigade and Le Cor's Portuguese brigade joined the fight, D'Erlon's two divisions fell back to Margarita. The extra space allowed General Alten to deploy Vandeleur's brigade and before long the whole of the Light Division had crossed the Zadorra and begun to attack Gazan's position on Arinez Hill.By mid-afternoon the French situation was precarious. Hill was threatening Gazan's left flank on the slopes of Puebla Heights, while the Light Division was gaining the upper hand in the fight for Arinez Hill. The 3rd Division was also forcing his right flank and Gazan had been obliged to withdraw all his troops from the area facing Nanclares, allowing General Cole's 4th Division to cross Puentes Nanclares unopposed and advance towards

The 15th Hussars crossing the bridge at Tres Puentes ready to support Kempt's riflemen.

Arinez village. This meant that he had British troops closing in from both flanks and to his front. Gazan was left with no option but to withdraw to

The Light Division advanced from Tres Puentes towards the top of Arinez Hill.

a new position anchored on Arinez Hill.

Unfortunately for the French commander, events overtook him when Vandeleur's brigade helped Picton's men to capture Margarita. This left D'Erlon's corps in serious danger of being outflanked and a second withdrawal had to be made. With difficulty, the French commanders extricated their battered divisions and tried to rally them on a new line between Gomecha and Lermanda. In some units withdrawal was mistaken for defeat and they began to fall back in disarray.

While Gazan and D'Erlon struggled to maintain order and deploy their units on a new line west of Vitoria, events were unfolding north-east of the town. By mid-morning General Graham's men were advancing across the hills north of the river Zadorra and preparing to attack the river crossings at Abechuco, Gamarra Mayor and Durana. The appearance of new troops moving down the Bilbao road had forced General Reille to redeploy many units to meet the threat, thus depriving Joseph of a large part of his reserve.

General Maucune had the furthest to travel but his troops arrived in time to stop General Longa's men crossing the Zadorra at Durana. General Reille was convinced that the Spanish were poorly armed guerrillas and so failed to post any of his troops on the north bank. It was a serious miscalculation. Longa's men were supported by artillery and while the infantry took up positions close to the bridge, the gun crews deployed close by in positions from which they could fire on traffic using the Bayonne road. Thus Joseph's preferred withdrawal route to San Sebastián and France was blocked by fire; his baggage would have to head east to Pamplona before making the long trek through the Pyrenean mountain passes.

North of Vitoria General Sarrut's division had crossed the Zadorra at Puentes de Yurre and intercepted the 1st Division as it advanced down the Bilbao road at Aranguiz and Abechuco. General Stewart's men were stopped in their tracks as they tried to reach Puentes de Arriaga. To the east General Lamartiniére's division took up positions around the village of Gamarra Mayor and blocked General Oswald's 5th Division's route to Puentes de Gamarra.

Wellington had instructed General Hill to be cautious, aiming to draw Joseph's reserves north of Vitoria, rather than making a full-scale attack on the Zadorra bridges. However, yet again it had taken longer than anticipated to get through the mountain passes and it was early afternoon before his troops were fully deployed. Graham eventually attacked Reille's positions during the early afternoon (many believe that he took too long to begin his attacks) and volley fire erupted all along the north bank of the Zadorra as the ranks of redcoats advanced. While the 1st Division advanced on Abechuco and the 5th Division attacked Gamarra Mayor, Graham's guns bombarded the two villages from the slopes overlooking the river. Heavy fighting followed in and around the two villages.

Despite repeated attempts, neither the 1st Division nor the 5th Division could reach the bridges and withdrew to reorganise, having failed to drive General Reille's troops from the north bank of the Zadorra.

While Graham was struggling to make any progress to the north of Vitoria, to the west of the town the allies were preparing to make the most of their advantageous position over the French. By late afternoon Gazan was busy rallying his tired divisions on D'Erlon's line in front of Vitoria when the 1/94th Regiment, led by Major Thomas Lloyd, captured the village of Lermanda, compromising the right flank of his new position. As the French troops wavered, Wellington realised that it was time to unleash the final part of his plan, a frontal assualt by the fresh 4th Division.

Picton's attack across the River Zadora viewed from the top of Arinez Hill.

General Lowry Cole's troops had already crossed the Zadorra at Puente Nanclares and were waiting near the foot of Arinez Hill. When the order to attack was given nearly 8,000 British and Portuguese troops advanced astride the road to Vitoria; to counter them, some eighty French guns opened fire while the French infantry waited for the onslaught. Anson, Skerrets and Stubbs led their brigades forward as the Light Division, 3rd Division and 7th Division advanced towards D'Erlon's and Gazan's crumbling corps. This was the final part of Wellington's plan, a plan that he had been forced to revise several times as the situation on the battlefield changed. He had the French exactly where he wanted them and it must have given him great satisfaction to watch the final stages of his plan unfold from the summit of the hill.

By late afternoon Joseph knew that his men had been pushed beyond their limits and he could ask no more of them. It was time to withdraw. But he was too late. As aides rode off with orders for an orderly withdrawal towards Vitoria, the 4th Division's attack hit home. Each time the French infantry had rallied back a new threat presented itself from a different direction. D'Armagnac's and Cassagne's divisions had been steadily pushed back along the banks of the river Zadorra by the combined efforts of Picton's, Dalhousie's and Alten's divisions and Gazan's corps had been left in a precarious position. As Lowry Cole's men closed in for the final assault the battered French divisions began to fall back towards Vitoria. Despite Joseph's orders, the withdrawal was not the orderly retreat he had asked for; it quickly turned into a rout as men turned tail and fled. What started as a trickle quickly turned to a torrent as thousands ran for their lives. The pharmacist Sébastian Blaze witnessed the chaotic scenes:

> I galloped along in the middle of a crowd of fugitives of whom the majority had flung away their arms so as to lighten their burden. None was better than the next, they had all run away rather than face the enemy, but all the same they still quarrelled with one another, calling one another cowards and poltroons, and even exchanging blows.

Despite the rout, Reille's corps managed to maintain discipline and his divisions conducted an orderly withdrawal to the Zadorra stream in front of Graham's troops. Sarrut's division had to abandon Aranguiz when Halkett's brigade scaled the hills to outflank the village and it fell back to Abechuco. It was, however, able to stop the 1st Division reaching the

Zadorra, where the British troops could cross by the Puente de Arriaga and a nearby weir.

The 5th Division renewed the attack on Gamarra Menor and Oswald's men eventually forced Lamartiniére's division back to Puente de Gamarra. There was heavy fighting along the river bank and in Gamarra Mayor, but the French infantry clung on grimly to the bridge until Robinson's brigade finally overwhelmed them. Sergeant John Douglas of the 1st Regiment described the fight for Puente de Gamarra Mayor:

> We reached the village, which we named Gomorrah as it was a scene of fire and brimstone. The enemy were driven over the river Zadorra. The light company entered a house at the end of the bridge, from the windows of which a very destructive fire was kept up, while as many as could pushed across and formed as they arrived by an old chapel.

Although the roads east of Vitoria — and thus the chance to cut Joseph's line of retreat — were within Graham's reach he was unable to force Reille back from the banks of the Zadorra stream. Critics say that Graham could have done more, or moved faster, to complete Wellington's victory, but several factors need to be considered in his defence. His three divisions were faced by equal numbers of French troops, and less than half of his 20,000 men were British. Reille's corps also held a strong line along the

Robinson's brigade attacking Gamarra Mayor.

Zadorra stream and the majority of the 11,000 French cavalry were waiting on the south bank ready to strike if any allied troops crossed; Graham had no cavalry of his own to counter them.

As Reille fought to hold off Graham, the rest of the Army of the Centre and the Army of the South were in full flight through Vitoria with over 7,000 British cavalry in close pursuit. However, once again their discipline left a lot to be desired as many took the opportunity to plunder the dozens of abandoned wagons and carriages. Some of the French cavalry squadrons had formed a screen and they took advantage of the disorder in the British ranks; staff officer Captain Thomas Browne was with the 18th Hussars in Grant's brigade when it caught up with the crowds of French troops:

> . . . in pursuit of the enemy, who were flying as fast as possible, we overtook a line of carriages and baggage, which offered so much temptation to many of the soldiers that they could not resist falling to the work of plunder, whilst others with their officers continued in pursuit. The squadron was thus considerably weakened in number.

When the French cavalry spotted the weakened squadron, they wheeled their horses round and charged, killing and wounding many; Browne himself was badly injured and taken prisoner.

Although the day was lost, some of the French officers managed to rally their men while the majority of the French cavalry bravely held their ground. William Hay was with a squadron of light dragoons with Anson's brigade when it ran into some French cavalry:

> On seeing our advance, advantage was taken of some broken ground to halt and form for our reception. As we approached this appeared madness, as their numbers did not exceed half ours. Our trumpet sounded the charge when their flanks were thrown back, and there stood, formed in squares, about 3,000 infantry.

Wellington's view of Arinez Hill.

Musket volleys stopped the light dragoons in their tracks and they could not resume the advance until a troop of horse artillery moved up to close range. A few rounds of grapeshot wreaked havoc in the squares and once again the French infantry were in full retreat.

The British cavalry carved their way through the crowds of French troops, cutting down hundreds as they ran, but many stopped to search the abandoned carriages and wagons for loot. As a result of this serious breakdown in discipline, only 2,000 of Joseph's troops were captured while around 58,000 escaped.

One of those who had a narrow escape was Joseph himself. He escaped the 14th Light Dragoons, but then Captain Henry Wyndham and Lieutenant Lord Worcester of the 10th Hussars reached his carriage; as they fired their pistols through a window, Joseph jumped from the opposite door, commandeered a horse and galloped off, leaving the rest of the hussars to fall upon his baggage train. One item seized was the royal silver chamber pot, a much-prized trophy, which was taken back to the regimental headquarters and christened 'The Emperor'.

Marshal Jourdan's baton was found by a corporal of the 18th Hussars, who handed over his trophy to Wellington, who forwarded it to the Prince Regent. In return Wellington was elevated to the new rank of field marshal and a new baton was made for him to signify the promotion. One cavalryman summed up the plunder to be found in the fields east of Vitoria with the phrase 'the wealth of Spain and the Indies seemed to be here'.

While the British cavalry scoured the fields east of Vitoria for loot, Wellington's infantry entered the town and went on the rampage, consuming large quantities of wine as they searched for plunder and women, many of the latter helpless camp followers abandoned by the French. Greed and indiscipline had ruined Wellington's chances of total victory and he was disgusted by their behaviour. He later described his army as the 'scum of the earth' in a letter to the Earl of Bathurst. As Joseph's men headed on foot into the Pyrenees, Wellington's men were in no condition to pursue. They were tired and the majority were drunkenly celebrating the victory in Vitoria.

Despite the lost opportunity, the amount of equipment taken was staggering and an indication of the rapid breakdown in Joseph's armies. In total, 151 (out of 153) guns, 100 military wagons and 415 caissons had been captured. Over 6,000 Frenchmen had been killed or wounded, while the allies had suffered around 5,100 losses. News of the victory had soon spread across Europe, strengthening the allies' resolve, and before long Austria had joined the fight against Napoleon. Meanwhile, in England there were wild celebrations across the country. After six long years of war Wellington and his allies had finally driven the French armies to the borders of Spain, leaving only a few enemy-held fortresses still to conquer. He would now have to concentrate on driving the French from the Pyrenees and into France.

Wellington's Army 79,000

General Hill's First Attack over the Puebla Heights

2nd Division General William Stewart **10,834**

Cadogan's Brigade	1/50th, 1/71st, 1/92nd, 1 Coy 5/60th
Byng's Brigade	1/3rd, 1/57th, 1st Prov Bttn, 1 Coy 5/60th (or Walker's Brigade)
O'Callaghan's Brigade	1/28th, 2/34th, 1/39th, 1 Coy 5/60th
Ashworth's Brigade	6th Portuguese Line, 18th Portuguese Line, 6th Caçadores
	Morillo's Spanish Division

The Final Central Attack around Nanclares

4th Division General Lowry Cole **7,826**

Anson's Brigade	3rd Prov. Bttn, 3/27th, 1/40th, 1/48th, 1 Coy 5/60th
Skerrets Brigade	1/7th, 20th, 1/23rd, 1 Coy Brunswick Oels
Stubbs's Brigade	11th Portuguese Line, 23rd Portuguese Line, 7th Caçadores

Northern Attack through Tres Puentes and Mendoza

Light Division General Charles Alten **5,484**

Kempt's Brigade	1/43rd, 1/95th, 3/95th, 1st Caçadores
Vandeleur's Brigade	1/52nd, 17th Portuguese Line, 2/95th, 3rd Caçadores

3rd Division General Thomas Picton **7,459**

Brisbane's Brigade	1/45th, 74th, 1/88th, 3 Coys 5/60th
Colville's Brigade	1/5th, 2/83rd, 2/87th, 94th
Power's Brigade	9th Portuguese Line, 21st Portuguese Line, 11th Caçadores

7th Division General Lord Dalhousie **7,287**

Barnes's Brigade	1/6th, 3rd Prov Batt. 1 Coy Brunswick Oels
Grant's Brigade	51st, 68th, 1/82nd, Chasseurs Brittaniques
Le Cor's Brigade	7th Portuguese Line, 19th Portuguese Line, 2nd Caçadores

General Graham's Northern Attack

1st Division General Kenneth Howard **4,854**

Stopford's Brigade	1/Coldstream, 1/3rd Guards, 1 Coy 5/60th
Halkett's Brigade	1st, 2nd, 5th Line KGL, lst, 2nd, Light KGL

5th Division General John Oswald **6,725**

Hay's Brigade	3/1st, 1/9th, 1/38th, 1 Coy Brunswick Oels
Robinson's Brigade	1/4th, 2/47th, 2/59th, 1 Coy Brunswick Oels
Spry's Brigade	3rd Portuguese Line, 15th Portuguese Line, 8th Caçadores

Other Troops

Pack's Brigade	1st Portuguese Line, 16th Portuguese Line, 4th Caçadores
Bradford's Brigade	13th Portuguese Line, 24th Portuguese Line, 5th Caçadores

Silveira's Portuguese Division

Da Costa's Brigade	2nd Line, 14th Line
A. Campbell's Brigade	4th Line, 10th Line, 10th Caçadores

Cavalry **7,424**

R. Hill's Brigade	1st and 2nd Life Guards, Horse Guards
Ponsonby's Brigade	5th Dragoon Guards, 3rd and 4th Dragoons
G. Anson's Brigade	12th Light Dragoons, 16th Light Dragoons
Long's Brigade	13th Light Dragoons
V. Alten's Brigade	14th Light Dragoons, 1st Hussars KGL
Bock's Brigade	1st and 2nd Dragoons KGL
Fane's Brigade	3rd Dragoon Guards, 1st Dragoons
Grant's Brigade	10th, 15th and 18th Hussars

Artillery

3,000 British (**78 guns**)   300 Portuguese (**12 guns**)

Joseph's Army 66,000
Cavalry 11,300 Artillery 153 guns

Gazan's Army of the South 31,450

Leval's Division	4,850	Daricau's Division	5,900
Villatte's Division	5,850	P. Soult's Light Cavalry	1,650
Conroux's Division	6,550	Tilly's Dragoons	1,900
Maransin's Division	2,900	Digcon's Dragoons	1,850

D'Erlon's Army of the Centre 16,750		*Reille's Army of Portugal 14,750*	
D'Armagnac's Division	4,450	Sarrut's Division	4,800
Cassagne's Division	5,200	Lamartiniére's Division	6,700
Casalpalacios (Spanish)	2,150	Mermet's Light Cavalry	1,800
Guards	2,350	Boyer's Dragoons	1,450
Cavalry	2,600		

Touring Vitoria

The E5-E80 motorway runs through the centre of the battlefield, to the north of Vitoria. Leave the motorway at the Nanclares exit 10 kilometres west of the town and take the road west towards the village, crossing the river Zadorra. Turn right into Nanclares after 1 kilometre and continue straight on at the roundabout, turning left for Epinal in the centre of the village. Follow the road up the hill past the church and a quarry to reach the stone tower at the summit. Wellington would have stood near this spot as the battle unfolded. From here he would have been able to see General Hill's attack over the Puebla Heights to the south and Picton's advance through Mendoza to the north, while monitoring the Light Division's movements around to Tres Puentes; the French positions around Arinez Hill to the east were also under his watchful eye.

Return to the centre of the village and turn left for Villodas, crossing the river Zadorra. Turn right at the T-junction and head south under the railway and then continue straight on at the roundabouts, passing under the motorway. Turn right beyond the motorway bridge for Subijana de Alvana, heading west to the centre of the village. Park near the church and walk to the west side of the village where it is possible to see the French view of the Puebla Heights and the gap through which General Hill's men moved to attack Gazan's right flank. General Maransin's division deployed on the low ridge halfway up the slope but was eventually driven back to Zumelu to the east.

Return to the motorway and pass under the bridge; at the first roundabout go straight on, but immediately turn right on to a rough track. There is a parking area at the top of the slope and a path leads to the top of Arinez Hill. The hill has two summits; go left at the fork in the tracks to reach the top of the western hill. Joseph and his staff had extensive views of the battlefield from the crucifix at the top. Developments began at Puebla Heights to the south-west and then the attacks from the north around Tres Puentes and Mendoza began; the final straw was General Graham's attack behind the French right flank. After Joseph had weakened his position on Arinez Hill by sending out his reserves, Wellington made his final frontal attack from Nanclares.

Return to the road and turn right, heading north at the two roundabouts and past Villodas. The road crosses the river Zadorra after 2 kilometres at Mendoza bridge, which Picton's division captured. Colville's troops forded the river to the east and the battle raged to and

The hidden bridge at Tres Puentes.

Gamarra Mayor church.

fro in front of Margarita, the village to the east beyond the railway.

Turn immediately left beyond the river to visit Tres Puentes and the hidden bridge crossed by Kempt's brigade. Then turn back to Mendoza bridge and take a left turn towards Mendoza village. It is possible to park in front of the village and look back to see Picton's view of Arinez Hill. To the north is the pass that Dalhousie's division was delayed in.

Continue straight on, following the road as it turns to the right and passes Estarrona; join the E5-E80 motorway and head east. Exit at junction 352 for the N240 Bilbao road. After 2 kilometres take the slip road to the right and continue straight on at the roundabout into Durana. Longa's Spanish troops used their artillery to fire at any wagons using the road across the river Zadorra, effectively closing it to traffic.

Turn round in the centre of the village and return to the N240, turning south for Gamarra Mayor, and cross the motorway. General Stewart's men suffered heavily in the village and it took all afternoon to capture the village and the bridge. Continue straight on at the roundabout in front of the church and cross the river Zadorra. Take the first right on the far bank and head west. Turn right at the roundabout for Abetxuko (Abechuco) after 2 kilometres and recross the river, bearing left at the roundabout in the village and head north-west across the motorway.

Arangiz (Aranguiz), the village that Barru's troops held, was bypassed by Halkett's brigade so that it could advance south to Abetxuko. However, Sarrut's troops were holding the village and the British were unable to cross the river. The N622 dual cariageway now cuts through the centre of Arangiz village and it is necessary to cross the bridge to visit the main part of the village and the church.

Return across the N622 and turn left, heading north for Mendiguren, the first village attacked by General Graham's men, 2 kilometres to the north. After turning round (the village is a dead end) head south back towards the E5-E80 motorway. While Stewart's division pushed south along the road towards Abetxuko, General Oswald's division made a sweeping march over the hills to the left (east) to reach Gamarra Menor and Gamarra Major; Longa's Spanish troops joined Oswald's men and headed for Durana.

Return to the E5-E80 motorway to complete your tour of Vitoria.

Chapter 9

THE FRENCH ATTACKS
IN THE PYRENEES

FOLLOWING THE BATTLE OF VITORIA, Wellington advanced quickly to the Pyrenees and his men eventually halted at the beginning of July having marched over 650 kilometres in forty days since leaving Portugal. His army only numbered 60,000 men but he had to spread them along a 80 kilometre front between Fonterrabia on the coast and Pamplona. He split the area into two and gave command of the coastal sector to General Hill, while General Cole controlled the passes north of Pamplona. Wellington knew that Marshal Soult could strike at any point and he had made arrangements to station outposts in the mountain passes so that the majority of his men could rest in reserve. His plan was for the outposts to delay any French threat long enough for him to be able to deploy his troops to counter it.

Marshal Soult was not a man to sit back and wait, and on 25 July his first blow fell in General Cole's area. He had chosen to break through at two points. The three divisions of D'Erlon's corps would attack the pass at Maya while Clausel and Reille used their five divisions to bludgeon their way through the Roncesvalles pass. All three corps would then march south through Sorauren, where the two mountain roads converged, heading to Pamplona to lift the siege.

DEFENDING THE MAYA PASS

The Maya pass was in the 2nd Division's sector, 6 kilometres south of Urdax. Two roads climbed to the summit above Maya before dropping steeply down to Elonzo on the Spanish side of the mountain range. General Stewart had deployed two of his brigades, one covering each of the roads, while Cameron's brigade was deployed to the west, astride the main road between Bayonne and Pamplona. While the 1/71st Regiment and 1/92nd Regiment covered the road, the 1/50th Regiment held the summit between the two brigades. A battery of four Portuguese guns had also been deployed in front of the summit of the pass, covering the road.

General Maransin's division advanced up the Urdax road to attack Cameron's brigade.

Pringle's brigade was deployed 1.5 kilometres to the east, astride the secondary road connecting Espelette and Maya, but the rough terrain here made it difficult to plan a good defensive position. Pringle was a newcomer to Spain and had only been given command of his brigade two days earlier, leaving him no time to become acquainted with his subordinates or the tactical situation. His naivety immediately caused problems when he chose to deploy only a single company of eighty men as an outpost on a knoll known as Mount Gorospil (or Aretesque) overlooking the pass. The outpost was supposed to raise the alarm if the French approached, but the pass was notorious for its poor weather and mountain mists which could reduce visibility to a few metres in a very short space of time. The outpost would have to be extremely vigilant to make sure that the alarm was raised in time.

Pringle had also chosen to place just 400 men from four light companies in close reserve south of the knoll, while the 2/34th Regiment was on standby on the lower slopes of the mountain. The rest of the brigade, the 1/28th and 1/39th Regiments, were camped south of Maya, and although they were only 3 kilometres from the front line, they would have to march rapidly up the steep slope before they could join any fighting.

At first light on 25 July D'Erlon's 21,000 men struck camp and advanced up the mountain roads towards the 2nd Division's positions in the Maya pass. To the west Maransin's 6th Division advanced up the winding main road towards Cameron's brigade in the pass. Meanwhile, to the east D'Armagnac's 2nd Division followed by Abbé's 3rd Division climbed the mountain road from Espelette and marched along the ridgeline towards Pringle's outpost. General Stewart had only 6,000 men to face this onslaught.

Pringle's brigade was in the most danger, as his men faced odds of over five-to-one, and by mid-morning D'Armagnac's division was approaching his outpost on Mount Gorospil. The rugged terrain hid the French troops for a considerable time and when the picquets finally spotted the approaching columns, the sounds of firing warned Pringle that he had a battle on his hands. He immediately moved up his light companies to reinforce the hill-top position but he still had fewer than 500 men facing 7,000 Frenchmen.

Although Pringle quickly alerted the rest of his brigade, his faulty deployment was his downfall. D'Armagnac's columns quickly

General D'Armagnac's division advanced along the ridge to the right to attack Pringle's brigade.

overwhelmed the outpost on Mount Gorospil. Joseph Sherer was captured in the fighting:

> In less than two hours my picket and the light companies were heavily engaged with the enemy's advance, which was composed entirely of voltigeur companies. These fellows fought with ardour, but we disputed our ground with them handsomely, and caused them severe loss. The enemy's numbers now, however, increased every moment: they covered the country immediately in front of and around us. The contest now was very unequal. I saw two thirds of my picket destroyed.

By the time the 2/34th Regiment was approaching the summit of the pass, French troops were already holding it in force. Pringle now panicked and rather than taking up defensive positions to contain the

The battle of the Maya pass 25 July 1813.

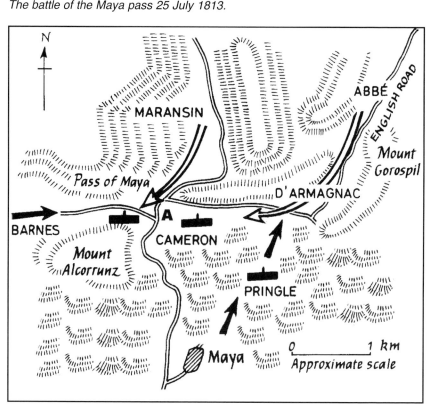

French until reinforcements arrived, he ordered his solitary battalion forward. Several French battalions lining the summit opened fire as soon as the exhausted men of the 2/34th came into range. The battalion was cut to pieces and fell back in disorder down the steep hillside. Pringle threw the 1/39th Regiment and then the 1/28th Regiment against the French hill-top position as soon as they arrived but they were unable to retake the summit of the pass.

Pringle had lost the pass and then squandered many lives trying to retake it, and he now proceeded to weaken the position astride the western road by moving troops east to engage D'Armagnac's flank. Even though Cameron objected, his experience was overruled by Pringle's seniority and the 1/50th advanced across the summit of the ridge only to be driven back in disarray by superior numbers. Five companies of the 1/92nd Regiment then moved forward and formed a support line across the plateau while the 1/50th Regiment rallied.

The 92nd Regiment's companies were virtually annihilated and they retired after suffering more than 300 casualties out of 400; their commander, Lieutenant-Colonel Cameron, was among the wounded. They had, however, stopped D'Armagnac's division from advancing along the plateau to attack Cameron's position. George Bell of the 34th Regiment later recorded how Cameron's men fought against tremendous odds to stop the French:

> It was death to go on against such a host, but it was the order, and on we went to destruction . . . The old half-hundred [50th] and 39th got a severe mauling. The 92nd were in line, pitching into the French like blazes and tossing them over. They stood there like a stone wall, overmatched by twenty to one. When they retired their dead bodies lay as a barrier to the advancing foe.

After several hours' fighting the French were obliged to reorganise after Cameron's brigade had fought them to a standstill. Despite still having overwhelming superiority, their sacrifice had made D'Erlon cautious and he ordered D'Armagnac to hold his position on the summit and wait for General Maransin's attack to develop against Cameron's brigade.

As the French regrouped, General Stewart returned to take over command and he ordered Pringle to call off any further attacks and take up defensive positions below the pass and stop D'Armagnac's division reaching Maya. Meanwhile, he also instructed Cameron to withdraw the men of his scattered brigade and deploy them around the summit of the pass where the Portuguese guns were covering the road.

General Maransin's division took a long time to climb the pass and he was unable to bring his full weight of numbers to bear owing to the rugged terrain. For the second time Cameron's depleted battalions had to fight off superior numbers while the noise of battle echoed around the smoke-covered slopes. The gun crews fired grapeshot and canister until the last moment and although they caused horrendous casualties among the advancing French battalions, they were unable to stop the onslaught. The horse teams were unable to reach the battery and for the first time in the peninsular campaign troops under Wellington's command had to abandon their guns (although Beresford had lost a gun at Albuera).

As the battered brigade fell back towards Elizondo, assistance finally arrived when Barnes's brigade approached from the west along Chemin des Anglais, having been sent by the 7th Division. The appearance of a fresh brigade behind the French flank unnerved Maransin and he was forced to redeploy to face the new threat. D'Erlon also wondered whether General Stewart was hoping to draw his men into a trap so they could be attacked in the flanks when it was dark. With evening approaching both D'Armagnac and Maransin were ordered to call off their attacks and regroup.

The French had taken the pass but it had cost over 2,000 men and the British were still blocking the two roads. However, the 2nd Division had lost over 1,300 men, a quarter of its strength, and the day's fighting had left it in a precarious position. General Hill arrived later that night and after surveying the battlefield and hearing Stewart's report was left in no doubt that the French could easily force the pass the following morning. The only option was to withdraw. As storm clouds drenched the hillside with rain, the British soldiers struck camp and marched south, leaving their dead behind to guard the pass.

Defending the Roncesvalles Pass

Marshal Soult's second attack on 25 July 1813 took place 25 kilometres to the east of Maya in the Roncesvalles pass. This pass was held by the 4th Division supported by the 2nd Division's third brigade, and General Sir Lowry Cole had been instructed 'to maintain the passes to the front of Roncesvalles to the utmost, but to disregard any wider turning movement to the allied right'.

The Roncesvalles pass is flanked by two parallel ridges that meet at the southern end of the horseshoe-shaped Carlos Valley (Val Carlos). In 1813 the main road ran along the eastern ridge, past Chateau Pignon to Leicar Atheca, before passing over the high point at over 830 metres, known as Altobiscar. On the morning of 25 July Clausel's corps was marching along the ridge with Vandermaesen's division leading and Taupin's division following. They were heading straight towards Lowry Cole's right wing. Meanwhile, Reille's corps was advancing along the narrow crest of Airola Ridge to the west, General Foy's division leading Maucune's and Lamartiniére's divisions. Soult had decided against sending troops up the valley, past the village of Val Carlos, suspecting that they would be vulnerable to artillery fire from the surrounding hills.

Lowry Cole had only 13,000 men and although they faced over 40,000 French troops they were in a strong position, blocking the only two roads passable through the mountains. The lack of roads in the area meant that Soult's troops had only eight small mountain guns for support while the British artillery had commanding fields of fire.

One of 2nd Division's brigades held the main road, and Brigadier Byng had posted his light companies on the knoll called Leicar Atheca to watch for troops approaching from the direction of St Jean Pied-de-Port. The

The view across Roncesvalles pass.

main force was deployed at the summit of the pass and the 1/3rd Regiment and the 1st Provisional Battalion (a number of companies from depleted battalions) were supported by Portuguese troops. The brigade's third battalion, the 1/57th Regiment, was deployed on the slopes below, in order to help Morillo's Spanish brigade cover the track through Val Carlos.

General Ross's British brigade covered the road to the west. The 1/20th Regiment had been deployed on the ridge as an outpost, while the 1/7th and the 1/23rd Regiments were positioned close by in support, out of sight on the reverse slopes. General Cole was also aware that Campbell's 2,000-strong Portuguese brigade was approaching from the west via the Alalosti pass.

At dawn on 25 July 1813 Soult's two corps set off along the two ridges towards the 4th Division. To the east Vandermaesen's division was soon brought to a halt by Byng's skirmishers and although the British were heavily outnumbered, the fire-fight lasted for over four hours. Clausel then allowed Vandermaesen time to reorganise for a second attack and for several hours there was a lull in the fighting while the French soldiers

The French troops advanced along two parallel ridges to get to the pass.

rearmed and deployed into columns. When a second attack was made in the afternoon the French finally drove the light companies back across the rocky slopes towards the rest of Byng's brigade at Altobiscar.

Meanwhile, Reille's three divisions were moving along the western ridge, passing the highest point at Laurigna before bearing down on Ross's brigade. The extensive column marched slowly forward along the narrow road and it was mid-afternoon before it engaged the British positions on the Linduz plateau. The ridge was narrow and the steep slopes made it impossible to deploy more than one battalion at a time and the 1/20th Regiment would have to withstand the full weight of Reille's corps on its own.

The French skirmishers swarming at the head of the column were soon engaging the thin line of redcoats and Colonel Ross's men returned fire as fast as they could. Dozens were killed and wounded but they stood fast until they ran out of ammunition. Although a French officer called on the 1/20th to surrender, Captain Tovey refused and ordered his company to

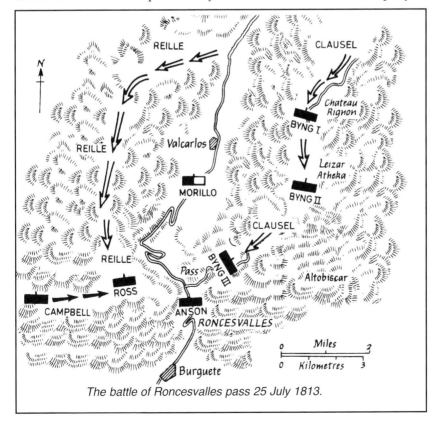

The battle of Roncesvalles pass 25 July 1813.

fix bayonets while the drummers prepared to sound the charge. They were heavily outnumbered but their heroic stand stopped the French for a short time; Ross's battalion lost 140 casualties in carrying it out.

As the 1/7th Regiment moved forward to take its place, Campbell's Portuguese brigade was approaching from the Atalosti pass to the west. To stop the French reaching the Mendichuri pass, outflanking Byng's position, The 1/57th Regiment and Morillo's brigade were ordered to withdraw from Val Carlos to take up positions on the summit of the ridge behind Byng's flank.

As both Reille's and Clausel's corps reorganised and prepared to drive the allies from the mountain passes, General Cole found that the weather was on his side. A thick mist descended, throwing the French into confusion.

The fog made it difficult for officers to keep in contact with their subordinates, who in turn had great difficulty in getting their bearings. With visibility restricted to a few metres, the attacks had to be called off to avoid a disaster and Soult was forced to admit defeat.

Casualties had been light, at about 200 French and 450 British, but General Cole was concerned that his men were holding an exposed position, and despite orders from Wellington to the contrary, his nerve wavered and he withdrew towards Pamplona.

The Battle of Sorauren, 28 July 1813

With darkness falling both General Stewart and General Cole came to the decision to abandon the passes and head south so they could join forces north of Pamplona. The mist and rain covered their retreat but morale plummeted as the two divisions trudged through the mountains. One soldier of the 28th later remembered the miserable night:

> Not a voice, not a sound was heard, save the slow step and casual murmur of the dejected soldiers, intermingled with the cries and groans of the wounded. In this state we kept moving the whole of this sad and sorrowful night amidst the mountains, the woods and the rain, the way being so deluged with mire that it was with difficulty we could wade through it. So entangled were we among carts, horses, mules, baggage and artillery broken down, together with artillery and other stores that lined the roads, that we could not extricate ourselves from these impediments.

As dawn broke on 26 July the French troops discovered that both passes had been evacuated during the night. The 4th Division continued to withdraw south along the Pamplona road, with Soult's two corps in close pursuit, and by the following morning had reached the village of Sorauren. General Cole knew he could not afford to withdraw any further and as his men took up positions along a steep ridge (later known as Cole's Ridge) to the south-east of the village, he was pleased to receive news that reinforcements were on their way.

Campbell's independent Portuguese brigade covered the division's left flank, deploying alongside a chapel overlooking Sorauren. Ross's brigade occupied the centre of the position while Anson's brigade held the summit of the ridge on the right flank, with Stubb's Portuguese brigade in close support. Spanish troops occupied the slopes to the east, overlooking the Arga valley, ready to stop the French turning the allied right. By nightfall Cole knew that his 18,000 men were in position and ready to face Marshal Soult's troops one more time.

A few hours later Marshal Soult's men approached Sorauren and he gave the order to occupy the ridge immediately north of Cole's position (later known as Clausel's Ridge) when it became obvious that the allies intended to stand and fight. Although General Clausel was anxious to attack before reinforcements reached Cole, Marshal Soult decided to wait for the rest of his troops to arrive. They took far longer than expected to reach Sorauren and it was nightfall before all his 50,000 men were in position on the sides of the steep valley opposite Cole.

Wellington did not learn of Cole's withdrawal from the Roncesvalles pass until the evening of the 26th. He rode south the following morning, accompanied by his military secretary, Major Fitzroy Somerset, to survey the 4th Division's new positions. As he sat on the bridge over the river Ulzama in Sorauren writing his orders to his Quartermaster-General, General Murray, he watched the French troops moving on to the ridge east of the village. Cole's withdrawal had brought Soult's army within two hours' march of Pamplona and major changes to the allied deployments had to be organised to stop the French reaching the city. As Somerset rode off with Wellington's orders, the allied commander was forced to gallop away on his trusty horse Copenhagen as French troops entered the village.

As Wellington rode up the steep hillside, Campbell's Portuguese troops spotted the unmistakable horseman approaching and before long their chant 'Douro! Douro! Douro!' echoed across the valley. The cheers continued as Copenhagen cantered along the 4th Division's line, lifting the men's spirits, and when he reached the summit of the ridge

Wellington rode along Cole's Ridge to the right to raise his troops' morale.

Wellington stopped to focus his telescope on Marshal Soult, who was watching the cheering soldiers from across the valley.

Captain Kincaid summed up how the men felt about their commander: 'We would rather see his long nose in the fight than a reinforcement of 10,000 men any day.' An unknown private was more down-to-earth, calling him 'that long-nosed bugger that licks the French'. Although Wellington's ride had provided the perfect antidote to the men's low morale after their difficult withdrawal from Roncesvalles, he later recalled the primary reason for his prominent ride: 'It will delay his attack to ascertain the cause of these cheers; that will give time for the 6th Division to arrive, and I shall beat him.'

Although Soult outnumbered the allies by nearly two-to-one, he had been unsettled by the reaction to Wellington's dramatic ride along Cole's Ridge and he was determined to allow his scouts time to reconnoitre the enemy positions properly before he finalised his plans. As the marshal took an unscheduled afternoon siesta, Clausel could not contain his frustration any longer and was seen 'leaning against an oak tree . . . beating his forehead with rage, muttering, "Who could go to sleep at such a moment?"'

As the hours passed, and Cole's men braced themselves for the imminent attack, the advantage was swinging in the allies' favour. Wellington was generally satisfied with Cole's deployment and the only change he made was to reinforce the Spanish brigade holding the slopes overlooking Zabaldica on his right flank with one of Anson's battalions, the 1/40th Regiment. Meanwhile, his plans to support Cole's position were being acted on and troops were already moving across the Pyrenees to reinforce the 4th Division. Two Spanish brigades, led by O'Donnell and Morillo, were moved to the San Cristobal Heights to cover the crossings over the river Ulzana at Villaba and Oricain to the south. General Picton had been ordered to march his 3rd Division south to Huarte to stop French troops crossing the river Arga behind Cole's right flank. General Pack had also been ordered to move his 6th Division, making sure that he avoided Drouet's corps. While one brigade marched south through the mountains to threaten Soult's flank at Sorauren, the rest of his men would block the road running parallel with the river Ulzana to support 4th Division's left flank.

Overnight a fierce thunderstorm drenched the hillsides and while the men huddled together to keep dry the British veterans remembered the stormy night before Salamanca and some took the bad weather to be a good omen. But as the sun rose on 28 July Wellington watched for movement across the valley, expecting the French to attack early. He was pleased to see redcoats moving along the Ulzana valley to the west; this meant that Pack's division was approaching and his left flank was secure.

Marshal Soult's plan was to engage both allied flanks in the hope that Wellington would reinforce them at the expense of weakening his centre. He would then make his main attack with three divisions, driving back Campbell's Portuguese brigade, so he could roll up the allied left flank. On the right Clausel's corps would send Conroux's division out of Sorauren village towards the Portuguese flank while Taupen's and Vandermaesen's divisions waited at a distance. Meanwhile, Reille had ordered Foy's division to move down the river Arga to try to outflank the allied position. Lamartiniére had been instructed to follow the Arga as far as Zabaldica so he could attack the allied right flank. Maucune's division was positioned at the highest point of Clausel Ridge, ready to attack Wellington's centre alongside Clausel's divisions.

Soult's first move was to threaten Wellington's left flank but as the men of Conroux's division advanced out of Sorauren and climbed the slopes towards Campbell's brigade, they came under fire from three sides. While the Portuguese troops fired from the upper slopes, one of Pack's brigades engaged the division's flank from the banks of the Ulzana. A concerned Conroux also spotted movement to his rear where a second of Pack's brigades was moving down the hillside towards Sorauren, after spending the night marching through the mountains. It was soon clear that his troops were in danger of being cut off, rather than threatening the allied flank. Heavy fighting continued late into the afternoon as the French and British troops tried to secure the village and one of the many casualties was the injured General Pack.

To the east, Foy's division had advanced down the Arga valley only to find that Picton's division was holding the slopes and rocky outcrops guarding the river crossings near Huarte, making an outflanking manoeuvre impossible. Meanwhile, Lamartiniére's division climbed the hillside above Zabaldica, heading towards the Spanish troops holding Wellington's right flank. The first advance was driven back by a round of steady volleys but the French rallied and a second attack drove the Spanish from the forward slopes. The elation of imminent victory quickly disappeared as they reached the crest of the hill (later known as Spanish Hill) only to find the 1/40th waiting for them in a two-deep line. Sergeant Lawrence remembered how effective the first volley was:

> Orders had been issued by our officers not to fire till we could do good work, but this soon came to pass, for the French quickly sallied up, and fired first, and we returned it. I never saw a single volley do so much execution in all my campaigning days, almost every man of their first two ranks falling, and then we instantly charged and chased them down the mountain, doing still further and more fearful havoc. When we had done, we returned to our old summit again, where the captain cheered and praised us for our gallantry.

It was an astonishing feat: 400 British infantry had driven back five times their number, and some of Wellington's staff cheered wildly as they watched the French infantry routed by the British charge. But Wellington himself stopped the celebrations, knowing that the 1/40th Regiment would have to face further attacks and he did not have reinforcements to spare to defend his right flank.

Two hours later Lamartiniére's men made a second attempt to seize Spanish Hill. Lawrence continues the story:

> Our likewise brave enemy tried again two hours later to shift us

but they were again sent down the hill. We were again praised by our commander, who said, 'I think they won't make a third attack in a hurry', but four hours had not passed before they were up again. Some of our men then seemed to despair but we reloaded and were then ready to meet them pouring another of our deadly volleys into their ranks and then going at them with our bayonets like enraged bulldogs.

Wellington had not had to reinforce his beleaguered flank and yet again Soult's men had failed to make him weaken his centre.

Shortly after noon Soult's main attack began as three divisions began marching down the slopes from Clausel's Ridge and up the opposite hillside towards the centre of Cole's division. Captain Thomas Browne of Wellington's staff was one of those impressed by the sight of over 20,000 troops advancing towards the allied lines:

These columns were very deep and moved steadily onwards in the most imposing masses I ever beheld. The enemy's grenadiers in their bear-skin caps with red feathers and blue frock coats appeared the most warlike body of troops possible. As they moved on they threw out their skirmishers, which were met by the British light troops, and thus the work of this bloody day began. I never remember to have witnessed so tremendous an onset.

Maucune's division reached the left of the allied line first and as it drew closer, Anson's brigade stood up and the 3/27th and 1/48th Regiments opened fire at short range. Several devastating volleys killed and wounded over 650 men in just a few minutes, routing the French columns. It was effectively the end of Maucune's division.

To the west Taupin's and Vandermaesen's divisions climbed the hill towards Campbell's brigade and in the fierce fighting that followed the Portuguese troops fell back, abandoning the chapel. Wellington, who was close by, realised that his flank was now in danger and he ordered Cole to move two of Anson's battalions down the hill to reinforce Ross's brigade and engage the French attack. The 3/27th and 1/48th quickly formed line and fired volley after volley into the flank of the dense columns, creating havoc, and one by one Vandermaesen's and Taupin's regiments turned and fled. Jac Weller watched as Anson's men defeated the two French divisions:

Never in the Peninsular War did two battalions accomplish so much so quickly. The 3/27th and 1/48th smashed each successive

Wellington directs his troops during the battle of Sorauren

enemy battalion, apparently by charging each after a short period
of fire. With remarkable tactical skill, Wellington contrived to gain
a two-to-one numerical advantage at each encounter, although he
was outnumbered in the general area by more than two to one.
The two battalions had defeated three divisions in turn but they had
suffered grievous losses: the 3/27th alone suffered over 300 casualties.

By mid-afternoon Soult's attack was over. He had lost around 4,000
men during the fighting on Cole's Ridge and his men were exhausted and
demoralised by their failure. More importantly, the allies still held the
road to Pamplona, but as Wellington later admitted to his Judge
Advocate, 'Why, at one time it was rather alarming, certainly, and it was
a close-run thing.' It had also cost his army over 2,600 casualties.

Both sides spent the 29th reorganising while their commanders
considered their next move. Wellington prepared for a second French
assault, and reinforced his position by moving additional artillery on to
Cole's Ridge to support the 4th Division. Meanwhile, Soult was planning
a new course of action, designed to outwit his enemy.

General Drouet's corps was about to engage General Hill's divisions at
Lizaso to the north-west, and Soult planned to disengage the two corps at
Sorauren so they could cut Wellington's army in two and then head west

towards San Sebastián. It was hazardous plan, fraught with danger. His army would have to march across Wellington's front and then head along the mountain roads while a rearguard kept the British at bay. On the night of 29 July Soult headed off to inform Drouet of the new plan, leaving his two corps commanders with orders to withdraw through Sorauren and head north-west. By dawn the next morning Clausel's corps was on its way, but as Taupin's and Vandermaesen's divisions marched along the Ulzama valley the British outposts raised the alarm and Wellington immediately ordered an attack.

Pack's replacement, General Pakenham, led three columns against Sorauren village and they were heavily engaged with Maucune's division for over two hours. The fighting blocked the obvious escape route and as Picton advanced north along Arga valley, in pursuit of Foy's and Lamartiniére's divisions, the 4th Division advanced on to Clausel's Ridge and hit them in the flank. Private William Wheeler later described how his brigade fell on the disorganised French columns:

> Fifty buglers were sounding the charge, and the drums were beating time to the music. A general rush was made by the whole brigade, accompanied by three British cheers. The concert was too powerful for the nerves of Monsieur and off they danced, the devil take the hindmost, down the hill to our right, the only way they had to escape. We followed them close to their heels and soon got them on a small level: they soon got huddled together like a flock of sheep.

The heavy fighting in Sorauren blocked Soult's escape route.

General Cole's men were outnumbered by two-to-one, and some French soldiers turned to fight in the hope of driving the British and Portuguese away. However, they were too few and too disorganised to put up a prolonged fight and the two divisions were scattered across the Spanish hills. Private Wheeler continues the story:

> This place was well studded with thick bushes of underwood, and here and there a cork tree. As we were galling them with a sharp fire, they summed up resolution to turn on us and threatened us with a taste of steel. Now the tug of war began. As they could only get away a few at a time many were the skulls fractured by the butts of firelocks. The enemy was soon thinned by some getting away and by their loss in killed and wounded, the remainder we made prisoners.

Drouet's three divisions, led by Abbé, D'Armagnac and Maransin, had driven Hill's three divisions back at Lizaso on the same day but their victory was to no avail. The French had fought their last battle in Spain and they had to withdraw to escape Wellington's troops as they pursued Soult's shattered army though the mountains. His preferred line of retreat, across the border to St Jean Pied-de-Port, had been cut, so they had to withdraw across rough mountain tracks to reach the Bidassoa valley. Fortunately for Soult, Wellington's men were equally exhausted by the short campaign and the majority rejoined their units to fight another day. However, over 12,000 Frenchmen had been killed, wounded or captured during the nine-day fight for the Pyrenees; many others deserted as morale plummeted in the face of defeat.

British Troops at Maya

Cameron's Brigade	1/50th, 1/71st, 1/92nd
Pringle's Brigade	1/28th, 2/34th, 1/39th, 2 Coys 5/60th
7th Division	1/6th, 1/82nd, Brunswick Oels

French Troops at Maya

Western Column	Maransin's Division
Eastern Column	D'Armagnac's Division, Abbé's Division

British Troops at Roncesvalles

Byng's Brigade	1/3rd, 1/57th, 1st Prov. Bttn (2/31st and 2/66th)
Ross's Brigade	1/7th, 1/20th, 1/23rd, 1 Coy Brunswick Oels
Campbell's Brigade	11th Portuguese Line, 23rd Portuguese Line, 7th Caçadores

French Troops at Roncesvalles

Western Column	Foy's Division, Maucune's Division, Lamartiniére's Division
Eastern Column	Vandermaesen's Division, Taupin's Division

Wellington's Army at Sorauren

3rd Division, General Picton, covering Huarte village

Brisbane's Brigade	1/45th, 5/60th (4 Coys), 74th, 1/88th
Colville's Brigade	1/5th, 2/83rd, 2/87th, 94th
Power's Portuguese Brigade	

4th Division, General Cole, along the ridge

Anson's Brigade	3/27th, 1/40th, 1/48th 2nd Prov. Batt. (2nd & 2/53rd)
Ross's Brigade	1/7th, 1/20th, 1/23rd, 1 Coy Brunswick Oels
Stubbs' Portuguese Brigade	

6th Division, General Pack, approaching from the south and west

Stirling's Brigade	1/42nd, 1/79th, 1/91st, 1 Coy 5/60th
Lambert's Brigade	1/11th, 1/32nd, 1/36th, 1/61st
Madden's Portuguese Brigade	

Soult's Army at Sourauren

Souraren Attack	Conroux's Division, Taupin's Division, Vandermaesen's Division
Zabaldica Attack	Maucune's Division, Lamartiniére's Division
Huarte Area	Foy's Division

VISITING THE PYRENEAN PASSES

The Maya and Roncesvalles passes and the battlefield of Sorauren are close to each other and an easy circuit joins the three together. However, the roads are steep and in places the hairpin bends are tortuous, and it is advisable to wait for good visibility to get the most out of your visit. The circuit starts at Pamplona on the Spanish side of the Pyrenees but could easily be started at St Jean Pied-de-Port on the French side of the mountains.

Sorauren Battlefield

Drive around Pamplona's northern bypass, turning on to the N121A at the north-east corner of the city. Head under the tunnel and go straight on at the roundabout at the far end, heading for Sorauren, 5 kilometres to the north. Turn off the village bypass and park in the large lay-by on the left before entering the centre of the old village.

Walk along the main road to the church and the rebuilt stone bridge over the river Ulzama (now the river Lanz) where Wellington sat to write his despatch before the battle. Go back to your car and cross the road. Walk between the houses just beyond the point where the mountain stream runs beneath the road. Climb the steep hill through the village, following the rough track on to the moorland beyond. The track climbs high above Sorauren, heading for the summit of Cole's Ridge. Although quarry waste has changed the shape of the lower slopes, it is easy to imagine the route that Wellington took as he cantered his horse along in front of his troops to the summit of Cole's Ridge to the right (south). Across the valley is Clausel's Ridge, a double ridge. The French deployed out of sight behind the lower ridge before emerging from cover to begin their attack. The slope down was steep and in full view of the allied guns but they marched on, sweating and cursing as they struggled up the slopes of Cole's Ridge.

The valley rises to the east and ends at the summit that Maucune advanced across to attack the allied right. To the west, above Sorauren, is the ridge that Pack's men climbed down to enter the battle for the village, outflanking Conroux's division as it scaled the slope you have just climbed to attack Wellington's left flank.

(Note: it is possible for cars to drive up to Sorauren's cemetery, at the highest point of the village, to obtain a distant view of the battlefield.)

Return to your car and retrace your route south past Orcain. Turn left at the roundabout, heading east through Arre, and take the left fork at the far end of the village. Leave by the slip road at the end of a cutting and turn left at the bottom on to the N135 and head north for Roncesvalles. Picton's division held the area behind the ridge immediately east of Huarte, stopping General Foy's division. Continue north along the N135 for 3 kilometres towards Zabaldica. Turn left just before Zabaldica's village sign into a large lay-by and picnic area, where the original bridge has been bypassed. Looking up it is possible to make out Spanish Hill, the wooded spur overlooking the river crossing, and it is clear what a difficult climb Lamartiniére's men faced to reach the Spanish position.

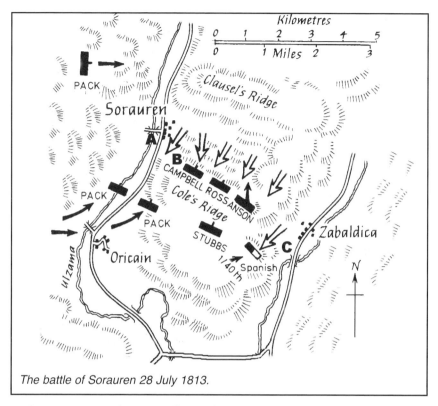

The battle of Sorauren 28 July 1813.

Continue on to the tiny village of Zabaldica, pausing in the small pull-in area to the right below the houses. Maucune's division crossed the crest of the ridge high above the village and the summit to the left is the highest point of Cole's Ridge.

Roncesvalles Pass

Head north-east along the N135 and Roncesvalles is 3 kilometres beyond Burguete. The village has a twelfth-century chapel and a large thirteenth-century Augustinian abbey. Continue driving up the steep mountainside to the summit of the pass, 2 kilometres to the north. Stop in the parking area to the right of the road alongside a small chapel. A memorial here remembers Roland, who led the Basque army when it overran Charlemagne's rearguard in 778.

To the north, the modern road now runs down the side of the Carlos valley, where Morillo held the centre of General Lowry Cole's position.

The bridge over the river Ulzama in Sorauren where Wellington wrote his orders.

Maucune's division had to negotiate this ridge to attack Wellington's right flank.

The original roads ran along the two ridges to the left and right. Clausel's corps used the right-hand ridge, driving the light companies from the pass of Leicar Atheca, 6 kilometres to the north-east. They fell back towards General Byng's position on the high plateau known as Altobiscar 3 kilometres to the east. There is a single track road up to Altobiscar and Leicar Atheca but it is an extremely precarious drive and the mountain mists can descend rapidly, just as they did in 1813.

Reille's corps advanced along the ridge to the west, driving the 1/20th back to the pass where the rest of Ross's brigade waited in support. The appearance of Campbell's Portuguese brigade over the crest to the west eventually stopped the French advance. It is possible to walk up the single track road for a short distance to get a better view of Roncesvalles Pass.

The Maya Pass

Drive down the steep road into the Carlos valley and head north along the N135 to St Jean Pied-de-Port, a walled town used as a French base during the Pyrenees attacks. Turn left for St Etienne-de-Baigorry and continue west for Elizondo, heading back up into the mountains. The road heads to the summit of the Maya pass, following the route of the original road used by Maransin's division. The 71st Regiment guarded the road until it was ordered to withdraw towards the summit of the pass, where the battery of Portuguese guns was deployed on the high ground to the right (west of the road).

Park your car at the summit, in the large turning area to the left, and cross the road to climb the footpath on to the lower slopes of Mount Alcorrunz. From here there are extensive views of Maransin's advance towards Stewart's position.

Return to your car and take the side road, heading west. This narrow road clings to the south (Spanish) side of the mountains and Maya village can be seen in the valley below. The road passes through a narrow cutting in the rock after 3 kilometres; stop in the parking area to the left where the pass opens out on to a small plateau. The original road came up behind the ridge to the right and D'Armagnac's troops had soon seized the high ground known as Mount Gorospil from Pringle's brigade. His reserves had to climb up the steep slopes from Maya and were so exhausted by the time they reached the plateau that they were quickly driven back. The 50th blocked the route to the west, stopping the French linking up with the second attack up the modern road.

Turn around and return to the main road at the summit of Maya pass. Either retrace your route north back into France or continue south into Spain to complete your tour.

Chapter 10

SECURING THE PYRENEES

THE SIEGE OF SAN SEBASTIÁN, JULY–AUGUST 1813

FOLLOWING THE BATTLE OF VITORIA, Wellington's army moved towards the French-held fortresses of San Sebastián and Pamplona. San Sebastián, a small coastal town with a harbour, stood on a narrow neck of land at the foot of a rocky headland called Monte Orgullo. The ancient La Mota castle stood on the summit of the hill and successive generations of military engineers had added fortifications and bastions to its defences, eventually building a wall around the town. The walls ran along the shore on the west and east sides, and the French, who had been in control of San Sebastián for five years by 1813, had added a series of earthworks, known as the Hornwork, across the neck of the isthmus. Now the 3,000-strong garrison was led by General Louis-Emanuel Rey, a resolute commander. He had sixty guns placed in strategic positions around the town walls and ships regularly brought supplies to the harbour.

Spanish troops had blockaded San Sebastián by 29 June 1813 and the siege began eight days later. Wellington was based nearby at Lesaca and

La Mota castle still looks down over San Sebastián.

Greater Breach

Lesser Breach

La Mota Castle

British attack

Portuguese attack

after studying the fortifications with his chief engineer, Colonel Richard Fletcher, came to the conclusion that General Thomas Graham should aim to breach the south-east corner of the fortress. Once the gap had been opened up, men could attack from two directions, with some moving along the isthmus, along the foot of the wall, while the rest waded across the river Urumea. The estuary was only fordable at low tide, however, and so this would affect the eventual timing of the attack.

Six batteries were set up on the high ground next to the convent of St Bartholomew, south of the town, and they started bombarding the Hornwork and the town's southern wall, giving support to the men digging the siege lines. As soon as redoubts had been built close to the Hornwork, two more batteries were brought forward, which started to batter the south-east corner of the walls. The engineers also supervised the digging of assembly trenches along the isthmus, so that the assault troops could get close to the walls. The work was difficult and dangerous and the French guns continued to fire at the British trenches. Colonel Sir Augustus Frazer's battery suffered heavy casualties in front of St Bartholomew's convent:

We were completely deluged with shot from the half-moon battery. Lieutenant Armstrong commanded the working party, who did their utmost to dig a hole for shelter from this incessant fire but to no purpose as the earth was battered down as soon as raised, and scarcely a man left unhurt. Those who escaped were assembled in the shelter of the walls, yet here was no safety as the shot flew through the windows and doors, and, rebounding off the walls, hurt many, while stones and mortar falling in every direction bruised some and blinded others.

Day after day the British gunners toiled in the hot sun firing their guns around the clock (each gun fired approximately three hundred rounds a day), chipping away at the widening gap. Many cannon-balls overshot their target and caused extensive damage among the narrow streets inside the walls.

By 22 July the breach was ready and many of the French guns had been silenced. Wellington had previously set the date of the assault for 24 July, but General Thomas Graham decided against attacking immediately, preferring to wait for twenty-four hours. Although the delay gave his men time to prepare, it also allowed the French to arrange some nasty surprises at the breaches.

When the tide was at its lowest, General Oswald's 5th Division (General Leith returned on 30 August but was wounded two days later) and Bradford's Portuguese brigade left the safety of their assault trenches around Santa Catharina and advanced north along the shoreline towards the breach. The garrison of the Hornwork fired at the troops as they moved along the narrow strip of land towards the breach, and casualties were increased when the town garrison threw missiles down on to the crowd of men below. The advance began to falter as they climbed the ruined wall, but when the Forlorn Hope discovered that there was a huge drop from the top of the breach into the street below, it came to a standstill. Men milled around helplessly on the rubble slope and many were killed trying to find a safe way down. Sergeant Douglas later recalled how the Royal Scots were driven back with heavy losses:

> Waiting for the tide to be sufficiently low to admit men to reach the breach, it was daylight 'ere we moved out of the trenches, and, having to keep close to the wall to be as clear of the sea as possible, beams of timber, shells, hand grenades and every missile that could annoy or destroy life were hurled from the ramparts on the heads of the men. Those who scrambled on to the breach found it was wide and sufficient enough at the bottom, but at the top, from thence to the street was at least twenty feet.

It was suicidal to go on and the officers recalled the survivors, forcing them to leave hundreds of dead and injured behind them; many of the wounded were later drowned when the tide rose.

On hearing the news that the attack had failed, Wellington rode to San Sebastián to investigate (which meant that he was not at his headquarters when Marshal Soult launched his attacks on the Pyrenean passes), and met a despondent General Graham assessing his losses. He also found to his dismay that his chief engineer Colonel Sir Richard Fletcher, the architect of the Lines of Torres Vedras, was among the dead. However, he was unable to concentrate his full attention on San Sebastián as the French were pushing large forces through the Pyrenees, so the siege was stepped down until the threat had passed.

After restoring order in the Pyrenees, Wellington was able to turn his attentions once more to San Sebastián and on 8 August gave the order to renew the siege with greater intensity; this time there would be two breaches. The French had spent the past three weeks repairing the existing breach, adding a second thick stone wall behind the gap. This meant that the British needed more siege guns, new battery positions and many more assembly trenches in front of the walls.

General Graham had also taken the decision to extend his siege lines across the river Urumea in order to extend the gap in the eastern wall. He could then send troops across the estuary, bypassing the problem of restricted access along the isthmus, and doubling the number of men who could reach the walls at the same time. After his infantry had cleared the fortified convent of San Francisco, his engineers moved in and digging began on the east bank. New batteries had to be sited in the Choffre Sandhills but the work was slow and many men were killed or injured by the French guns sited on San Sebastián's walls. The soft sand made it difficult to build revetments and tracks in the dunes and it took until 26 August to get all thirty guns into position. But once in place, they returned fire across the estuary, aiming at the temporary wall behind the old breach. Once this had been demolished, the gun crews concentrated on extending the gap and over the days that followed it had grown to more than 100 metres wide; a second smaller breach was also made. The walls could not endure the relentless bombardment. Following a reconnaissance of the breach on 29 August the decision was taken to prepare for an assault. The men would advance an hour before low tide on the 31st.

Tension mounted as the men gathered in their assembly trenches. The guns opened fire at dawn, and a cheer was raised when one lucky shot exploded a mine buried below the breach, sending a shower of rubble and dust into the air. The signal to advance was given a few minutes before 11am and the three Forlorn Hopes, formed from 750 volunteers from the 1st, 4th and Light Divisions, clambered out of their trenches and charged towards the breaches, followed by Oswald's 5th Division and Bradford's brigade.

The French had installed guns behind and to the sides of the breach and they fired round after round of grapeshot at Oswald's men. As the Forlorn Hopes scaled the breaches, men on top of the walls fired muskets and threw grenades into the crowd below. Once at the top of the rocky slopes, the assault parties again faced a steep climb down the rubble to get to the street below and many were killed or wounded as they shied away from the edge. The survivors fell back out of sight of the guns and were forced to crowd together in a ditch at the foot of the breach. Once more it looked as if the assault had failed. Sergeant John Douglas of the 3/1st Regiment was lucky to escape back to the ditch:

Lieutenant Macguire of the 4th Regiment leads the Forlorn Hope to the breach.

Contrary to my expectations, I gained the trench which was a dreadful sight. It was literally filled with the dead and dying. 'Twas lamentable to see the poor fellows here. One was making the best of his way minus an arm; another his face so disfigured as to leave no trace of the features of a human being; others creeping along with the leg dangling to a piece of skin; and, worse than all, some endeavouring to keep in the bowels.

Casualties were horrendous. Most of the Forlorn Hope volunteers had been killed or injured on the rubble-strewn slopes, while Robinson's Brigade had lost over seven hundred men, many of them cut off in the narrow streets with no means of escape.

Forty minutes after the 5th Division's attack started, Bradford's Portuguese brigade began wading across the estuary in two columns, moving quickly through the surf even though the water was thigh-deep in places. The French gunners had a clear sight of their targets, firing roundshot and canister into the water below, but the Portuguese forged on. One column clambered up the shore and climbed up to the smaller breach, only to find, once again, that the drop at the far side was too high and it was impossible to enter the town. The men were forced to take cover where they could find it around the breach, forming a small

Portuguese troops waded across the estuary to reach the Lesser Breach.

foothold in the shadow of the walls. The second column, seeing the problem at the smaller breach, veered south towards the main breach in the hope of finding a way into the town, but their arrival only added to the congestion in the crowded ditch.

By midday both attacks had ground to a halt and it looked as if the assault was going to fail for a second time with heavy losses. But General Graham was determined that his men would not die in vain when they were so close to entering the fortress and he ordered his artillery commander, Colonel Dickson, to fire at the curtain wall to the south of the main breach. For twenty minutes the gun crews fired over the heads of the British and Portuguese troops huddled in the breaches, causing casualties among the French defending the walls, and then the moment Graham had been hoping for came. A shell hit a large magazine, killing or stunning many of the garrison as large quantities of gunpowder exploded.

All along the siege lines gun crews heard the order to cease fire as the infantry renewed their assault. This time there was no holding Graham's men back and they were soon clambering through the breach and scrambling into the debris-strewn streets beyond. The Royal Scots led the way and Graham later commended the men of the 1st Regiment for their bravery: 'I conceive our ultimate success depended on the repeated attacks made by the Royal Scots.' This time the French garrison was unable to hold back the British and Portuguese troops, who were soon swarming through the town at the start of a rampage of violence. There was fierce hand-to-hand fighting in the narrow streets as soldier and civilian alike were put to the sword. The French soldiers knew they were fighting a losing battle and many fell back towards the foot of Monte Orgullo; Lieutenant Gethin, a volunteer of the 1/11th, captured a Colour in the confusion.

General Rey led the survivors up the steep ramp into the castle and locked the gates behind them, leaving the people of San Sebastián to the mercy of the allied soldiers. Few escaped as yet again Wellington's men went on the rampage, plundering the city below while their officers tried in vain to regain control. Subaltern Gleig was one of many disgusted by the behaviour of his comrades:

> As soon as the fighting began to wax faint, the horrors of plunder and rapine succeeded. Fortunately there were few females in the place, but of the fate of the few which were there I cannot even now think without a shudder. The houses were everywhere ransacked, the furniture wantonly broken, the churches profaned, the images dashed to pieces; wine and spirit cellars were broken open, and the troops, heated already with angry passions, became absolutely mad by intoxication. All good order and discipline were abandoned.

Fires began burning out of control as strong winds fanned the flames and large parts of the town were burnt to the ground. Later on Wellington would learn that London was disgusted by the behaviour of the British troops and the damage they had done to the city, while the Spanish government in Madrid was quick to accuse him of deliberately encouraging the destruction so that it could not be used to trade with France in the near future.

As the allied officers slowly regained control of their men, their commanders were studying the next problem: La Mota castle itself, where 1,300 determined Frenchmen awaited their fate. General Rey was hoping that Marshal Soult would try to relieve his men but the latter's attempts to cross the river Bidassoa were stopped at San Marcial (San Martzial) and Vera (Bera) on 1 September. Four days later Rey opened surrender

The entrance courtyard to La Mota castle where General Rey surrendered his command.

negotiations, knowing full well that his limited stocks of water and food would not last long.

A plan was drawn up to keep intact General Rey's reputation as a resolute commander, and on 8 September over sixty guns and mortars opened fire on the citadel to give observers the impression that he was still determined to put up a fight. When the guns fell silent two hours later the commander met senior British officers in the entrance courtyard and officially handed over control of the castle. The garrison marched out of the gates with full honours soon afterwards. After a prolonged and costly siege, San Sebastián had fallen. It had cost the lives of over 850 allied soldiers while another 1,500 had been injured in and around the city walls.

The British Troops at the Storming of San Sebastián

Hay's Brigade   3/1st, 1/9th, 1/38th

Robinson's Brigade 1/4th, 2/47th, 2/59th, 2 Coys Brunswick Oels

Spry's Brigade   3rd Portuguese Line, 15th Portuguese Line,
                    8th Caçadores Volunteers

1st Division: Guards Brigades and the KGL Brigade

4th Division: Ross's and Anson's Brigades, Stubbs's Portuguese

Light Division: Kempt's Brigade, Skerrett's Brigade, Portuguese Caçadores

Bradford's Brigade 13th Portuguese Line, 24th Portuguese Line, 5th Caçadores

VISITING SAN SEBASTIÁN

Exit the E70 following signs for San Sebastián town centre. The town has grown tremendously in the last 200 years. The river Urumea has been channelled and the area around the Old Quarter (Parte Vieja) is built up. Follow the road along the west bank of the river heading for the old town and park around the Breach Market (La Bretxa Market), which was built on the site of the main breach. The foundations of the southern wall were unearthed when the nearby underground car park was built and they

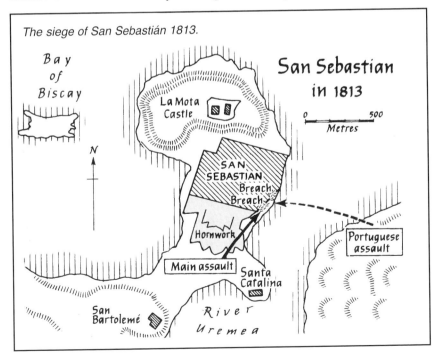

The siege of San Sebastián 1813.

The narrow streets of San Sebastián.

have been preserved.

Walk through the narrow streets of the old town to the church, which still bears scars from the siege. Although much of the old town was destroyed by fire during the siege, many of the ground-floor façades are original. The only street to survive the fire is now called 31 de Agosto and a walk through the old town is poignant as you imagine Wellington's soldiers racing through the dark, narrow alleyways. On every anniversary of the battle the people fill the streets and hold a silent candlelit vigil.

A walkway leads up Monte Orgullo and the steep cobbled ramp to the entrance courtyard where General Rey finally surrendered La Mota

San Sebastián's battered memorial.

Remembering the unknown soldiers who died in the Napoleonic Wars and the Carlist Wars.

castle. Despite the heavy bombardment the castle grounds and fortifications are worth exploring. There are extensive views of the city from the castle at the summit, where a museum has displays covering the history of the city, including the siege.

The Cementerio de los Ingleses (English Cemetery) is on the seaward side of Monte Orgullo but the graves date from the Carlist War in 1836—37. Nearby are several monuments, including one to the engineers and another to the men who died in the siege.

Walk back down the hill and return to your car. Drive across the river and along the seafront, heading east (alternatively walk along the promenade). Turn left at the end of the beach and stop in the parking area. As you look back along the sea front towards the castle, you are seeing San Sebastián as the Portuguese did when they waded across the estuary.

THE FRENCH ATTACK ACROSS THE BIDASSOA, 31 AUGUST 1813

While the final preparations for the assault on San Sebastián were taking place, Marshal Soult was making a desperate attempt to relieve the fortress. Spies reported that French troops were preparing to cross the river Bidassoa (Bidasoa) in strength and advance along the coast to threaten the siege lines, forcing Wellington to divide his attention between the border and the siege. Although he knew the attack was imminent, the question was where and when would it take place?

The river Bidassoa ran through a 8-kilometre-long gorge between Vera and Irun near the coast, making it almost impossible to move large numbers of troops forward. The village of Vera stood in the centre of a valley, where its small bridge was vulnerable to attack and it was possible to ford the river. General Alten's Light Division was covering the area around the village. Downstream of Irun the river flowed into a wide valley as it neared the coast. Although the bridge at Behobie had been destroyed, the shallows and the mudflats were fordable in several places.

Wellington believed that Soult would attack along the coast road: this was the easiest place to cross the river and opened the way to the shortest route to San Sebastián. He knew it would be impossible to defend the river bank but a high ridge, topped by the San Marcial Hermitage, overlooked the road. The steep slopes ran down to the south bank of the river, forming an ideal defensive position with extensive views of the French deployment area. Wellington had seen to it that his men had fortified the crest of the ridge and he had chosen to defend it with General Manuel Freire's Corps of three Spanish divisions. General Howard's 1st Division and Aylmer's independent brigade were deployed in support to steady them.

Soult's options were severely limited by the rugged terrain, but he planned to attack the allied line at the two points Wellington expected, hoping to split the allied reserves. D'Erlon's two divisions were given the task of holding the river bank and mountain passes south of Vera on Soult's left flank, and it was expected that they would have little to do. Reille's three divisions would attack on Soult's right flank, making the expected crossing at Irun near the coast. Although this would force the Spanish and British troops to defend the coast road, it would not be the main attack. Reille's orders were simply to pin the Spanish troops on San Marcial Hill.

Soult had assembled Clausel's four divisions near Sare and they had orders to capture the ford at Vera. Once across the Bidassoa, they would turn north and advance parallel to the river, scattering the Light Division as they advanced towards the coast road. The two-pronged assault would pin General Howard's 1st Division to the coast road, and as soon as this had been cut off and destroyed, the two French Corps could advance side-by-side towards San Sebastián. It was an ambitious plan that depended on good coordination between the French commanders to make Wellington think that the coastal attack was the main threat.

On 31 August nature intervened in Soult's plans for an early attack. The Bidassoa valley was wrapped in a thick morning mist at daybreak and Reille was forced to wait two hours for it to clear. To add to his frustration, the attack then began badly when his three divisions moved down to the river bank before the artillery was in position, and they were already wading across the river when their guns opened fire. This left the French infantry in an exposed situation as the Spanish guns fired freely at the dense columns below. The lack of French artillery fire also allowed General Freire to order his own divisions forward down the slopes of San Marcial Ridge, ready to engage the French. The skirmishers took their toll on the French as they formed up on the riverbank, and then fell back to allow the lines of Spanish infantry to open fire. Volley after volley slammed into the ragged French columns and before long all three of Reille's divisions were falling back in disarray towards the river, having suffered heavy losses.

While the troops rallied, the artillery eventually began firing across the valley but the range was too great to disrupt General Freire's thin lines of infantry. A second French attack at midday had more success, driving some of the Spanish back up the slopes towards the Hermitage. When General Villatte's division eventually reached the summit, General Freire asked Wellington for reinforcements, only to be politely refused: 'If I send you the English troops you ask for, they will win the battle; but as the French are already in retreat, you may as well win it for yourselves.' Wellington really wanted the Spanish to win the day for themselves. His assessment that the French were beaten was correct and Villatte's exhausted men were quickly driven off the hilltop by counter-attacks.

Soult wanted Reille to make a third attack but his divisional commanders were unable to rally their men; over 2,500 Frenchmen lay dead or wounded on the slopes of San Marcial Ridge and the survivors were exhausted by their exertions. The Spanish army had come a long way since the start of the peninsular campaign; although they had lost over 1,650 men during the battle they had held the important ridge without needing to call on British help.

Some 12 kilometres upstream at Vera, Clausel's four divisions had started to cross the river Bidassoa at dawn but they were moving slowly through the mist. As one division moved to engage the Light Division the rest marched west, heading towards the coast in an attempt to cut off the allied troops fighting on San Marcial Ridge.

Although the advance was going to plan, Clausel was distracted by the news that his own flank was under attack. As soon as news of the French attacks reached the British headquarters, Wellington ordered General Dalhousie to advance down the Maya pass and attack the town of Urdax (Urdazubi) behind Clausel's flank. When Clausel learnt that Reille's attack had failed and his flank was being threatened, he was forced to reconsider his situation. He was already in a difficult position and the further his divisions advanced along the west bank of the Bidassoa, the easier it would be for Wellington to cut them off from their supply lines. Yet again nature intervened as heavy rain drenched the area and the Bidassoa began to flood. Clausel had no choice but to order a withdrawal.

Three of the divisions forded the river around Vera, but

Captain Cadoux's bridge.

Vandermaesen's division, numbering 10,000 men, found that their ford was impassable. As the floodwaters rose, scouts searched desperately for a crossing and eventually came across a narrow stone bridge near Vera. Unfortunately for the French, it was held by an outpost of the 95th Rifle Regiment under Captain Cadoux. Despite the overwhelming odds, Cadoux refused to withdraw and for two hours the small outpost held Vandermaesen's skirmishers at bay. The French division was trapped in a vulnerable position but General Skerrett, the Light Division's acting commander, refused to send assistance. Cadoux was eventually killed and the survivors of the outpost were forced to abandon the bridge, leaving behind 17 dead. Another 46 had been wounded. The French division then withdrew across the narrow bridge to the safety of the north bank, having lost over 230 casualties, including General Vandermaesen who had been killed. Skerrett's inaction had allowed an entire division to escape and he was sent home in September; he subsequently left the army.

In all, some 1,300 Frenchmen had been killed or injured trying to cross the Bidossoa and the allies had suffered 850 casualties keeping them at bay. Soult's offensive had failed. Although he couldn't have known it, this was the last time that French troops would try to enter Spain: Pamplona's garrison would have to fend for itself.

THE ALLIES CROSS THE BIDASSOA, 7 OCTOBER 1813

By the end of August the situation south of the Pyrenees had swung completely in the allies' favour. San Sebastián had fallen, Pamplona was ready to surrender and Soult had failed to cross the river Bidassoa. As Wellington made his plans to attack, Marshal Soult was forced on to the defensive. Wellington wanted to cross the river and advance deep into France, clearing the Pyrenees before the winter rains turned the roads into impassable quagmires. Throughout September the French dug in and waited north of the river while spies reported on their movements. Meanwhile, to the south the allies reorganised and rested as they prepared to attack.

Soult was determined to hold the river line and his men had spent the autumn building fortifications along the north bank. Although he had 47,000 men organised into three corps, they were spread thinly along the 25-kilometre front stretching between the coast and the Maya pass. Soult based his defensive scheme on several assumptions made as a result of his own experiences along the river. He believed that the allies could not cross the estuary owing to rising river levels brought on by the autumn

Troops wade across the river estuary.

rains. Reille's corps had been reduced to two divisions and only numbered 10,500 men. They were divided between Maucune's and Boyer's divisions and were dug in along the north bank of the river, covering the Behobie fords.

The centre was the strongest part of the French line, but here Clausel had chosen not to hold the river line itself, but deployed his 20,000 men on a high rugged ridge called the La Grande Rhune. The ridge stretched east of Vera towards Sare and four divisions led by D'Armagnac, Abbé, Conroux and Taupin had been hard at work fortifying the ridges and valleys. Soult's left flank was covered by D'Erlon's corps, with orders to stop the allies breaking out of the Pyrenean passes. Maransin, Daricau and Villatte had posted over 22,000 men around Urdax and St-Etienne-de-Baigorry.

However, Soult's belief that Wellington's infantry could not cross the estuary was incorrect. Local shrimpers who knew the river well had told Wellington that they could lead his men across at very low tide, and the next one was due on 7 October. They were also confident that men would be able to wade across at Behobie. This was just what the British commander wanted to hear. An attack near the coast would allow him to hit the French lines where they were weakest.

Wellington's plan involved sending two divisions across the river simultaneously. General Andrew Hay's 5th Division would wade across the estuary, while General Howard's 1st Division would cross at the

Bidassoa River estuary today.

Behobie fords. Aylmer's British brigade and Wilson's Portuguese brigade would follow in support. Freire's Spanish divisions and Bradford's Portuguese brigade had been given the task of holding the Bidassoa Gorge to the south, linking the coastal attack with the Light Division's attack at Vera. General Alten's men had the hardest task, for after crossing the Bidassoa they had to capture the La Grande Rhune. The plan was that they would advance up two parallel ridges to the summit, rolling up the French line, while two Spanish divisions carried out feint attacks. To the south General Stewart's 2nd Division probed the French positions in the pass at Maya, while General Clinton's 6th Division watched the road through the mountains at Roncesvalles.

The attack began at Fuenterrabia during the early hours of 7 October when the 5th Division waded out into the Bidassoa estuary in three columns, the shrimpers leading the way. There were a few tense moments as the seawater rose up to the men's waists but their fears subsided as they clambered out on to dry land on the far bank, having crossed the 500-metre wide expanse of water. The shrimpers had been right, and Wellington had a division on the north bank before it was light. What's more, it was right under the French noses, where they least expected an attack.

Mist again covered the valley and this time it worked in the allies' favour, assisted by good planning and excellent discipline among the assault troops. As soon as the skies cleared the allied guns fired across the river, targeting the French fortifications, while General Hay's men climbed the slopes and moved in to the attack. Even though Reille's men outnumbered General Hay's men by two-to-one, many of the Frenchmen were raw recruits while the veteran British and Portuguese soldiers had experience and determination on their side. Disciplined volleys followed by charges cleared each redoubt in turn and the two French divisions were soon falling back; only a few troops stood their ground.

Upstream General Howard's men waded across the mist-shrouded mudflats at the Behobie fords and yet again the French were unaware of the crossing until it was too late. They had no inkling that they were under attack until the lines of redcoats emerged from the fog as they climbed the slopes. Ensign Gronow's account describes how the two Guards brigades advanced towards Reille's positions:

We commenced the passage of the Bidassoa about five in the morning and in a short time infantry, cavalry and artillery found

French fortifications

Light Division

The Light Division climbed this ridge to reach the French fortifications.

themselves upon French ground. The stream at the point we forded was nearly 4 feet deep, and had Soult been aware of what we were about, we should have found the passage of the river a very arduous undertaking. Three miles above we discovered the French army and 'ere long found ourselves under fire. The sensation of being made a target is at first not particularly pleasant, but 'in a trice, the ear becomes less nice'.

By mid-morning Reille's two divisions had been driven out of their coastal fortifications and were falling back towards Bordegain hoping to escape across the river Nivelle ahead of the British. Soult had ridden all the way from Ainhoa when he first heard that the British were attacking his coastal sector but he arrived too late to prevent the withdrawal becoming a rout. He was dismayed to find that his men had surrendered an important defensive position and his flank had been turned; worse still, they were now in full retreat, abandoning their guns and a large part of their baggage. As Wellington ordered his men to secure their bridgehead, he was pleased to hear that the two divisions had only lost 400 men; the French had lost around 450.

In Clausel's sector Taupin's and Conroux's divisions had built an impressive range of earthworks and redoubts on La Grande Rhune Ridge, north-east of Vera. At dawn the Light Division waded across the Bidassoa and overran the French outposts on the north bank of the river before starting the long, steep climb. General Longa and General Giron ordered their men to deploy while their artillery fired at the French across the valley. Although it looked like they were preparing to advance it was only a hoax. And it worked. While Clausel's men waited for the Spanish to attack, the riflemen of the Light Division were already advancing up the ridges towards the crest of the La Grande Rhune.

On the left flank Colborne's brigade scrambled up a 3-kilometre-long narrow spur called La Bayonnette, heading towards Star Redoubt, the first of the many fortifications they would encounter. As the 52nd Regiment approached it deployed into line and charged the redoubt, clearing the way for the rest of the brigade. Rifleman Leach of the 95th Regiment later described what lay ahead of Colborne's men:

> During these operations Colonel Colbourne's brigade had a much more arduous task to perform. His opponents could not be taken in flank and he was therefore obliged to advance straight against them, entrenched up to their chins. A succession of redoubts were carried by the bayonet, and those who defended them were either shot, bayoneted or driven off the mountain.

As General Longa's Spanish troops engaged the French outposts in the valley between the ridges, Kempt's brigade followed a narrow track on to a large hill called the Hog's Back. The brigade advanced on a broad front, the six battalions deployed in lines across the summit as they clambered up the rocky slopes. Rifleman Leach's account explains how the light infantry overran one of the French redoubts:

> The business commenced by our third battalion climbing a small mountain on which the French had a small advanced post. After a sharp conflict the enemy was driven from it and General Kempt's brigade was enabled, by a movement to its right and a flank fire on their engagement, to dislodge a strong force of French infantry,

who must have been made prisoners if they had not bolted like smoked foxes from their earths.

Heavy fighting continued throughout the morning as the two brigades cleared the line of earthworks but by midday they had reached the crest and linked up. With their advantage lost, the French began to withdraw, leaving the hill in allied hands. As Alten's men reorganised and took stock of their position, Ensign Gronow of the Guards was impressed by the state of their bivouacs:

> The French army, not long after we began to return their fire, was in full retreat, and after a little fighting, in which our division met with some loss, we took possession of the camp of Soult's army. We found the soldiers' huts very comfortable: they were built of branches of trees and furze and formed streets which had names placarded up, such as Rue de Paris and Rue de Versailles.

Even though they had outnumbered the British troops in places, Marshal Soult's conscripts' low morale and lack of experience had led to their defeat. They had lost a strong defensive position despite a relatively low casualty figure of just 1,700 troops; the allied casualties had been even lower, numbering only 1,200 killed and wounded. As the French troops fell back disheartened, Wellington's troops were in high spirits: after five years of campaigning across Portugal and Spain they were ready to advance deep into France.

Wellington's Army along the Bidassoa

Left Flank on the Coast

1st Division General Howard 6,900

Maitland's Brigade	1/1st Guards, 3/1st Guards, 1 Coy 5/60th
Stopford's Brigade	1st Coldstreams, 1st Scots, 1 Coy 5/60th
Hinuber's Brigade	1st, 2nd, and 5th Line KGL, 1st and 2nd Light Bttns KGL

5th Division General Hay (acting) 4,550

Robinson's Brigade	3/1st, 1/9th, 1/38th, 1 Coy Brunswick Oels
Greville's Brigade	1/4th, 2/47th, 4th Prov. Bttn, 1 Coy Brunswick Oels
De Regoa's Portuguese Brigade	Wilson's Portuguese Brigade
Aylmer's Independent Brigade	Bradford's Portuguese Brigade

Centre around Vera

Light Division General C. Alten **4,950**

Kempt's Brigade	1/43rd, 1/95th, 3/95th, 1st Caçadores
Colborne's Brigade	1/52nd, 2/95th, 3rd Caçadores, 20th Portuguese

Spanish Divisions General Freire

Longa's (2,600)   Giron's (7,850)

Right Flank along the river Bidassoa to Elixondo

2nd Division General Stewart **8,450**

Byng's Brigade	1/50th, 1/71st, 1/92nd, 1 Coy 5/60th
Walker's Brigade	1/3rd, 1/57th, 1st Prov. Bttn, 1 Coy 5/60th
Pringle's Brigade	1/28th, 2/34th, 1/39th, 1 Coy 5/60th
Ashworth's Portuguese Brigade	

6th Division General Colville **6,700**

Pack's Brigade	1/42nd, 1/79th, 1/91st, 1 Coy 5/60th
Lambert's Brigade	1/11th, 1/32nd, 1/36th, 1/61st
Douglas's Portuguese Brigade	

Soult's Army along the Bidassoa

Reille's Corps on the Coast
Maucune's Division 4,000
Boyer's Division 6,500

Clausel's Corps in the Centre
D'Armagnac's Division 4,400
Abbé's Division 6,050
Conroux's Division 4,950
Taupin's Division 4,750
Villatte's Division 8,000

D'Erlon's Corps in the Passes
Foy's Division 4,650
Maransin's Division 5,550
Daricau's Division 4,100

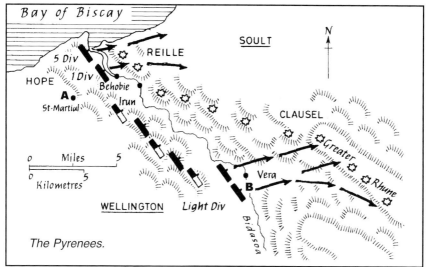

Bay of Biscay

SOULT

N

5 Div
REILLE

HOPE   1 Div
Behobie
A
Irun
St-Martial
CLAUSEL

Miles   5
0

Vera
B

Kilometres
0   5

WELLINGTON   Light Div

Greater

Rhune

Bidassoa

The Pyrenees.

TOURING THE BIDASSOA RIVER

Exit the E70 motorway at the Behobie turning, on the Spanish side of the border crossing. Turn left at the roundabout after 300 metres, following signs for Mendipe. Drive through the industrial estate, heading straight on at the first roundabout and turning left at the second. Follow the narrow lane alongside the motorway, turning sharp left (a U-turn) in front of the cemetery. Drive up the steep hill and stop in the parking area near the top. Walk along the pathway to the church, which was built to commemorate the defeat of a French invasion in 1522. There are extensive views of the river Bidassoa from the terrace in front of the church. While shrimpers led General Hay's 5th Division across the estuary at Hondarribia (known as Fuenterrabia in 1813), the 1st Division crossed at the Behobie fords where the river widens out around a series of islands. Retrace your route back down the hill to the motorway and drive underneath it, following the N121 for Bera (Vera de Bidassoa).

The road winds through a narrow gorge and steep rocky slopes drop down to the river. A new road is in the process of being built through the valley but it is still possible to see why neither Wellington nor Soult wanted to attack in this area.

Vera is 8 kilometres upstream. Go into the village and drive through the centre, turning right at the roundabout at the south end. After crossing the Nivelle by the modern bridge, turn immediately right and

5th Division

French fortification

1st Division

While the 5th Division waded across the mouth of the estuary, the 1st Division crossed at the Behobie fords.

The Rifle Brigade's memorial.

park near the narrow, stone bridge after 400 metres. Vandermaesen's division had waded across the river but rising floodwaters made it impossible for them to return the same way and this was the only bridge in the area. Captain Cadoux's small outpost held the French at bay for two hours, until it was clear that reinforcements were not going to arrive. There is a memorial to these brave riflemen on the centre of the bridge.

Return across the river and turn left at the roundabout back into the centre of Vera. In the centre of the village turn right along the D406, signposted for Sare, to visit the river Nivelle. Head east for 10 kilometres, crossing the frontier and continue straight on to Sare. La Grande Rhune is to the north of the road and the Light Division had to climb up the steep ridges to reach the summit.

Chapter 11

THE ADVANCE TO BAYONNE

THE BATTLE OF THE NIVELLE, 10 NOVEMBER 1813

ONCE WELLINGTON'S ARMY had crossed the river Bidassoa, Marshal Soult was forced to abandon the Pyrenees and withdraw his army towards the fortress of Bayonne. He was determined to make the most of the rolling terrain south of the town and had decided to hold a line west of the Nivelle river, fortifying a series of hills between St Jean-de-Luz on the coast and the town of Urdax 30 kilometres to the east.

Wellington's army spent October reorganising on the north bank of the Bidassoa, while the French built redoubts and waited for the next blow to fall. Yet again Soult had to spread his divisions thinly to try to guard against all possible attacks, but 63,000 men were just not enough to cover the whole area in strength. He believed that the main British attack would be made along the coast road, on the direct route to Bayonne, and to counter this General Reille's four divisions had built a line of fortifications along the south bank of the river Nivelle. The rest of the line was held by only five divisions and Clausel's corps had dug in along La Petite Rhune, a low ridge running parallel to the La Grande Rhune, between Ascain and Sare. D'Erlon's corps held another low ridge overlooking the villages of Amotz and Ainhoa on the east bank of the river Nivelle.

La Grande Rhune viewed from the north.

The starving French garrison in Pamplona finally surrendered at the end of October, releasing the two Spanish divisions that had been surrounding the city, and Wellington could now turn his full attention to the French fortifications along the Nivelle. As he studied Soult's positions from the La Grande Rhune, he was fully aware that his hand was not as strong as he might have liked: some 22,000 of his 82,000 troops – more than a quarter – were new Spanish recruits who had never before been in battle – a factor that had caused problems in earlier battles.

As Wellington made his plans General Colborne passed comment on the difficulties faced by his men, only to hear his commander's assessment of the strategic situation:

> Ah, Colborne, with your local knowledge only, you are perfectly right. It appears difficult, but the enemy have not men to man the works and lines they occupy. They dare not concentrate a sufficient body to resist the attacks I shall make upon them. I can pour a greater force on certain points than they can concentrate to resist me.

It was an accurate assessment of precisely the problem that Soult was trying to overcome.

After studying the area and listening to reports from spies, Wellington decided to make feint attacks against both of Soult's flanks, forcing Reille and D'Erlon to man all their fortifications and deploy their reserves. Meanwhile, the main attack would be made against Clausel's position in the centre. Once La Petite Rhune had been taken, his right flank could advance along the east bank of the Nivelle, joining a general advance north-west towards the coast. If the plan worked, a large part of Soult's army would be driven back towards Bayonne, and the line of retreat of Reille's corps cut off.

General Sir John Hope (Graham was sick with eye trouble) took the command between the coast and Serres, leading 19,000 men; they faced approximately 23,000 French troops led by General Reille. The plan was for Howard's 1st Division and Hay's 5th Division to feint an attack towards the river Nivelle, while Freire's two Spanish divisions deployed in front of Fort Nassau and the fortifications covering Ascain village, threatening the French line at Serres.

General Beresford, commanding the centre of Wellington's line, had the difficult task of breaking through Clausel's corps. To this end he had 36,000 men grouped into the 3rd, 4th, 7th and Light Divisions and two

Skirmishing in front of the French redoubts along the river Nivelle.

Spanish divisions, all supported by twenty-four guns. General Alten's Light Division was ordered to take a line of redoubts on the summit of La Petite Rhune facing Beresford's left flank, thus driving the French towards the village of St Pée-sur-Nivelle and its two narrow bridges over the river Nivelle. General Le Cor's 7th Division held his centre, and was tasked with taking the village of Sare and then advancing towards the bridge at Amotz, where it would link up with Hill's men on the far bank. The 3rd Division had to advance along the west bank of the Nivelle towards Amotz and General Colville had to coordinate his attack with General Clinton's 6th Division across the river.

General Hill held Wellington's right flank and had been given the task of seizing a series of redoubts covering the ridge north of Ainhoa that was held by D'Erlon's corps. He had 26,000 men and 9 guns organised into the 2nd and 6th Divisions, and they were supported by Morillo's Spanish division and Hamilton's Portuguese brigade.

The attack was planned for 10 November. As dawn broke across the hills south of Bayonne, Wellington watched and waited with General Beresford on the crest on La Grande Rhune for the Light Division's attack to begin. Although the lower slopes were passable, the rocky spurs became impassable towards the top and on the eastern side; the only way

French fortifications

Light Division

The Light Division advanced up this valley to reach the summit of La Petite Rhune.

to reach the top was from the west. The allied plan was to use stealth to cover as much ground as possible under cover of darkness and the riflemen clambered down the slopes during the night, assembling at the bottom of La Petite Rhune before dawn.

Guns on Mount Atchubia signalled the start of the assault as General Alten's men advanced up the valley between the Grande and Petite Rhunes. The first redoubt covering the road was attacked by the 43rd and 95th Regiments before the garrison had time to react and Rifleman Harry Smith later described how his comrades overran the French position: 'Nor did we ever meet a check, but carried the enemy's works by one fell swoop of irresistible victory.' Kempt's and Colborne's brigades then advanced across the steep gorse-covered slopes towards the top of the pass, moving across the front of the French redoubts on the summit of the ridge. General Taupin's men watched the lines of men picking their way up the hillside, knowing that they could not attack them without giving up their earthworks. Once at the top Kempt's brigade headed east and attacked King Louis XIV Fort, before advancing along the summit. General Maransin and General Conroux were powerless to stop their men falling back in front of the Light Division and after only two hours of fighting the final redoubt at the eastern end of the ridge, known as the Donjon, had fallen.

Meanwhile, Colborne's brigade had crept on to the adjacent plateau and the 52nd and 95th Regiments captured a large star-shaped redoubt before the garrison had raised the alarm. The rest of the French began falling back, fearing that they were in danger of being cut off, and before long Colborne's men had seized the whole plateau. The first stage of Wellington's plan was complete; General Alten's men had taken the key position in the centre of the French line, and casualties had been light. The main attack could now begin and thousands of allied troops moved forward to sweep Soult's men before them.

Five allied divisions moved forward side-by-side along the banks of the river Nivelle, driving a defeated army before them. The village of Sare quickly fell to the 4th Division and General Cole's men advanced on to La Petite Rhune beyond. The 7th Division advanced to the east of the village, and pushed General Maransin's division from the slopes overlooking the village of Amotz. The 3rd Division advanced along the west bank of the river Nivelle and Campbell's brigade also cleared La Sare redoubt. Joseph Donaldson of the 94th later gave an account of his regiment's advance on to La Petite Rhune:

> The enemy having been driven from the redoubts in front of Sare, we advanced to the attack of the enemy's main position on the heights behind it, on which a line of strong redoubts was formed with abattis in front. Colonel Lloyd, having pushed his horse

The 4th Division drove Maransin's division from this ridge.

forward before the regiment, advanced cheering with the most undaunted bravery, but before he reached the summit he received a mortal wound in the breast, and was only saved from falling off his horse by some of the men springing forward to his assistance. When this was perceived by the regiment, regardless of everything, they broke through all obstacles, and driving the enemy from their position, they charged through their burning huts without mercy.

The 74th Regiment cleared the village of Amotz before seizing the nearby bridge with the help of the 1/45th and the 94th. Although Colonel Lloyd later died of his wounds, his stirring courage had inspired his men to advance at all costs, effectively cutting the French army into two.

To the east of the river, General Hill ordered his two divisions forward to the ridge between Amotz and Ainhoa. The men of General Henry Clinton's 6th Division advanced along the east bank of the river Nive, coordinating their attack with the 3rd Division on the opposite bank, while General William Stewart's 2nd Division advanced north from Ainhoa. Walker's brigade led the attack towards the redoubts north of the village, driving General Abbé's men back from the crest of the ridge.

Soult tried to counter Hill's attack by ordering General Foy to cross the river Nive at Bidarray to the east before moving south towards Maya. This manoeuvre threatened General Hill's exposed right flank but the opportunity to wreak havoc across the British lines of communication was lost when three Spanish battalions stoutly stood their ground; the

The Amotz gap.

French withdrew after seizing a few transport wagons. Soult failed to reinforce the raid and Foy was eventually forced to withdraw to Cambo and recross the river Nive before his own escape route was cut. This venture was the only highlight during an otherwise disastrous day for the French.

By early afternoon the centre of Marshal Soult's line had been broken by General Beresford's attack, and his army was in full retreat, falling back across the Nivelle at St Pée. Inglis's brigade led the 7th Division's advance, capturing several fortifications on the rear slopes of La Petite Rhune, including Herastaguia Redoubt, but the Light Division's advance stalled in front of Signal Redoubt. The 52nd Regiment attacked twice, losing many men to volley fire, and for a while it appeared as if the French line would hold. The brigade commander, Colonel John Colborne, decided to try to trick the redoubt commander and went forward under a flag of truce to parley. He knew that the French were terrified of being captured by Spanish troops because of their reputation for mistreating prisoners, and he shouted out: 'See you are surrounded on every side. There are Spaniards to your left. You had better surrender at once.' The ruse worked and the commander surrendered, handing over his sword to Colborne with the words 'There, Monsieur, is a sword that has ever done its duty.'

On the coast, Reille took the bait offered by General Hope's feint attack and 23,000 Frenchmen languished near the coast while the rest of Soult's army fell back in disarray. Wellington's men had driven the French from the fortified line of hills south of the river for the loss of less than 2,500 men; in contrast, over 4,300 Frenchmen had been killed, wounded or captured. The historian Napier neatly summed up the victory: 'The plains of France were to be the prize of battle, and the half-famished soldiers, in their fury, were breaking through the iron barrier erected by Soult as if it were a screen of reeds.'

Although Wellington had originally planned to allow Beresford to pursue Clausel's corps north-west towards the coast, cutting off Reille's corps, his men first needed to reorganise on the far side of the river, and it would take time before the 6th Division could advance beyond the bridge at Amotz. The light was beginning to fail and following Soult towards Bayonne in darkness was a dangerous proposition. To Wellington's frustration, the French had to be allowed to withdraw unmolested behind the barrier of fortifications surrounding the city and across the river Nive. He later expressed his disappointment to his brother: 'I did not do as much as I had wished; if there had been more daylight and less mud, I should have given Soult a terrible squeeze. As it is, they are more frightened than hurt.'

Visiting the Battlefield of the Nivelle

Enter Sare along the D406 from the west. (If appropriate, this can be a continuation of the tour along the Bidassoa river.) The 4th and 7th Divisions cleared the line of redoubts held by General Maransin's troops on the low ridge to the north of the village. The centre of Sare has changed little over the past two hundred years and the large church tower stands tall over the market place.

Head west along the D4 to Ascain, a distance of 8 kilometres, and the road climbs to the Col d'Ignace. La Grande Rhune is the high rocky ridge to the left (south) of the road, while La Petite Rhune rises to the right (north). Beyond the summit the road drops steeply to Ascain. General Taupin's men were holding a series of redoubts on the ridge to the north. Once General Alten's men had cleared a large redoubt at the foot of the pass, they advanced rapidly up the slopes astride the road. Having cleared the summit at the head of the pass, they then spread out on to the crest of the ridge, outflanking the French redoubts. There is a track to the right halfway down the pass, and it is possible to walk up it to see the French view of the Light Division's attack.

Continue into Ascain and turn right at the end of the village, on the far side of the Nivelle, taking the D918 for St Pée-sur-Nivelle. Stop in the centre of the village, near the church, and walk down to the river to visit the original stone bridge that Clausel's corps had to cross after losing the summit of La Petite Rhune, the ridge to the south. There would have been a huge mass of men and wagons trying to squeeze across this narrow crossing, and Wellington was frustrated by his inability to get his army to take advantage of the confusion to trap the French.

Continue to the east end of St Pee and turn right across the Nivelle on to the D3, heading south through Amotz. There is a gap in the range of hills at Amotz and the bridge there was an important crossing point, linking the two attacks on either side of the river. Picton's 3rd Division advanced along the west bank while General Clinton's 6th Division moved up the east bank to squeeze the French out of the pass.

Turn left about a kilometre south of the village on to the N121 and cross the river Nivelle. D'Erlon's corps held the low ridge of hills to the left (north) of the road and was attacked by General Hill's two divisions.

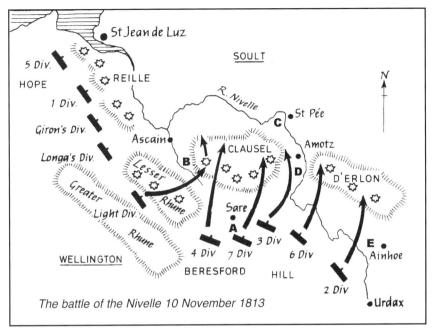

The battle of the Nivelle 10 November 1813

Continue 2 kilometres east, turning left on to the D305. General William Stewart's 2nd Division advanced up the slope to the left of the road to attack General Abbé's redoubts. Turn left after 3 kilometres, at the entrance to Ainhoa village, and head north along the D20, heading for Cambo-les-Bains to visit the river Nive.

THE BATTLE OF THE RIVER NIVE, 9–12 DECEMBER 1813

After losing his line along the Nivelle river, Marshal Soult withdrew his army, now numbering 63,000 men, north towards Bayonne, a strongly fortified town which had served as a major supply depot for the French army throughout the Peninsular War. The ancient citadel on the north bank overlooked the large Vauban fortress south of the river, while new earthworks had been dug around the city. The citizens had also been fiercely loyal to Napoleon thoughout his campaigns and for once the French soldiers were made welcome.

While part of Soult's army deployed in the fortifications south of Bayonne, the rest crossed the river Nive at Cambo-les-Bains and Ustaritz and deployed along the riverbank where they could threaten Wellington's flank as he advanced towards the city. Any advance against

General Hill's troops attacked this ridge.

Bayonne was hampered by the terrain and Wellington's movements were further restricted by the sea to the west and the river Nive to the east. Soult's troops could watch and wait in their entrenchments while the British infantry had to contend with a labyrinth of walls, streams and woods as they advanced across the rolling hills. The winter weather had also turned the fields in front of Bayonne into a muddy wasteland.

Wellington planned to approach Bayonne from two directions, attacking the flanks of the French army. Rather than confront Soult head on, the British commander wanted to threaten his lines of communication. He now had over 8,000 cavalry, over ten times the number under Soult's command, but there were few opportunities for them in the rough terrain south of the city. If he could get them across the river Ardour to the east of Bayonne and into the open countryside beyond, the town would be isolated.

Wellington's plan called for two divisions to move north along the coast road, threatening the French positions around Anglet. In the centre, the Light Division would hold a line of outposts on the hills around Arcangues, connecting the two flanks of the army. The rest of the army would cross the river Nive, south-east of the city, and capture the hills on the far bank, as the start of an outflanking move designed to cross the river Ardour. It was an ambitious plan and Wellington knew that he would have to advance quickly because his army would be separated by the river Nive at a time when the winter weather could cause it to flood.

Marshal Soult had deployed five divisions south of Bayonne and they were well dug in. His remaining four divisions were holding the east bank of the river Nive, where they could threaten Wellington's flank as he approached Bayonne. D'Erlon's corps held a strong position on the heights overlooking Villefranque, south-east of the city, while

D'Armagnac's division covered the crossing at Ustaritz and Foy's division held the bridge at Cambo.

As the allied troops prepared to move against the city, Wellington was forced to reconsider his situation when Spanish troops under his command began to rebel. The authorities had failed to pay many of them, while the logistics chain frequently broke down, leaving the men starving and with no means to buy food. As troops began to plunder villages, taking out their frustration on the local population, the British commander was forced to order the majority of his Spanish troops back across the Pyrenees. Although the order reduced Wellington's army to 64,000 troops, and cost him his superiority in numbers, he knew that the French population could easily turn against his men, and he did not want to have to contend with guerrilla bands as the French had had to in the peninsula. He summed up the situation in November 1813:

> If I could now bring forward 20,000 good Spaniards, paid and fed, I should have Bayonne. If I could bring forward 40,000, I do not know where I should stop. Now I have both the 20,000 and the 40,000 at my command, but I cannot venture to bring forward any for want of means of paying and supporting them. Without pay and food, they must plunder; and if they plunder, they will ruin us all.

Morillo's division would continue to serve alongside the British and Portuguese soldiers but only after the Spanish commander had been lectured on how his men must behave once they had crossed the border: 'I did not lose thousands of men to bring the army under my command into the French territory, in order that the soldiers might plunder and ill-treat the French peasantry, in positive disobedience of my orders.'

General Hill's troops began offensive operations on 16 November and drove General Foy's outposts from the west bank of the Nive in front of Cambo, but then the weather closed in. Heavy rains turned the roads into quagmires, soaked the men's powder and turned the river Nive into a raging torrent. Engineers were unable to launch their pontoon bridges into the floodwaters at Ustaritz in General Beresford's sector, while the fords in Hill's sector became impassable. The only advantage for the allies was that the French outposts had to withdraw before they were cut off. It was the start of a prolonged period of bad weather and while the allied troops searched for shelter, Wellington contemplated the risks involved in the forthcoming operation. For the next three weeks the rain poured down as the two armies huddled miserably beneath their tents on either side of the flooded river.

The skies eventually cleared at the beginning of December, and as the floodwaters receded the allied troops made their final preparations for the attack. The advance on Bayonne began on 9 December when 15,000 men advanced from St Jean-de-Luz astride the coastal road towards Bayonne. General Hope's 1st Division led with Hay's 5th Division following, alongside Aylmer's, Bradford's and Campbell's independent brigades. After crossing the river Tanque where it cut through a deep valley, the British troops advanced on to the heights beyond, forcing the French outposts back to their earthworks around Anglet. By nightfall the 1st Division had established a line of picquets on the slopes overlooking the village, but Reille's position was never in danger. General Hope decided that the 1st Division was capable of holding Anglet on its own and the 5th Division was ordered to withdraw 5 kilometres to the south and camp for the night; the independent brigades were allowed to return to St Jean de Luc. As the advance went to plan on the left flank, the Light Division moved forward in Wellington's centre on to the heights overlooking Arcangues village, maintaining contact between the two wings of his army.

The main attack was to take place along the river Nive. More than 13,000 men under General Hill's command were roused from their billets in front of Cambo while it was still dark and moved down to the river bank. At dawn the sight of a beacon burning brightly against the grey sky signalled that the battle was about to commence. To the south, Morillo's Spanish division crossed the river at Itzatza (Itxassou) and climbed the slopes towards General Paris's troops holding Mount Ursouia. This was only a feint attack but it was enough to stop the French moving north to threaten the crossing at Cambo.

In the centre, General Hill's 2nd Division and General Le Cor's Portuguese division headed down to the river bank north and south of Cambo, and officers shepherded their companies as the men queued up to cross at three fords. General Foy had posted a strong guard around the bridge in the centre of the village but the floodwaters meant that he had not been able to maintain outposts at the fords. As the British and Portuguese troops waded into the chest-deep torrent they held their powder and muskets above the freezing water. General Foy's infantry maintained a heavy fire from the far bank but the two divisions quickly deployed on the far bank and returned fire before charging. The village of

Cambo and its bridge were soon in allied hands, and as cavalry and artillery poured across the bridge the French began to withdraw. The daring crossing had been a total success and Wellington was able to order an advance north along the river bank.

Wellington's main attack was in the centre around the village of Ustaritz, which sat high on a ridge overlooking the wide, open river valley. General D'Armagnac had been unable to establish a strong defensive line on the east bank and the allied guns posted on the heights kept the French at bay while the engineers launched their pontoon bridge. General Beresford ordered Picton's 3rd and Clinton's 6th Divisions across and they fanned out on the far bank, driving the French before them. The experienced British soldiers advanced rapidly against the green French troops and by the time Cole's 4th and Walker's 7th Divisions had crossed, over 26,000 men were on the far bank.

The three French divisions were powerless to stop Hill and Beresford and by nightfall their two footholds had expanded to form a single 8-kilometre-wide bridgehead on the east bank of the river Nive. Marshal Soult chose to abandon Mount Ursuoia and withdraw from the high ground overlooking the British positions so he could concentrate his

Ustaritz overlooks the river Nive where the 3rd and 6th Divisions crossed a pontoon bridge.

troops around Villefranque. Although he had lost this battle, Soult was determined to win the campaign. The withdrawal north towards Bayonne was seen by many as a sign of defeat but as Wellington's troops settled down for the night, the French divisions were on the move once more.

The French commander believed that Wellington had made a mistake in moving so many troops to the east bank of the Nive and he was determined to make him pay for it. As rain fell across Bayonne over 25,000 troops left their camp fires burning and marched into the city. Five divisions moved through the dark streets and deployed south of the city ready to attack in a bold move to strike back at Wellington's weakened left and centre. Soult wanted to attack quickly before the British commander could move his troops back to the west bank of the Nive.

Despite the appalling weather some 50,000 French troops were in position before dawn on 10 December and ready to attack. Reille's corps was waiting to advance down the coast road towards Hope's position around Anglet while Clausel's corps faced the Light Division. D'Erlon's corps was poised to advance down the west bank of the river Nive, cutting the British army in two. Wellington, however, was unimpressed by the marshal's plan and confidently stated that he 'has lost his numerical advantage by extending himself in this manner and I intend to attack him in the false position he has adopted'.

General Reille's corps led the attack down the coast road towards the 1st Division and soon drove the Guards picquets from Anglet, forcing General Hope's men to fall back in confusion across the river Tanque, where they made a stand alongside Campbell's and Bradford's Portuguese brigades. Although French dragoons overran the 1st Portuguese Line, another more solid line was soon formed and Reille's men were stopped in front of Chateau Barrouillet, the home of the Mayor of Biarritz.

Undeterred, Reille ordered the rest of his corps forward. While General Villatte's division reinforced the attack down the coast road, General Foy advanced inland through the village of Pacho and forded the upper reaches of the river Tanque to outflank General Hope's precarious position. As soon as this manoeuvre was spotted by British outposts, Wellington was notified and he ordered General Hay to move his 5th Division forward to counter the move. Lord Aylmer's brigade arrived just as the French were about to attack the 1st Division's flank and Wellington galloped up to the 85th to offer them encouragement: 'You must keep your ground, my lads. Charge! Charge!' The two lines of redcoats did exactly what was asked of them, opening fire as the French infantry closed in and charged. The 85th stopped Foy's attack in its tracks, giving the 1st Division time to reorganise and prepare for the next onslaught. This was, however, the high point of the French assault: Reille had lost the advantage. General Hope was able to cover the south bank of the river Tanque and turn his right flank at an angle to face Foy's attack. Time after time the three French divisions tried to break the British but the line repeatedly triumphed over the column and after several hours' fighting Reille gave the order to withdraw.

While the 1st Division was fighting for its life, the Light Division faced the full weight of Clausel's corps. The picquets fell back in front of the three French divisions, abandoning the high ground around Bassussarry, as General Alten checked the deployment of his troops around Arcangues, 3 kilometres to the south. He had chosen a strong position and the French found marshy ground blocking the way forward in many areas. It would have been suicidal to push columns forward on the flanks and Clausel ordered them to wait until the Arcangues ridge had been taken.

The 43rd Regiment was deployed around Arcangues church and stood directly in the path of the French onslaught. Alten's riflemen took cover where they could, some using the churchyard wall and the headstones for cover. Others broke into the church and lined the galleries inside, smashing the windows to get a better shot at the French. Clausel needed to deploy his gun batteries as close as he could to the 43rd to give his men the advantage they needed but as soon as the gun teams appeared on the ridge around Arcangues chateau, the riflemen opened fire. They were some 400 metres away, at extreme range for riflemen, but dozens of French artillerymen and horses were shot down as they tried to take aim, firing roundshot at the church. It was an unequal fight but the Goliath of the duel was eventually forced to retire and Clausel's horse teams withdrew to a safe distance, leaving twelve guns abandoned on the ridge.

By the afternoon of 10 December, Soult's ambitious plan was in tatters but General D'Erlon was ordered to make a final attempt to drive a wedge between the two wings of Wellington's army. D'Armagnac's division was ordered forward and advanced along the west bank of the Nive, aiming to outflank the riflemen holding Arcangues. Again the outcome was the same. The outposts abandoned their positions near Villefranque and fell back towards Ustaritz. The French columns found

General Le Cor's 7th Division waiting for them on the far side of a stream and once again the lines of British and Portuguese troops stopped the columns in their tracks.

As the light began to fail, Soult had to admit that his plan had failed; his men were exhausted after their long night march followed by a frustrating battle in the heavy rain. The situation did not improve during the night for the French when three battalions of German troops deserted after hearing news that Napoleon had been defeated at Leipzig in October.

Meanwhile, Wellington spent the night deploying his army, shifting troops from west to east to counter further attacks. The 4th and 7th Divisions moved to St Jean de Luc to help General Hope defend the coast road. The 3rd and 6th Divisions had also crossed the river Nive to reinforce the Light Division and took up positions north of Ustaritz.

By the morning of 11 December the advantage had shifted in the allies' favour. Wellington knew where the French were likely to attack and French morale had plummeted after two days of fighting and marching without success. Even so, Soult was determined to continue and Reille renewed the attack across the river Tanque, taking the 1st Division by surprise. The British picquets were overrun and as they fell back General

Arcangues church.

Riflemen lined the galleries inside the church to shoot at the French guns.

Hope found himself on the defensive. His battalions suffered over 400 casualties in the opening attack and they fell back over 1.5 kilometres, losing the village of Barrouillet and its chateau. Despite the initial shock, the 1st Division rallied on the 4th and 7th Divisions, bringing Reille's attack to a halt.

Soult's options were running out and a final attack on 12 December ended in failure when Reille's exhausted corps fell back from the river Tanque to the fortifications around Anglet. Casualties had been high – around 1,500 on each side – but the French commander refused to accept defeat. Although his attempt to break the allied positions on the west bank of the river Nive had failed, Marshal Soult had not given up trying to drive Wellington's troops back from the outskirts of Bayonne. He would once again move his men through Bayonne and shift his attack to the opposite flank.

British Troops Engaged during the Battles of the Nive

1st Division General Sir John Hope

Howard's Brigade	1/1st Guards, 3/1st Guards, 1 Coy 5/60th
Stopford's Brigade	1/Coldstream, 1/3rd Guards, 1 Coy 5/60th
Hinuber's Brigade	1st, 2nd and 5th Line KGL
Halkett's Brigade	1st and 2nd Light Battalions KGL

2nd Division General Stewart

Barnes's Brigade	1/50th, 1/71st, 1/92nd
Byng's Brigade	1/3rd, 1/57th, 1st Prov. Bttn (1/31st and 2/66th)
Pringle's Brigade	1/28th, 2/34th, 1/39th
Ashworth's Brigade	6th Portuguese Line, 18th Portuguese Line, 8th Caçadores

5th Division General Leith

Greville's Brigade	3/1st, 1/9th, 1/38th
Robinson's Brigade	1/4th, 2/47th, 2/59th, 2/84th
Lord Aylmer's Brigade	2/62nd, 76th, 85th
De Regod's Brigade	3rd Portuguese Line, 15th Portuguese Line, 8th Caçadores

6th Division General Clinton

Pack's Brigade	1/42nd, 1/79th, 1/91st, 1 Coy 5/60th
Lambert's Brigade	1/11th, 1/32nd, 1/36th, 1/61st
Douglas's Brigade	8th Portuguese Line, 12th Portuguese Line, 9th Caçadores

Light Division General Alten

Kempt's Brigade	1/43rd, 1/95th, 3/95th
Colborne's Brigade	1/52nd, 2/95th
Portuguese Brigade	1st and 3rd Caçadores, 17th Line

Portuguese Division General Le Cor

Da Costa's Brigade	2nd Line, 14th Line
Buchan's Brigade	4th Line, 10th Line, 4th Caçadores
Bradford's Brigade	13th Portuguese Line, 24th Portuguese Line, 5th Caçadores
Campbell's Brigade	1st Portuguese Line, 16th Portuguese Line, 4th Caçadores

Cavalry 13th Light Dragoons, 14th Light Dragoons, 16th Light Dragoons

TOURING THE BATTLEFIELD OF THE NIVE

Heading north from Ainhoa, turn right on to the D918 after 4 kilometres and bypass Espelette. Cross the D932 before Cambo-les-Bains and drive straight on into the centre of the village to visit the river. Cambo sits on a ridge, high over the river, and beyond the far bank is a wide, flat, open flood plain. It was impossible to dig strong fortifications so close to the British guns and when the time came, it was easy for Wellington's men to establish a foothold on the far bank, and hold it until the engineers had built their pontoon bridge. General Hill was then able to order his troops to head north so they could meet General Beresford's men at Ustaritz.

Return to the D932 and turn right, heading north for Ustaritz. Turn right into the village after 5 kilometres. Again the village stands on a high ridge overlooking the river and the far bank is an open flood plain, expanding to nearly a kilometre wide in places. It was impossible to build strong defences on the east bank once the British had driven the French outposts from the heights. Once General Beresford's men had waded across they linked up with Hill's bridgehead to the south.

The bridge in Ustaritz is in the centre of the village, to the north of the church. Cross over to the east bank and turn left on to the D137 for Villefranque beyond the railway. Turn left in the centre of the village to visit the parking area overlooking the river. Wellington's troops held the west bank at Villefranque until Hill and Beresford had cleared the heights. The river was impassable when the river levels rose and once the bridge of boats at Villefranque had been swept away, Hill's troops on the east bank were isolated. Return to the centre of the village and turn left, heading north for St Pierre.

The coastal area attacked by Soult's troops between 10 and 12 December is now heavily built up and there is little to see of relevance to the French counter-attack. The only discernible landmark is the river Tanque and the deep valley where General Hope's 1st Division crossed and forced the French outposts back towards Anglet; his men in turn were forced back to the river. A modern bridge carries the N10 high above the valley and Biarritz railway station covers the area where the original crossing was made.

Arcangues church, the site of the Light Division's stand, is worth visiting. Head north along the D932 from Ustaritz and turn left on to the D755 and head through Bassussarry. Arcangues church is at the south end of the village in the centre of a golf course. After parking your car, follow the driveway to the walled cemetery where the church stands on the low hill. The inside of the church has hardly changed and the building would have been filled with smoke as the riflemen fought the French to a standstill. The men of the 43rd lined the two tiers of balconies to fire out of the windows at the French guns on the ridge to the north; there is a memorial to the men buried in the churchyard to the left of the entrance.

It is possible to see glimpses of the chateau during the walk back down the driveway.

Retrace your route through Bassussarry back on to the D932 and return to Ustaritz to cross the river and visit the battlefield of St Pierre.

THE BATTLE OF ST PIERRE, 13 DECEMBER 1813

Following the French attack west of the river Nive on 10 December, Wellington had moved a large number of his troops to the west bank, leaving General Hill to hold the hills south of Bayonne. Beresford's four divisions, the 3rd, 4th, 6th and 7th, had crossed the river to reinforce the left and centre of the allied line but the redeployment had seriously weakened the allied position on the east bank. General Hill had been left with Stewart's 2nd Division and Le Cor's Portuguese division: only 14,000 men and 14 guns.

By nightfall on 10 December Soult had realised that Wellington must have transferred a large number of troops across the river Nive. He decided it was the ideal time to turn his attentions to General Hill's positions on the right bank, aware that the poor weather could jeopardise the link between the two allied flanks. His opportunity came forty-eight hours later, on the night of 12 December, when heavy rains flooded the river Nive and swept away the bridge at Villefranque; the bridge of boats at Ustaritz was also in danger of being destroyed. This meant that General Hill would be isolated for the next few hours and Marshal Soult was going to take the opportunity to attack and overrun his troops before reinforcements could reach him.

General Beresford had been given orders to return to the right bank but the floods meant that he would have to wait until the engineers could repair the bridges. To the north, Marshal Soult was making the most of Wellington's difficult situation and was moving troops through Bayonne on to the east bank of the river Nive. Fortunately for General Hill, his troops were deployed in a strong defensive position between the river Nive and the river Ardour. They held three low ridges that were separated by woods, streams and lakes, and would split the French attack into separate columns. The 2nd Division numbered some 8,500 men, and General Stewart had deployed his brigades on the ridges. Pringle's brigade held the westerly ridge overlooking the Nive, while the 34th, the 39th and the 28th had been deployed side-by-side, blocking the narrow summit in front of Chateau Larraldea. The central ridge had a wide flat summit around the village of St Pierre d'Irube and General Hill had made

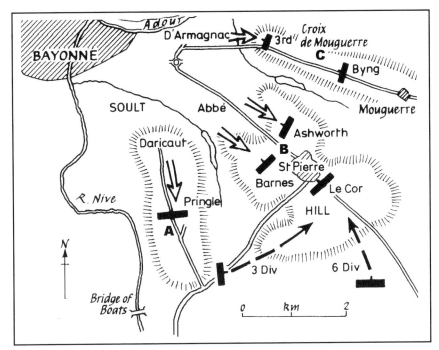

The battle of St Pierre 13 December 1815.

sure that it was strongly defended. Barnes's brigade, with the 50th, 71st and 92nd, was deployed to the west of the road to St-Jean-Pied-de-Port, while Ashworth's Portuguese brigade was to the east. Hill had also ordered ten gun crews to unlimber their guns astride the road so they could sweep the flat summit with canister and grapeshot. Le Cor's Portuguese division had 5,000 men and both Da Costa's and Buchan's brigades were placed in reserve on the central ridge.

The narrow eastern ridge was the weak point in Hill's line, but Stewart had chosen to position a strong outpost at the northern end, in the hope of disrupting the French advance. The 3rd Regiment was deployed at Partouhirie, protecting a bridge over a stream, about a kilometre in front of the rest of Byng's brigade. General Hill hoped that the advance guard would disrupt the French advance and give him time to decide how to deploy the rest of Byng's brigade. The 57th and the 1st Provisional Battalion were positioned near Mouguerre village, from where they would be able to support the 3rd Regiment at Partouhirie or join the fight for St Pierre in the centre where Hill expected the main French attack to fall.

At first light on 13 December artillery fire began targeting the allied positions while the columns of French infantry left Bayonne and marched towards the three ridges. Marshal Soult had amassed around 35,000 men organised into six divisions, and over twenty artillery pieces had been brought forward to support the attack, but they all had to cross the single bridge across the Nive before they could deploy.

As the mist lifted across the hills south of Bayonne, General Hill could see for the first time the strength of the French attack. Each of his three positions would have to face attacks by at least one French division and hold it at bay until reinforcements could find a way across the swollen river Nive. It was going to be a race against time and the British and Portuguese troops silently watched and waited as the noise of drums, bugles and cheers of '*Vive l'Empereur*' in the valley below grew louder.

On the western ridge General Daricau's division, numbering over 5,500 men, advanced towards Castello de Villa, where Pringle's three battalions were positioned. Some 1,800 redcoats waited as the French columns climbed the narrow ridge, confident that their flanks could not be turned as long as they could hold the summit. Although Pringle's men were outnumbered by three-to-one, Daricau's men struggled to find a way through the woods and enclosures and kept stopping to reorganise, giving the British skirmishers time to pick off the French officers. Pringle's men opened fire as the columns drew closer but the French charged. Heavy fighting followed but the British stood their ground and forced the Frenchmen back into the woods, closing their ranks ready for the next onslaught. George Bell later recalled how Colonel Brown rallied the men of the 28th with cries of 'Dead or alive we must hold our ground'.

On General Stewart's right flank, the 3rd Regiment faced General D'Armagnac's entire division, nearly 6,000 men. Although Hill did not expect the outpost to hold the eastern ridge, they did stop the French from crossing the stream for several hours.

The main French attack fell where General Hill expected, in his centre, as General Abbé's 6,000-strong division deployed on the ridge in front of St Pierre. Once again, walls and rough scrub disrupted the dense columns and Stewart's skirmishers and the British guns added to the French problems. The summit eventually erupted in musket and artillery fire as the two sides steadied their ranks ready for the inevitable charge. George Bell watched from the western ridge as the French guns bombarded

Stewart's exposed position: 'Every point was attacked to weaken our force and keep us separate, their guns keeping up a terrific fire, knocking the dust out of Saint Pierre ploughing up the side of the hill, thinning our ranks, and playing Old Harry, having no regard for life or limb.' The fighting continued unabated for several hours, with the French falling back to rally after each charge, but eventually their weight of numbers began to tell and Ashworth's Portuguese brigade began to retire east of the road.

Barnes's brigade was standing fast but its position was compromised when the 71st Regiment's commanding officer ordered his men to abandon their positions after severe hand-to-hand fighting. Colonel Sir Nathaniel Peacock had only just joined the regiment from England and his inexperience led him to believe that all was lost. It was a severe setback and General Hill eventually found the cowering officer pretending to escort Portuguese ammunition carriers forward. Hill cursed when the situation was explained to him and Wellington later commented: 'Well; if Hill is starting to swear, we must all mind what we are about.' However, the situation was restored by General Stewart and after rallying the 71st, he led them back to their positions west of the guns while General Barnes guided the 92nd forward to help Ashworth's brigade.

Several hours had passed since the first shots were fired and the weight of French numbers was now beginning to take effect on Stewart's exhausted brigades. Regiments were beginning to fall back on either side of St Pierre and some of the artillery crews had to abandon their guns or risk capture. Both Ashworth and Barnes had been wounded, leaving junior officers in command of their brigades, and General Hill realised that it was time to deploy his reserve if he were to stop General Abbé's division overrunning his centre.

On the eastern ridge the 3rd Division had eventually been forced to withdraw to Mouguerre village but General D'Armagnac's advance had been slow and poorly organised. The rest of Byng's brigade had been able to support Ashworth's beleaguered troops in front of St Pierre while General Le Cor had also been ordered to send Buchan's brigade forward.

Marshal Soult knew that victory was within reach if he could break General Hill's centre before Wellington could bring his reserves across the river Nive. The wise option would have been to withdraw General Abbé's division to make way for one of the three divisions waiting in reserve on the outskirts of Bayonne, but time was running out. To the disgust of the men who had spent all morning fighting around St Pierre, they were ordered to attack again. Although the troops were tired, angry and disheartened, they went forward one last time as the British and Portuguese soldiers again prepared to defend St Pierre ridge.

General Hill and General Stewart had rallied every available man they could find in the hope of holding the smoke-wreathed ridge. As the French columns advanced to the sound of drums and bugles, the two mounted officers rode along the lines cheering the men as they opened fire on the approaching ranks. The men rose to the challenge but casualties were high and every single member of General Stewart's staff was killed or wounded as they milled around the thick of the fighting. To the west of St Pierre village the sound of a solitary piper playing 'Cogag na shee' led the 92nd Regiment forward; nearly 200 of Colonel Cameron's men were killed or wounded restoring the line.

By midday the fighting had began to die down. General Abbé's men had reached their limit of endurance but Soult hesitated over sending reserves forward to take St Pierre and the French began to fall back. The tide of the battle had turned in favour of the allies and General Hill was given news that the 6th Division was crossing the river Nive at Ustaritz with Wellington at its head. Fresh reserves were at hand as the columns of redcoats approached from the south, and St Pierre had been saved. Meanwhile, British engineers had repaired the bridge of boats at Villefranque and the 3rd, 4th and 7th Divisions had started to cross.

General Hill was delighted to see Wellington and offered to hand over his command to his superior officer. Wellington refused, being more than satisfied with Hill's handling of the situation, and replied: 'My dear Hill, the day's your own', leaving his subordinate to organise the inevitable counter-attacks.

Hill's first instructions were sent to Byng's brigade, which was ordered to advance against Mouguerre village to regain control of the northern ridge, but when Hill's aide-de-camp reached the brigade, he could not find any senior officers, all having been either killed or wounded, and so the aide found himself leading the crucial attack. Byng's men advanced and by mid-afternoon the brigade was pushing General D'Armagnac's division back along Mouguerre ridge towards Bayonne. This was just the first of many successes. The French troops engaged on the centre and southern ridges had also begun to fall back, leaving General Hill master of the St Pierre ridges.

As the fighting died down the survivors counted their blessings and their casualties. Some 14,000 allied troops had held over 35,000 French troops at bay. Hill's troops had suffered over 5,000 casualties, the majority of them on the centre ridge, and the historian Napier was later to describe the battle as 'the most desperate of the whole campaign'.

Although Hill's position around St Pierre could have been overrun on several occasions, his men had stoutly fought against overwhelming odds until reinforcements had been able to cross the swollen river Nive. For a second time Soult had used the advantage offered by the bridges in Bayonne and had concentrated the majority of his troops faster than Wellington could. But despite his strategic success, he was denied the tactical success he had hoped for by a combination of the difficult terrain, the reluctance of his own troops to push home their advantage and the steadfastness of the British and Portuguese soldiers.

Marshal Soult had seen enough and he withdrew most of his troops east along the river Adour, leaving a large garrison of 10,000 troops under General Thouvenot to defend Bayonne. The battle was over, and Wellington was left in command of the area around Bayonne. Although the fighting on 13 December was officially part of the battle of the Nive, it is often called the battle of St Pierre by the British after the village in the centre of General Hill's line. The French usually call it the battle of Mouguerre after the small village on the northern ridge where Marshal Soult's memorial stands.

VISITING ST PIERRE

Head north from Villefranque and turn left to visit Pringle's Ridge some 500 metres beyond the turning to Quartier Bas. After 500 metres follow the left-hand fork to the turning area at the end. Although it is possible to see the centre ridge and St Pierre to the east, it is not possible to see Bayonne from here.

Turn around and return to the main road, turning left for St Pierre; you arc following the route taken by the reserves heading from Villefranque to join General Hill. Go straight on at the roundabout and right at the T-junction into the centre of the village where the main battle was. The area is now covered in housing but Barnes's brigade held the area to the right (west) of the road while Ashworth's Portuguese brigade held the ground to the left (east). Time after time General Abbé's men tried to take the summit but each attack was driven back.

Turn left at the roundabout and follow the road as it drops down the hill. Go straight on, signposted for Bayonne, at the large roundabout at

The French memorial to those who fought on French soil during the 1813–14 campaign.

the foot of the slope and turn right after 400 metres signposted for Mouguerre Bourg. The road crosses the bridge at Partouhirie where the 3rd Regiment held D'Armagnac's division at bay for several hours; it eventually fell back up the slope to the summit. The memorial is on the crest of the ridge, 2 kilometres further along on the left, where there is a parking area. It was erected by the French to honour Marshal Soult and his men who 'with inferior forces, foot by foot, defended this country for seven months against the army of Wellington'. There are extensive views of the area from the memorial: Bayonne and the Adour are to the north-west, with the Nive and the Pyrenees to the south-west. It is possible to see St Pierre ridge but Pringle's ridge is obscured.

The view across Bayonne.

Bayonne City

Bayonne Citadel

Chapter 12

THE FINAL CAMPAIGN
IN FRANCE

THE BATTLE OF ORTHEZ, 27 FEBRUARY 1814

W ELLINGTON'S ARMY left the Bayonne area on 24 February 1814 and the columns of British and Portuguese soldiers crossed the river Gave d'Oloron on a 24-kilometre-wide front, aware that they were heading deep into French territory. Marshal Soult had already withdrawn his troops towards the small town of Orthez and they had started to cross the river Gave de Pau in order to prepare to meet

General Soult's army crossed the river Gave de Pau via Orthez's ancient bridge.

the British advance. By the following morning over 36,000 men and 48 guns had used the town's ancient bridge to reach the north bank and had deployed on a long ridge, running parallel to the river.

The French positions ran in a wide arc starting at Orthez to the east and curving along the summit of the ridge to the village of St Boes. It was a strong position, and any allied attack would be further limited by the terrain. Three spurs that wound their way down from the crest towards the river Gave de Pau were passable, but the dense undergrowth, streams and marshy ground between the spurs would split the allied attack into four separate narrow columns. It would take great skill to coordinate the attacks; any delays and the French would be able to deal with each column in turn.

Reille's corps held Soult's east flank with over 10,000 men, with General Taupin's division centred on St Boes village, looking west at the top of a wide, inviting spur, and General Rouget's division deployed facing south towards the river. General D'Erlon's corps had a similar number of men deployed along the ridge on the French left flank. General D'Armagnac's men held a strong position covering the head of the marshy gulleys but General Foy's division was more exposed, facing west on the gentle slopes connecting Orthez to the ridge.

Although Marshal Soult knew it was a strong position, he was concerned that the British would be able to concentrate on his right flank and drive Taupin's division from St Boes, outflanking Reille's corps. Rather than wait for the attack to begin, he had already ordered General Clausel to withdraw from Orthez village to a second ridge to the north. But the order came too late. While Villatte's division was already deployed on the high ground north-east of the village, covering the road to Mont-de-Marsan, General Jean-Isidore Harispe's division was still close to the river when Wellington launched his attack.

By the morning of 27 February Wellington's army of 48,000 men and 42 guns was closing in on Orthez from all directions. He already had five divisions and two cavalry brigades, around 31,000 men, north of the river, deployed at the foot of St Boes Ridge. The rest of his men were still searching for a ford across the river Gave de Pau to the east of Orthez but Wellington decided he would attack immediately. As he sat on a rock writing his orders, wrapped in a white winter cloak, an officer sadly remarked to Colborne: 'Did you see that old White Friar sitting there? I wonder how many men he is marking off to be sent into the next world.'

The main assault was to be made by General Beresford, and it would take place exactly where Soult expected. General Cole's 4th Division would lead the advance along the ridge to St Boes with General Walker's 7th Division following. General Alten's Light Division would make the second attack, advancing from Baight village up a second ridge to attack St Boes from the south. Wellington's final attack would be made by the 3rd Division against D'Armagnac's and Foy's divisions in the centre of Marshal Soult's line. Picton's men would have to advance up two separate spurs because of the marshy ground and it would take great skill to coordinate their attacks properly. The 6th Division would wait in reserve near the river, ready to exploit any breakthrough made by General Picton's men.

To the east of Orthez the allied plans took a new turn when General Hill's troops found a ford across the river Gave de Pau and began to cross. Stewart's 2nd Division and Le Cor's Portuguese division, around 13,000 men, would soon be able to pin Harispe's division in the village, stopping it from withdrawing as General Clausel had planned.

The allies used the first few hours of daylight to move into position, and while Wellington's divisions prepared to advance up the slopes of St Boes Ridge, Hill's men continued to cross the river. The first attack was made against St Boes and Ross's brigade scored an early success by capturing the church. However, Anson's brigade was unable to drive the French from the rest of the village and attack General Taupin's main position on the summit of the ridge. Roundshot and canister swept the open spur, causing horrendous casualties among Cole's men, and they eventually withdrew to a safe distance to regroup as the French prepared to counter-attack.

The Light Division was also having difficulties to the south. Once Alten's men advanced beyond a Roman camp about halfway up the spur, artillery and musket fire from Rouget's division forced them to withdraw to a safe distance. It was a similar story to the east where Picton's 3rd Division had to advance in columns until it was close to the French line due to the poor terrain. Crossfire from D'Armagnac's and Foy's divisions stopped Keane's and Brisbane's brigades in their tracks, killing and injuring over 500 before they fell back down the slopes. It was a disastrous start. After only an hour of fighting, three of Wellington's divisions were falling back to the foot of the ridge.

The attack against St Boes was renewed by the 7th Division before noon and General Walker's men were soon engaged on the summit of the ridge as they tried to clear the village. For a second time the British troops were driven back by artillery fire, but this time Taupin's division followed them, leaving their hilltop position. Wellington was anxiously watching the new attacks from the Roman camp and he spotted a gap opening in General Reille's line as the French surged forward. It was the opportunity he had been waiting for. The 52nd Regiment was ordered to advance towards Taupin's flank and followed a gulley to stay hidden from the French battalions.The lone regiment soon reached the top of the ridge and found itself in the centre of Reille's line, behind both Taupin's and Rouget's flanks.

While the French infantry redeployed to meet this unexpected threat, Wellington led the 3rd and 6th Regiments in the footsteps of the 52nd. Before long there were over 1,500 men in the centre of Reille's lines and the combined firepower of their musket volleys created havoc in the French ranks.

The fighting was severe but Wellington remained at the critical point, laughing when his Spanish aide, General Alava, called out that a spent bullet had hit him on the buttocks and mocking that he had been 'ofendido' or wounded. A few minutes later Wellington himself was also hit, and Alava responded with a laugh, saying it was a punishment for laughing at him. In fact, it was no laughing matter. A spent musket ball had hit Wellington's hip, driving his sword hilt into his side, and he was unable to ride for a week.

As Taupin tried to recall his battalions from St Boes to counter the threat, General Beresford ordered the 7th Division to renew its attacks and General Walker's men were soon driving the French from the burning village. The 6th Division had also moved up from reserve and advanced up the centre spur where the 3rd Division had failed earlier. Clinton's attack stopped D'Erlon from reinforcing Reille and before long his men were heavily engaged on the summit against D'Armagnac's and Foy's divisions.

For the next two hours the fighting swung backwards and forwards as the British and French attacked and counter-attacked, wreathing the ridge in smoke. The breakthrough eventually came when Fririon's brigade was unable to withstand the weight of Picton's attacks and fell back from the east end of the ridge. The retreat had exposed the French line of withdrawal to the east, leaving Reille's and D'Erlon's men in a dangerous position. Even a counter-charge by French cavalry, which cut down around 200 men of the 1/88th, could not stop Brisbane's and Keane's men.

Picton's division had to advance either side of this gulley to reach the summit of the ridge.

The French line was being rolled up from two directions. General Beresford's men were advancing along the summit from the direction of St Boes, while General Hill had also deployed on the north bank of the river and was moving forward from the ford at Souars around the French left flank. The twin attacks left Marshal Soult with only one option: to retreat before the withdrawal turned into a rout.

Harispe's men formed up across the highest point on the road to Mont-de-Marsan, while Villatte and D'Armagnac deployed their divisions on the ridge to the north. These three French divisions stopped the British pursuit in its tracks, while Reille's and D'Erlon's men withdrew to the bridge over the Luy do Bearn stream. Wellington's men were exhausted after the long battle and they followed at a safe distance while the last of Soult's men conducted an orderly withdrawal; the bridge was destroyed after the majority of the French soldiers had passed over.

Although Soult had managed to extricate a large part of his army from a difficult situation, he had lost over 4,000 men and had been forced to leave 1,300 prisoners and 6 guns behind. In contrast, there had been around 2,150 allied casualties, a low return for an attack against a strong defensive position.

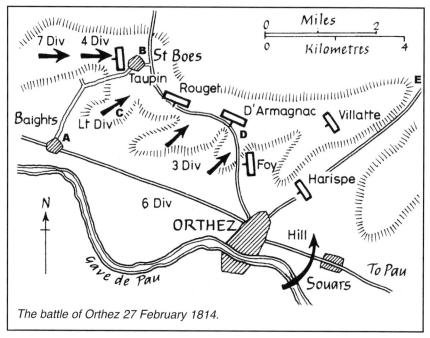

The battle of Orthez 27 February 1814.

Touring Orthez

Orthez is 50 kilometres east of Bayonne, along the A64. Leave the motorway at junction 8 and follow signs for Centre Ville, crossing the river Gave de Pau to enter the main square. The original river bridge is to the west of the modern road bridge and Soult's soldiers would have recognised the sentry tower in the centre. Turn left and leave the square with the Hotel de Ville to the right and turn right at the traffic lights, following the road around the church. Carry straight on at the second set of traffic lights to visit Wellington's deployment area.

Head west for Baights de Bearn on the allied left flank, and the road rises and falls over the spurs where Picton's men deployed to the right of the road and the reserve waited near the river, to the left. Turn right into Baights de Bearn after 5 kilometres and go straight on at the crossroads in the centre of the village. Head north along the D315, turning right for St Boes after 3 kilometres. The road follows the crest of the spur used by the 4th Division followed by the 7th Division as they tried to take the village; a radio mast on the horizon marks their objective. The ridge to the right was used by the Light Division to reach the village.

The ridge used to attack St Boes, viewed from the Roman camp.

St Boes was demolished after the battle and rebuilt 500 metres to the east but the church and a few scattered farms mark the site of the main fighting. Continue through the village where it is possible to park next to the Marie and walk down the road to the right, signposted for the Roman camp, to see where the Light Division was engaged.

Return to your car and continue to drive through St Boes, turning right at the T-junction. The road swings to the left, heading west along the ridge held by Soult's men. The 52nd climbed up the gulley to the right, appearing near the bend between Rouget's division and Taupin's division.

The road turns to the right after 3 kilometres and there is a monument to General Foy's division on the left-hand side of the road. It is possible to park at the bend and walk back to get a good view across the undulating spurs crossed by Picton's men. After the fall of St Boes, three French divisions took the side road, heading east, to escape to the second defensive line north-east of Orthez. Continue south down the slope towards Orthez, noting the memorial to the French army on the left-hand side after 2 kilometres.

Turn left at the traffic lights in Orthez and follow the road around the church, turning left at the second traffic lights to enter the main square. Take the road heading north out of the square, signposted for Mont-de-Marsan. The French fell back to the low ridge which intersects the road at right angles after 4 kilometres. Turn around at the first opportunity to return to Orthez. (Note: the road crosses the ridge and although you get a good view of the position, the land is private and there is nowhere to stop safely.)

The memorial to General Foy's men.

Remembering the French soldiers who died for France during the battle.

THE BATTLE OF TOULOUSE, 10 APRIL 1814

Following the battle of Orthez, Soult withdrew his battered divisions east towards Toulouse, and his weary men eventually reached the fortified city on 24 March 1814. The river Garonne ran through the centre of the city, separating the suburb of St Cyprien on the east bank from the rest. The Languedoc Canal ran around the perimeter, around a kilometre outside the walls. The majority of the inhabitants lived inside the walls but there were two suburbs outside the walls, St Etienne to the east and St Michel to the south.

Marshal Soult had 42,000 troops and 100 artillery pieces to defend Toulouse and the population had helped to build earthworks at strategic points covering the approaches to the city, turning it into a fortress. The key to any attack was the capture of the Calvinet Heights, a long ridge overlooking the east side of the town. Over half of the French soldiers had been positioned on the hill and many were deployed behind the earthworks that lined the summit. The French gun batteries were deployed in three large artillery redoubts and the crews were going to be well protected from allied artillery fire. The Great Redoubt covered the northern approaches to the ridge, while the Sypiére Redoubt occupied the southern end; Augustins Redoubt stood in the centre.

Marshal Soult deployed General Daricau's division on the north-west side of the Toulouse, along the Languedoc Canal, and his brigades held bridgeheads at Pont Jumeaux and Pont des Minimes. To the north of the city General D'Armagnac's division was deployed on the far bank of the canal at Pont de Matablau and his brigades covered the northern approaches to the Calvinet Heights. The heights were held by two divisions, General Harispe's men occupying the northern end, between the Great Redoubt and Augustins Redoubt, and General Villatte's troops covering as far south as the Sypiére Redoubt. General Pierre Soult, the marshal's brother, had been ordered to cover the southern approaches to the ridge and his cavalry, numbering around 2,700 men, was stationed near Sypiére farm. General Taupin's division was deployed close behind the crest of the ridge, while General Travot had command of 7,000 conscripts held in reserve in the St Etienne suburbs and along the city walls. Marshal Soult had deployed his remaining division, led by General Maransin, on the west bank of the river, defending St Cyprien.

After the battle of Orthez Wellington had gathered his troops, a force of 49,000 men, including 10,000 Spanish and 50 guns, at the town of Tarbes. They then marched east following Soult's army and by 26 March they were closing in on Toulouse. The waterways around the city severely limited his plans for an assault: an attack from the west was impossible due to the river Garonne, while the Languedoc Canal protected the north side of the city; the river Hers also limited movement to the east. Instead, Wellington decided to approach the city from the south and on 27 March British engineers started to construct a pontoon bridge over the river Garonne, 16 kilometres south of Toulouse. But the scheme quickly ran into trouble: the river was too wide and the engineers did not have enough equipment and material to reach the far bank. A second bridge was completed 1.5 kilometres further downstream three days later and General Stewart's 2nd Division and General Le Cor's Portuguese division crossed over. General Hill soon found to his cost that the road network was virtually non-existent and it was impossible to move his men and guns towards the city.

As the 13,000 men returned to the west bank of the river Garonne, Wellington was forced to concede that he would have to find another way to attack Toulouse. His only remaining option was to cross the river north of the city and then approach from the north and the east, where Soult's defences were strongest. A smaller contingent would attack the French troops holding the fortifications on the west bank.

By 4 April British engineers had built a bridge across the river Garonne 24 kilometres north of the town and General Beresford's troops started to cross the following day. Yet again bad luck struck: as they headed towards Toulouse, the spring rains flooded the river and washed the bridge away. Wellington's army was cut in two and for the next three days he watched and waited anxiously until the floodwaters subsided and the crossing had been repaired. The only consolation was that Soult did not learn of the British engineers' troubles and the rest of Beresford's men were allowed to cross unmolested.

On 8 April the bridge was again open and Wellington joined Beresford on the east bank of the Garonne with Picton's 3rd Division and Alten's Light Division. This brought the total of British and Portuguese soldiers poised to attack Toulouse to over 20,000, while General Freire led another 10,000 Spanish troops. Wellington's troops marched east before turning south and the following day they seized a bridge over the river Hers at Croix d'Orade and Beresford's men began to cross. Before long his troops were deploying around Toulouse, forming a tight circle around the city, pinning the French to their positions. This allowed General Beresford to prepare for the main attack against Calvinet Ridge. Once the ridge was in his hands, the allied guns could start to shell the city and bombard its garrison into submission.

Events unfolded rapidly as Wellington's army moved into position around Toulouse and Picton's 3rd Division and Alten's Light Division moved towards the Languedoc Canal to threaten the northern side of the city. To the north-east General Beresford had to lead Cole's 4th Division and Clinton's 6th Division along the west bank of the river Hers, at the foot of Calvinet Ridge, before they could turn and advance up the slopes towards the French fortifications. Meanwhile, General Freire's Spanish troops deployed opposite the northern end of the ridge as Gruben and Somerset led their cavalry regiments south to cover Beresford's flanks. West of the river Garonne, General Hill prepared to attack the fortifications protecting the suburb of St Cyprien. Wellington's plan was for Beresford and Freire to make the main attack, while Hill and Picton made feint attacks, pinning down as many French troops as possible. It was a complicated plan, one that was forced on Wellington by the difficult terrain.

As Soult and Wellington prepared for the forthcoming battle, neither of them knew that events in Paris had made it unnecessary. Allied troops had entered Paris on 31 March and by the time the first shots were fired at Toulouse, Napoleon was in the process of abdicating. However, before first light on Easter Sunday, 10 April, General Hill's troops began their attack and General Stewart's 2nd and General Le Cor's Portuguese divisions began engaging the French troops holding the earthworks around St Cyprien. Both generals had been given orders to advance cautiously, aiming to prevent General Maransin withdrawing troops from the west bank of the Garonne; it was the start of a prolonged fight that in the end cost only 80 allied lives.

On the east bank of the river Picton had also been instructed to limit his attacks against the Languedoc Canal, forcing General Daricau to keep his reserves at Pont Jumeaux and Pont des Minimes. To begin with Picton's men engaged the two French bridgeheads, and Colville's British and Power's Portuguese brigades maintained a safe distance. However, when General Picton sensed that the bridgehead at Pont Jumeaux was wavering, he ordered Brisbane's brigade to attack the earthworks. It was a costly order. The unfortunate brigade failed to take its objective, losing many men in the process.

To the east the main attack had also run into difficulties. General Beresford's men had come under fire from the north end of Calvinet Ridge where the French guns were protected by the Great Redoubt. The British infantry and their supporting artillery struggled to advance along the swampy banks of the river Hers and the gun crews were eventually ordered to unlimber their weapons and return fire.

General Freire's troops were supposed to attack the north end of the ridge at the same time as Beresford attacked the southern end, but the sound of British guns firing led the Spanish general to believe that the attack was already under way. His two divisions advanced prematurely towards the Great Redoubt where D'Armagnac's and Harispe's divisions were waiting. The attack was poorly supported and the French gun crews wreaked havoc among the dense columns before the infantry fired a devastating volley. The Spanish lost around a thousand casualties, including four generals, before they turned tail and fled down the slopes. Wellington's plan was falling apart and as he watched the Spanish rout, he was heard to remark that he 'had never before seen 10,000 men running a race'.

The Spanish defeat had repercussions all along the allied front and Wellington was forced to change his plans. General Alten had to order the Light Division to fall back from the Languedoc Canal and deploy to cover the gap left by Freire's rout. They formed a line in front of the bridge at Croix Daurade, so the Spanish could rally in safety. Picton also had to be ordered to move Colville's British and Power's Portuguese brigades along the north bank of the canal to cover the ground vacated by General Alten's withdrawal.

As the right of Wellington's line reorganised, Beresford's men continued to march south along the banks of the river Hers while Somerset's cavalry covered his flank and Gruben's cavalry harried the French cavalry across the river. It was an audacious advance, involving 11,000 men marching across the face of the French positions on Calvinet Ridge. But Wellington was confident that the French troops would wait and watch from their fortifications rather than attempt to attack; it was an indication of his contempt for the fighting qualities of Soult's troops. Eventually, after marching 5 kilometres, the two divisions were ready to turn west and duly deployed in front of General Villatte's division which was waiting at the top of Calvinet Ridge around the Sypiére Redoubt.

Both the 4th and 6th Divisions advanced in lines up the muddy slopes

General Picton's men try to force their way across the Languedoc Canal.

while Gruben's and Somerset's cavalry covered their south flank. General Villatte was outnumbered by over two-to-one and the weight of numbers quickly began to tell. Rey's brigade was soon driven from Sypiére farm and Gabquet's brigade was forced out of the neighbouring redoubt, but as the French fell back down the slopes towards St Etienne help was at hand. General Taupin deployed two of his brigades in columns and personally led the counter-attack until he fell. His sacrifice helped to stop Beresford's men in their tracks and gave the French a temporary respite as the British fell back to the top of Calvinet Ridge. As they reorganised on the summit, Beresford's gun crews had to manhandle their pieces up to the top of the muddy ridge, ready for the next attack.

Despite the success on Calvinet Ridge, by mid-afternoon Wellington was facing a difficult situation. His troops had been driven back in many places and while they reorganised all around Toulouse, he visited General Beresford to explain that the outcome of the battle lay in his hands. Freire's Spanish troops were a spent force and the rest of the British divisions were fully occupied containing the French inside Toulouse. His men had to drive the French from the northern end of Calvinet Ridge or the battle was lost. Once the ridge was in British hands, his guns could shell the garrison into submission.

As General Hill's troops continued to pressurise Maransin's troops on the western bank of the Garonne, Picton launched further attacks along the Languedoc Canal to prevent General Daricau sending troops south to reinforce Calvinet Ridge. Again Brisbane's men failed to seize the French bridgeheads and were forced to withdraw having suffered over 400 casualties for no gain.

Following Wellington's visit, Beresford issued new orders to General Clinton, instructing him to turn north to clear the rest of the summit of the ridge while General Cole's men stopped the French retaking the Sypiére Redoubt. The 6th Division advanced under heavy fire from the French guns and drove General Harispe's men from Augustins Redoubt, but a counter-attack forced them to retire. Fierce hand-to-hand fighting broke out as first the British and then the French charged into the redoubt; it would change hands five times during the course of the afternoon's fighting.

As casualties mounted (the 6th Division suffered 1,500 casualties during the fighting for the ridge) Beresford was forced to order Clinton to withdraw his men and make way for Cole's 4th Division. The fresh wave of attacks swung the fighting in the British favour, and by the late afternoon the French had started to withdraw, abandoning their fight for Augustins Redoubt and the Great Redoubt. Sensing that a calamitous end was in sight if he did not break off the engagement, Soult ordered his generals to pull back their men across the Languedoc Canal to regroup in Toulouse. He had lost over 3,200 casualties, the majority in the fight for the redoubts on Calvinet Ridge.

Although Wellington now had the advantage he had hoped for, he was in no position to exploit the French withdrawal. His own army had suffered over 4,500 casualties and Picton's division was still spread thinly north of the town. The troops on Calvinet Ridge had reached the end of their endurance after their prolonged engagement and he did not dare to commit the Spanish to another possible defeat. He was also facing a supply problem as his wagons had to make the circuitous route across the Garonne and Hers rivers. The British did, however, possess the heights overlooking the city and would soon be able to bombard the city.

The British success had left Soult in a predicament, and by nightfall he faced a difficult decision: he had to decide whether to counter-attack or abandon the city before he was trapped inside its walls. A day-long stand-off followed as Wellington waited for his men to be supplied and Soult made preparations to leave. His army abandoned Toulouse during the night of 11 April, and nearly 40,000 men slipped silently away through the suburb of St Michel and headed south to Carcassone. Although Soult had managed to extract his battered army, he had been forced to leave behind nearly a hundred guns. The following morning Wellington's picquets found that their opposite numbers had fled and British patrols discovered that the earthworks surrounding Toulouse were deserted; the only soldiers left were 1,600 wounded and sick who had been too ill to move.

It had been a good day. Toulouse was in British hands and Soult's battered army was retiring, leaving its artillery behind. Later that afternoon the mood at Wellington's headquarters improved dramatically when Colonel Frederick Ponsonby of the 12th Light Dragoons reported in. He had ridden all the way from Paris with the news that Napoleon had abdicated. After six long years the war with France was over.

VISITING TOULOUSE

The area of the battlefield has been completely built over since 1814 and there is little to see relating to the battle. The narrow streets and brick buildings are centred around the huge Place du Capitole, with its impressive Hotel de Ville, and St Sernin Basilica. Small sections of the sixteenth-century walls are still standing and these give some indication of the scale of the fortress facing Wellington. By the time his army arrived the local population had helped the French soldiers build a network of gun emplacements and trenches covering many of the parks and road junctions.

The obelisk commemorating the battle stands on the summit of Calvinet Ridge (also known as Mont Rave) in the north-east suburbs of the city. Drive across the Canal du Midi on the Allee Jean Jaures next to the statue of Pierre-Paul Riquet, the canal's architect, and pass Matabiau railway station heading up the hill past the huge red-brick arch housing the media centre. Turn right for the observatory at the top of the hill and follow the road around the grounds, finding a parking place near the obelisk. The obelisk is a memorial to the French soldiers who fell on 10 April 1814 and to the people of Toulouse; from it there are extensive views to the north and west across the city. The nearby orientation panel gives a large amount of detail on the French fortifications and troop movements during the battle.

The Languedoc Canal still runs around the old town, although it is now called the Canal du Midi. The Pont des Minimes has been rebuilt but the bridges and locks around the canal basin at Pont Jumeaux have changed little, apart from an extra bridge added in 1834. The river Garonne flows through the western suburbs of the city and Pont Neuf is one of the three bridges leading into the suburb of St Cyprien, where a large part of the city wall still stands. Maransin's division had dug entrenchments in front of the walls to stop the British bringing their artillery close enough to destroy the walls.

THE FRENCH SORTIE FROM BAYONNE, 14 APRIL 1814

When news of Napoleon's abdication reached Wellington's headquarters he sent a messenger to Soult asking for a truce. The marshal agreed, and at last Wellington was able to stand his troops down, bringing hostilities across France to an end. As stories of the armistice spread across the allied army, the men relaxed and began looking forward to going home after many seasons of campaigning. However, General Pierre Thouvenot, the French Governor of Bayonne, did not believe the news. He rejected the reports and dismissed them as rumours put about in an attempt to trick him into surrendering the city. He refused to cooperate and gave orders for his men to prepare for a long siege.

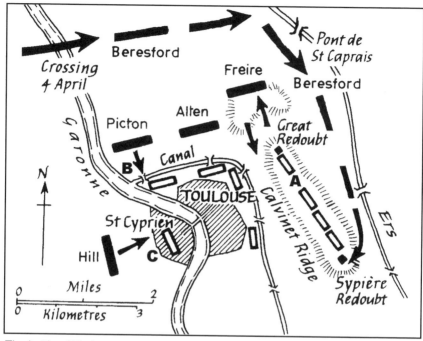

The battle of Toulouse 10 April 1814.

Thouvenot's besieged garrison numbered 14,000 troops. Many held the fortress on the south bank of the Adour and the surrounding entrenchments, while others were based in the citadel on the north side of the river. Nor was the French commander content to sit inside his fortifications and wait, and when it became clear that Wellington's army was fully engaged in chasing Soult's army into Toulouse, he planned a sortie out of the city. Originally he planned to break through the British lines on the south bank of the river and head west along the river bank to seize the bridge of boats that connected the 1st Division's camp around le Boucau with the south bank. His men would then cross over and take the 1st Division's lines in the rear as the citadel's garrison attacked from the front. This overly-ambitious idea was eventually scaled down and the plan to take the bridge was abandoned; instead, General Maucomble's men would carry out a spoiling attack from the citadel at dawn on 14 April, overrunning the allied picquets around St Etienne before turning on General Howard's billets.

Above: A small section of Toulouse's citadel walls remains in St Cyprien.

Left: This tall, brick-faced obelisk stands near the site of the Great Redoubt at the northern end of Calvinet Ridge.

Below: Picton's division made several unsuccessful attempts to take Pont Jumeaux.

Lieutenant-General Sir John Hope commanded the 18,000 British troops manning the siege works around Bayonne, with General Hay's 5th Division to the south of the river, facing the French entrenchments. General Howard's 1st Division was on the north bank with one of the 5th Division's brigades and they held the siege lines facing the citadel. The line of picquets ran from the Adour at St Bernard's Mill, west of the citadel, through the village of St Etienne to the river bank east of Bayonne; a single cavalry brigade formed the reserve. Maitland's 1st Guards Brigade held the area west of the citadel while Stopford's 2nd Guards Brigade occupied St Etienne, in the centre of Howard's line. Greville's Brigade from the 5th Division was to the east with Hinuber's German Brigade in support.

While the French were making their final preparations for the attack during the early hours of 14 April, two French deserters were captured by one of the British picquets and taken to Major-General Hay, the General Officer of the Night. As he was unable to understand them, they were taken to the headquarters of the King's German Legion brigade, where Major-General Hinuber heard their story about the impending dawn sortie. Unfortunately, General Hay dismissed the warning and the prisoners were taken to the rear while the British picquets continued to watch the French lines, unaware of the storm that was about to break. Only General Hinuber believed the two messengers and he alerted his

Bayonne's citadel overlooks the river Ardour.

men before passing the word on to General Hope.

Meanwhile, behind the French lines General Thouvenot was furious to learn that the two deserters had crossed over to the British lines and ordered his subordinates to attack as soon as they were ready. The first French attack began around midnight. This was a feint made by Lieutenant-General Baron Abbé's men and they left the entrenched camp south of the river to advance against Anglet and Bellevue, drawing General Hope's attention away from the real threat north of the river Adour.

Three hours later, as the British waited for the attack to develop on the south bank, the main attack started on the north bank. Some 3,000 men emerged in silence from the citadel and the surrounding entrenchments, taking many of the British picquets by surprise and making many of them prisoner.

The picquets covering Greville's brigade camp to the east were quickly overrun and the men of the 95th Regiment were soon moving quickly through the streets of St Etienne, finding many British sleeping in their billets. As the British fell back in disorder Major-General Hay belatedly rose to the challenge and ordered Greville to hold the village 'to the last extremity'. It was the last order he gave, as he was one of many to fall in the hand-to-hand fighting as the French surged through St Etienne. Before long, virtually all of the village was in French hands; only a single house at the north end of the village still remained in British hands, held by a resolute group of men of the 38th led by Captain Forster. As the 2nd Guards Brigade fell back from St Etienne, their woes increased when their commanding officer, General Stopford, was wounded. Colonel Guise then took over command of the Guardsmen and as they rallied, the French attack was brought to a standstill.

On hearing the news of the attack, General Hope rode forward, accompanied by his aide Lieutenant Moore (a nephew of Sir John Moore) and Captain Herries from the Quartermaster General's Department, to assess the situation. As the three officers rode along the 2nd Guards Brigade line, they discovered to their cost that some Guardsmen had fallen too far back, allowing the French to infiltrate behind their line of picquets. Sergeant-Major Pigeon's group of twenty men from the 82nd Regiment ambushed the three horsemen and the struggle that followed was later described by Napier:

A shot struck him [the General] in the arm, and his horse, a large one, as was necessary to sustain the gigantic warrior, received eight bullets and fell upon his leg; his followers had by this time escaped from the defile, yet two of them, Captain Herries and Mr Moore, a nephew of Sir John Moore, seeing his helpless state, turned back and endeavoured amidst the heavy fire of the enemy, to draw him from beneath his horse.

Both Moore and Herries were badly wounded as they tried to reach their commanding officer, and he was carried off by Sergeant Beregeot and Voltigeur Bonencia towards the citadel.

While the battle of St Etienne surged back and forth, the left-hand French column advanced along the river bank west of the citadel supported by gunboats. Yet again the picquets were overrun quickly and the French fell on the 1st Guards Brigade's camp near St Bernard's Mill. Buglers hastily sounded the alarm and Colonel Maitland's men clambered from their tents but the surprise was complete and many were taken prisoner in the initial confusion. In the mêlée that followed the Guards' officers organised their men and gave orders to open fire, stopping the attack in its tracks. Maitland's men had prevented the French reaching the bridge of boats but many had been killed or injured in the darkness.

For a time it appeared as if the 1st Division's camps would be overrun but the 2nd Brigade eventually rallied north of St Etienne while the 1st Brigade recovered from its initial shock and formed up along the river bank. The battle was tipped in favour of the British by General Hinuber, who had rapidly organised his alert brigade and led his troops into St Esprit, where they launched an attack that threatened the French position in St Etienne.

As the sky above Bayonne began to grow light, Thouvenot knew that it was time to call off the attack and he ordered his troops to withdraw, aware that the two British brigades were preparing to counter-attack.

The allies had lost over 800 men, the majority of them Guardsmen who were taken prisoner and marched to Bayonne citadel. The Coldstream Guards lost 246 men around St Bernard's Mill while the 3rd Foot Guards lost 203 in the fighting for St Etienne. Despite the advantages of launching a surprise night attack, the French had not had it all their own way; over 900 had been killed, injured or captured in the fighting.

The prisoners did not have to spend long in captivity as attempts to persuade General Thouvenot to surrender continued. They succeeded on 26 April when he finally accepted news of the armistice and the men were allowed to file out of the citadel. It was the final act of the six-year-long peninsular campaign between France and the allies.

VISITING BAYONNE

The old city is on the south bank of the river Adour, while the citadel stands proudly on the opposite side of the river. Head north across the Adour on the N10 road bridge, and the citadel can be seen on the north bank, to the west of the bridge. The huge fortress has changed little since 1814 and it is still an active military barracks.

Continue north along the N10, turning right in front of the railway station and heading through St Esprit. Follow the right fork at the first mini-roundabout and head straight on at a second to a crossroads at the top of the hill, next to a water tower. St Etienne is to the east (right) of the crossroads and the built-up area occupies high ground overlooking the river. The church and chateau mark the area where the fighting was heaviest.

Return to the crossroads by the water tower and turn right, heading north. Turn left after 800 metres, signed Inglis Cementerio (English Cemetery), and park near the crossroads after 300 metres in the suburbs. Walk straight on, following a grassy path through the houses and the 3rd Guards Cemetery is hidden in the woods after 200 metres. The cemetery contains a small number of graves, including those of Captains Mahon, Holburne, White and Shiffner, who all died during the French sortie.

Head back to the crossroads and the water tower, turning right 200 metres before the traffic lights on to Chemin de Laharie. Take the first left signposted for the English Cemetery and turn right after 1.5 kilometres. Park after 200 metres and follow the path across the fields to the Coldstream Guards cemetery. There are around a dozen officer graves here, including General Hay's, and a similar number of plaques. Visits made by Queen Victoria, Edward VII and the 8th Duke of Wellington are also remembered.

Turn around and turn right, heading down the hill to the Adour. Turn right and head north along the river bank, passing St Bernard's Mill on the right, and park next to Boucau's small harbour. The Coldstream Guards and 3rd Foot paddled across the river in small boats on 23 February 1814 while salvoes of rockets hit the east bank. British engineers eventually built a bridge of boats at Boucau, allowing the British troops to close the circle around Bayonne.

The secluded 3rd Guards Cemetery.

The Coldstream Guards Cemetery.

FURTHER READING

Ascoli, David. *A Companion to the British Army* (London, 1983)
Brett-James, Anthony. *Life in Wellington's Army* (London, 1972)
Bryant, Arthur. *Years of Victory. 1802—1812* (London, 1944)
Bryant, Arthur. *The Age of Elegance. 1812—1822* (London, 1950)
Bryant, Arthur. *The Great Duke or the Invincible General* (London, 1971)
Chandler, David. *Napoleon's Marshals* (New York, 1987)
Chandler, David. *Dictionary of the Napoleonic Wars* (Simon & Schuster, 1993)
Esdaile, Charles. *The Spanish Army in the Peninsular War* (Manchester, 1988)
Esdaile, Charles. *The Duke of Wellington and Command of the Spanish Army* (London, 1990)
Esdaile, Charles. *The Peninsular War* (Penguin Books Ltd, Allen Lane, 2002)
Fletcher, Ian. *Craufurd's Light Division* (Tunbridge Wells, 1994)
Fletcher, Ian. *Fields of Fire: Battlefields of the Peninsular War* (Sarpedon, 1994)
Fletcher Ian. *Wellington's Regiments* (Spellmount, 1994)
Fletcher Ian (ed.). *The Peninsular War: Aspects of the Struggle for the Iberian Peninsula* (Spellmount, 1998)
Fortescue, Sir John. *History of the British Army, 13 volumes* (London, 1899-1920)
Gates, David. *The Spanish Ulcer. A History of the Peninsular War* (Pimlico, 2002)
Glover, Michael. *Wellington as Commander* (London, 1968)
Glover, Michael. *Legacy of Glory, the Bonaparte Kingdom of Spain* (New York, 1971)
Glover, Michael. *Wellington's Army in the Peninsula* (Newton Abbott, 1977)
Glover, Michael. *The Peninsular War, 1807—1814* (Penguin, 2001)
Grehan, John. *The Lines of Torres Vedras* (Spellmount, 2004)
Griffiths, Paddy. *Wellington — Commander* (Chichester, 1986)
Harris, Rifleman, *Recollections of Rifleman Harris* (1848)
Haythornthwaite, Phillip. *Wellington's Military Machine* (Tunbridge Wells, 1989)
Haythornthwaite, Phillip. *The Armies of Wellington* (Brockhampton Press, 1996)
Haythornthwaite, Phillip. *The Peninsular War Almanac* (Brassey, 2004)
Holmes, Richard. *Redcoat* (HarperCollins, 2002)
Holmes, Richard. *Wellington. The Iron Duke* (HarperCollins, 2003)
James, L. *The Iron Duke. A Military Biography of Wellington* (London, 1992)
Kincaid, J. *Adventures in the Rifle Brigade and Random Shots from a Rifleman* (1981)

Longford, Elizabeth. *Wellington. The Years of the Sword* (London, 1969)

McGuigan, Ron (ed.). *Inside Wellington's Peninsular Army, 1808—1814* (Pen & Sword, 2006)

Myatt. *British Sieges of the Peninsular War* (Tunbridge Wells, 1987)

Napier, William. *History of the War in the Peninsula and in the South of France from 1807 to 1814*, 6 volumes (London, 1889)

Oman, Charles. *A History of the Peninsular War*, 7 volumes (Greenhill, 1995—1997; (written 1903—1930))

Oman, Charles. *Wellington's Army, 1809—1814* (London, 1913)

Paget, Julian. *Wellington's Peninsular War* (Leo Cooper, 2005)

Parkinson, Roger. *The Peninsular War* (Wordsworth, 2000)

Read, J. *War in the Peninsula* (London, 1977)

Richards, D. *The Peninsula Years. Britain's Red Coats in Spain and Portugal* (Pen & Sword, 2002)

Robertson, Ian. *Wellington at War in the Peninsula* (Leo Cooper, 2000)

Rogers, H. *Wellington's Army* (London, 1979)

Ward, S. *Wellington's Headquarters* (Oxford, 1957)

Weller, Jac. *Wellington in the Peninsula 1808—1814* (Greenhill Books, 1999)

Wellington, Duke of. *Wellington's Despatches*, ed. J Gurwood (London, 1852)

The Osprey series of campaign books included titles on Vimeiro, Buçaco, Fuentes de Oñoro, Salamanca and Vitoria. The same publisher also produces a wide range of books covering uniforms, organisations and tactics of the Napoleonic Wars, including titles specific to the Iberian peninsula.

Websites

www.napoleon-series.org

www.hstmil1805—14.com

www.peninsularwar.org

www.napoleonguide.com

www.britishbattles.com

INDEX

Abbé, General Louis 249, 264, 300, 303, 316, 317, 318, 319
A Coruña see La Corunna
Agueda river 171, 199
Ainhoa 303, 312
Alcobaça 36
Alcuescar 165, 166
Alicante 228
Algeciras 132, 138
Almaraz 83, 92, 170
Almeida 97, 98
  siege of 103
  touring 103
Alten, General Sir Charles, Count von 201, 202, 232, 234, 235, 238, 282, 288, 291, 297, 298, 299, 302, 309, 323, 330, 331
Amotz 295, 297, 299, 300, 301, 302
Andaluciéa 10, 13, 14, 15
Anglet 304, 306, 308, 311, 313, 319
Arcangues 306, 309, 313
Ardour river 304, 314, 339, 341
Arroyo Dos Molinos
  battle of 165-167
  touring 167-168
Ascain 295, 296, 302
Astorga 55, 59
Austria 7, 92, 242
Badajoz 24, 25, 26, 92, 125, 131, 140, 152, 158, 170
  sieges of 184-196
  order of battle at 195
  visiting 196-198

Bailén 10, 35
Baird, General Sir David 52, 53, 62, 63, 65
Barcelona 9, 14, 227
Barrié, General 172, 174
Barrosa
  battle of 133-137
  order of battle at 138
  touring 138-139
Bayonne 9, 231, 236, 247, 295, 296, 297, 301, 303, 304, 306, 308, 311, 314, 316-321
  battle of 335-341
  touring 341
Behobie 287, 288, 293
Bembibre 56
Benavente 54, 55, 59
Beresford, General William 11, 76, 141, 152, 153, 154, 155, 156, 157, 158, 170, 185, 186, 209, 210, 296, 297, 301, 305, 307, 313, 314, 322, 324, 325, 330, 331, 332, 333
Betanzos 58
Bidarray 300
Bidassoa (Bidasoa) river 264, 277
  British attack across 286-291
  French attack across 282-286
  order of battle along the 291-293
  touring 293-294
Blake, General Joachim 152, 153, 154, 157, 163, 170, 171
Bonaparte, Joseph, King of Naples and Spain 9, 10, 14, 27, 84, 86, 87, 91, 92, 189, 199, 218, 227, 228, 229, 230, 231, 232, 236, 238, 239, 241
Bonaparte, Napoleon 7, 8, 9, 10, 13, 54, 55, 59, 92, 98, 124, 169, 189,

199, 227, 228, 303, 310, 331, 334, 335
Bonnet, General Jean-Pierre 205, 209, 210
Boyer, General Joseph de Rebeval, Baron 287
Braga 74
Brennier, General Antoine-François, Count 43, 45, 46, 49, 204, 205, 206, 208, 216, 217
British Army 10-11
Bucellas 120, 122
Buçaco 11, 12, 76
  battle of 105-115
  order of battle at 118
  touring 115-119
Burgos
  siege of 218-225
  visiting 225-226
Burrard, General Sir Harry 35, 42, 47

Cacabelos 57
Cadiz 92, 131, 132, 133, 137
Cambo-les-Bains 303, 305, 306, 307, 312
Campbell, General Alexander 85, 88, 95, 106, 142
Campbell, General H 106, 202, 219
Cantabrian mountains 229
Carlos VI, King 7, 8
Castaños, General Francisco 152, 161
Cassagne, General 230, 234, 238
Chaves 74
Chiclana 132, 133
Cintra, Convention of 47, 51
Ciudad Rodrigo 97, 140, 141, 147, 160, 167, 170
  siege of 171-181
  order of battle at 181

touring 182-184
Claparéde, General 146
Clausel, General Bertrand Count 205, 206, 209, 210, 215, 227, 230, 247, 253, 254, 256, 258, 259, 261, 263, 269, 283, 284, 287, 290, 295, 296, 301, 302, 308, 309, 322, 323
Clinton, General Sir Henry 200, 202, 204, 209, 210, 215, 288, 297, 300, 302, 307, 324, 330, 333
Côa river
  battle on the 97-103
  touring 104-105
Coimbra 39, 75, 76, 105, 106, 141, 142
Columbeira 37, 41
Colville, General Sir Charles 190, 297
Conroux, General Nicolas 146, 230, 232, 233, 259, 260, 266, 287, 290, 298
Constitution, 1812 218
Continental System 7, 8
Copenhagen 7
Corps of Royal Engineers (British) 23
Craufurd, General Sir Robert 97, 98, 99, 101, 102, 103, 105, 106, 112, 116, 141, 145, 176, 179, 180, 181

Dalhousie, General Sir George Ramsey 165, 167, 168, 231, 232, 254, 256, 259, 268, 297, 305, 306
Dalrymple, General Sir Hew Bart. 35, 47
Daricau, General Augustin 230, 231, 287, 316, 329, 331, 333
Delaborde, General Henri 36, 37-39, 40-41, 42-45, 62, 66, 74, 78
D'Armagnac, General Jean 249, 251, 270, 307, 309, 316, 317, 318, 320, 322, 323, 324, 325

D'Erlon, General Jean Baptiste 142, 146, 147, 230, 234, 235, 236, 237, 238, 247, 249, 251, 252, 283, 287, 295-297, 302, 304, 308, 309, 322, 324, 325
Dorsenne, General Jean-Marie 172
Douro river 74, 76-80, 92, 223, 229
Drouet, General 124, 165, 259, 262, 264
Dubreton, General Jean-Louis, Baron 218, 221
Dupont de l'Etang, General Pierre 10

El Burgos (O Burgo) 58, 61
Elonzo 247
Elvas 51, 186, 198
Elviña 61, 62, 65, 66
Erskine, General Sir William, Bart.141
Esla river 229
Espoz y Mina, Francisco 227
Extremadura 14, 51, 92, 140, 165, 181, 186, 195, 199

Fernando, Prince 8
Ferey, General 112, 142, 143
Figueira da Foz 35
Fletcher, Lieutenant-Colonel Richard 120, 129, 174, 272, 273
Fonterrabia 247
Foy, General Maximilien 78, 111, 116, 201, 202, 205, 210, 211, 253, 259, 260, 263, 266, 300, 305, 306, 308, 309, 322, 323
Fraser, General Alexander 62, 64
Freire, General Benardino 36
Freire, General Manuel 283, 284, 288, 296, 330, 331
French Army 13-15

Fuentes de Oñoro
   battle of 140-147
   order of battle at 148-149
   touring 147-151

Garonne river 328, 329, 330, 331, 333, 334, 335
Gave de Pau river 321, 323, 326
Gazan, General Théodore 230, 231, 232, 233, 234, 235, 236, 237, 238
Gerona 10
Gibraltar 132, 138
Girard, General Jean-Baptiste 153, 165, 166, 167
Gizan, General 153
Godoy, Manuel de 7, 8, 9
Gordon, Colonel James 224
Guadiana river 165, 185, 186, 189, 194, 198
Graham, General Sir Thomas, Lord Lynedoch 106, 131, 132, 133, 134, 136, 137, 187, 229, 230, 231, 236-240, 272, 273, 274, 276, 296
Guerrilla warfare 26-28

Hay, General Andrew 287, 288, 293, 296, 306, 308, 338, 339, 341
Hamilton, General 155
Harispe, General Jean Isidore 322, 323, 325, 329, 331, 333
Herrasti, General Andrés 97, 171, 183
Heudelet de Bierre, General Etienne, Count 109, 110, 111, 112, 142
Hill, General Sir Rowland, Viscount 14, 38, 40, 43, 62, 66, 76, 78, 83, 85, 86, 87, 95, 107, 108, 165, 167, 187, 223, 225, 229, 231-233, 237, 247, 252, 262, 264, 297, 300, 302, 305, 306, 307, 313, 314,

315-319, 323, 329, 331, 333
Hope, General Sir John 61, 62, 66, 71, 202, 204, 301, 306, 308, 309, 310, 313, 339
Houston, General William 141, 144, 150, 151
Howard, General Kenneth, Earl of Effingham 165, 168, 231, 283, 287, 288, 296, 336, 338

Irun 282, 283
Itzatza (Itxassou) 306

Jena, battle of 7
John, Prince Regent of Portugal 8
Jourdan, Marshall Jean-Baptiste, Count 87, 199, 232, 241
Junot, Marshal Jean Andoche, Duke of Abrantes 8, 11, 35, 36, 42, 43, 44, 45, 46, 47, 114, 120, 123, 142, 144

Kempt, General Sir James 191, 234, 290, 298

La Corunna (A Coruña) 35, 52, 54, 73, 120, 229
    retreat to 54-59
    touring the retreat 59-61
    battle of 61-68
    order of battle at 72
    touring 68-71
Lamartiniére, General 230, 237, 239, 253, 266
Languedoc canal 328, 334, 335
La Peña, General Manuela 131, 132, 137, 138, 139
Lapisse, General Pierre 89, 90, 96
Latour-Maubourg, General Marie 154, 156, 157

Le Cor, General 235, 297, 306, 310, 314, 315, 317, 323, 329, 331
Lefebvre-Desnouettes,Marshal Charles, Comte 55
Leith, General Sir James 62, 65, 66, 107, 198, 202, 204, 206, 207, 209, 215
Leipzig, Battle of 310
Le Marchant, General John 21, 204, 206, 207-209
Leval, General Jean François 88, 132, 133, 134, 137, 230
Lisbon 8, 14, 35, 36, 42, 74, 75, 108, 112, 113, 115, 119, 120, 122, 123, 140, 185, 195, 229
Liverpool, Robert Banks Jenkinson, Earl of 185
Lizaso 262, 264
Loison, General Louis Henri, Comte 36, 37-39, 42, 43, 48, 98, 101, 112, 113, 142-144, 146
Los Arapiles 201, 202, 203, 204, 205, 209, 210, 213
Lowry Cole, General Galbraith 106, 153, 157, 231, 238, 252, 253, 256, 264, 268
Lugo 57
Luisa, Queen María 9

Macdonald, Marshal Jacques, Duke of Tarentum 27
Mackenzie, General Sir Alexander 75, 84, 85, 89, 90
Madrid 8, 9, 10, 14, 52, 54, 84, 87, 91, 92, 170, 195, 211, 218, 219, 223, 277
Mafra 120, 122
Maransin, General Jean Pierre 45, 249, 251, 252, 264, 287, 298, 329, 331

Marchand, General Jean Gabriel, Comte 98, 112, 113, 114, 142, 143, 144, 148, 150

Marmont, Marshal Auguste, Duke of Ragusa 169, 170, 171, 172, 175, 181, 187, 189, 190, 199, 200, 201, 202, 203, 204, 205, 206, 209, 210, 211, 214, 215, 216,

Massena, Marshal André, Duke of Rivoli, Prince of Essling 11, 30, 105, 106, 107, 108, 112, 114, 115, 116, 119, 122, 124, 129, 169, 184, 201, 206, 210, 224, 261

Master-General of Ordnance (British) 23

Maucune, General Antoine 204, 205, 206, 207, 208, 217, 259, 263, 266, 287

Maya Pass 247
battle of 247-252
order of battle at 264
touring 269-270

Medellién 165

Medina de Riéo Seco 10

Mendizabal, General Gabriel 185

Mérida 73, 75, 83, 165, 166, 167, 189

Merle, General Pierre, Count 62, 63, 65, 74, 111, 116, 142,

Mermet, General Julien 63, 65, 70, 74, 142, 144

Moncey, Marshal Bon Adrien Jeannot de, Duke of Conegliano 10

Mondego river 35, 107

Montbrun, General Louis-Pierre, Comte 144

Monte Agraco 121, 122, 127

Moore, General Sir John 14, 47, 51, 52, 53, 54, 55, 56, 57, 58, 59, 61, 62, 63, 64, 65, 67, 68

Morillo, General Pablo

Mortier, General Edouard, Duke of Treviso 92

Mouguerre 315, 319, 320

Murat, Marshal Joachim, Prince and King of Naples 9

Murray, General Sir John 76, 79

Napier, Lieutenant-Colonel William 131, 145, 158, 301, 319, 339

Ney, Marshal Michel, Duke of Elchingen 73, 83, 97, 101, 103, 108, 112, 115, 169, 171, 183

Nive river
battle of 303-311
order of battle at the 312
touring 312-314

Nivelle river 289, 294
battle of 295-302
touring 302-303

Obidos 36, 39

Ocaña 92

Olivenza 185, 186

Oporto see Porto

Orthez
battle of 321-325
touring 326-327

Oswald, General John 231, 237, 239, 246, 273, 274

Paget, General Hon. Henry, Lord 53, 56, 57

Paget, General Hon. Sir Edward 58, 62, 64

Pakenham, General Sir Edward 118, 202, 204, 205, 206, 209, 215, 217, 224, 263

Palafox y Melzi, General José, Duke

of Zaragoza 10
Pamplona 52, 230, 236, 247, 256, 257, 262, 266, 271
Paris 330, 331, 334
Paris, General 306
Phillipon, General Armand, Baron 187, 189, 190, 194
Picton, General Sir Thomas 106, 107, 108, 110, 111, 112, 116, 119, 141, 145, 147, 175, 176, 177, 180, 190, 191, 198, 231, 234, 235, 236, 238, 259, 260, 263, 307, 323, 324, 326, 331, 332, 333, 334
Porto
battle of 76-80
touring 81-83
Portuguese Army 11-12
Prussia 7
Pyrenees 9, 11, 13, 15, 32, 247, 259, 264, 273, 286, 295

Reille, General Charles 230, 236, 237, 238, 239, 240, 247, 253, 255, 256, 259, 269, 283, 284, 287, 288, 289, 295, 296, 301, 306, 308, 309, 310, 311, 322, 324, 325
Rey, General Louis-Emanuel, Baron 271, 277, 278, 281
Reynier, General Jean Louis, Comte 108, 109, 111, 112, 116, 123, 142, 144
Rhune, La Grande 287, 288, 290, 294, 295, 296
Rhune, La Petit 295, 296, 297, 298, 299, 301, 302
Rio Maior 124
Roliça
battle of 36-39
order of battle at 50

touring 39-42
Roncesvalles Pass
battle of 252-256
order of battle at 265
touring 268-269
Rouget, General 322, 323, 324, 327
Royal Military Artificers (British) 23
Royal Navy 76, 131, 138
Royal Sappers and Miners (British) 25
Royal Staff Corps (British) 23
Ruffin, General François 86, 90, 91, 132, 133, 136, 137
Russia 7, 8, 13, 14, 169, 199, 227

Sahagun 53-54
Santander 229
Sare 283, 287, 295, 297, 299, 302
St Boes 322, 323, 324, 325, 326, 327
St Etienne-de-Baigorry 269, 287
St Jean-de-Luz 295
St Jean Pied-de-Port 315
St Pée-sur-Nivelle 302
St Pierre d'Irube
battle of 314-319
touring 319-320
Salamanca 11, 14, 21, 27, 51, 52, 53, 92
battle of 201-211
campaign of 200-201
capture of the city 199-200
order of battle at 212-213
touring 213-218
San Marcial (San Martzial) 277, 283, 284
San Sebastián 25, 227, 236, 263
siege of 271-278
order of battle at 279
visiting 279-282
Santarém 124

Sarrut, General 205, 209, 210, 230, 236, 238, 246
Sébastiani, General 14, 84, 86, 87, 88, 89, 92, 94
Seville (Sevilla) 152
Sherbrooke, General Sir John 79, 83, 85, 86, 88, 95
Skerrett, General 285
Siege warfare 23-26
Sierra de Guadarrama 54
Sobral 121, 123, 124, 127
Solignac, General 230, 234, 235, 236, 238, 247, 249, 251, 252, 283, 287, 295, 297, 304
Sorauren
    battle of 256-264
    order of battle at 265
    touring 266-268
Soult, Marshal Nicolas Jean-de-Dieu, Duke of Dalmatia 14, 15, 53, 54, 57,   58, 61, 62, 63, 65, 66, 73, 74, 75, 76, 78, 79, 83, 87, 92, 125, 131, 141, 152, 153, 154, 157, 158, 160, 163, 185, 186, 190, 199, 218, 223, 228, 247, 252, 254, 256-259, 261, 263, 264, 273, 277, 282, 283, 286, 287, 289, 291, 295, 296, 299, 301, 303, 304, 307, 308, 310, 314, 316, 317, 319, 321, 322, 323, 325, 328, 329, 330, 332, 334, 335
Spanish Army 12-13
Spencer, General Sir Brent 35, 106, 115, 141, 145
Stewart, General Sir William 107, 152, 153, 154, 156, 157, 158, 164, 236, 246, 247, 249, 251, 252, 256, 270, 288, 300, 303, 314, 315-318, 323, 329, 331
Suchet, General (later Marshal)

Louis-Gabriel, Duke of Albufera 170, 171, 223, 228
tactics, artillery 22-23
tactics, cavalry 20-22
tactics, infantry 15-20

Tagus river 84, 85, 92, 120, 122, 123, 129, 185
Talavera de la Reina 10
    battle of 83-92
    order of battle at 93
    touring 94-96
Talleyrand, Count 8, 9
Tanque river 306, 308, 309, 310, 311, 313
Tarifa 131, 132, 138
Taupin, General 253, 261, 263, 287, 290, 298, 302, 322, 323, 324, 327, 329, 333
Thomiére, General Jean 44, 48, 204, 205, 206, 217
Thouvenot, General Pierre 319, 335, 336, 339, 340
Tilsit treaty 7
Tormes river 92, 200, 201, 202, 203, 211, 214, 216
Torres Vedras, Lines of 11, 12, 39, 42, 48, 115, 119-130, 184, 228, 273
Toulouse
    battle of 328-334
    touring 334-335
Treaty of Fontainebleau 8
Trafalgar 7, 131
Travot, General 329

United States 7
Urdax 247, 284, 287, 295
Ustaritz 303, 305, 307, 309, 310, 313, 314, 318

Valencia 10, 13, 14, 170
Valladolid 10
Vandermaesen, General 253, 254, 259, 261, 263, 285, 294
Venegas, General 87, 91
Vera (Bera) 282, 283, 285, 287, 288, 290, 293, 294
Victor, Marshal Claude 14, 73, 75, 76, 83, 84, 85, 86, 87, 91, 92, 131, 132
Vigo 56, 73
Villafranque 304, 308, 313, 318, 319
Villatte, General 90, 132, 133, 139, 230, 284, 287, 308, 322, 325, 329, 332, 333
Vimeiro
    battle of 42-47
    order of battle at 50
    touring 48-50
Vitoria 11, 13, 15
    advance to 227-229
    battle of 230-242
    order of battle at 242-243
    touring 244-246

Walker, General 307, 323, 324
Wellesley, Arthur 10, 11, 14, 35, 36, 41, 42, 43, 44, 45, 47, 48, 51, 75, 76, 77, 78, 80, 81, 82, 83, 84, 85, 86, 88, 89, 90, 91, 92
Wellington, Duke of 92, 105, 106, 107, 108, 109, 111, 112, 113, 114, 116, 119, 120, 122, 124, 126, 127, 131, 140, 141, 142, 143, 144, 146, 147, 152, 154, 158, 160, 167, 170, 171, 172, 174, 175, 177, 180, 181, 184, 186, 187, 189, 190, 194, 196, 199, 200, 202, 204, 205, 206, 207, 209, 210, 211, 214, 215, 218, 219, 220, 221, 223, 224, 225, 227, 228, 229, 230, 232, 233, 234, 237, 239, 241, 244, 247, 252, 256, 257, 258, 259, 260, 261, 262, 263, 266, 271, 273, 277, 282, 284, 287, 290, 296, 297, 301, 304, 305, 307, 308, 310, 314, 317, 318, 319, 322, 324, 329, 330, 331, 333, 334

Zaragoza 10, 28, 52